That Day with God

THAT DAY WITH GOD

Edited by
William M. Fine

Foreword by Richard Cardinal Cushing

McGraw-Hill Book Company
NEW YORK TORONTO LONDON

THAT DAY WITH GOD

Library of Congress catalog card number 64-66265

First Edition

20925

The other members of the

family and I are deeply

grateful for this tribute

to my son in your book

That Day with God.

Rose Kennedy

(MRS. JOSEPH P. KENNEDY)

HYANNISPORT,
MASSACHUSETTS

September, 1964

FOREWORD

All of us recall Friday, November 22, of last year as a day of national tragedy. It is consoling to remember now that Sunday, November 24, became spontaneously a day of national prayer. It is estimated that more people responded on that Sunday to the urge to pray for the martyred President of the United States by attending the church of their choice than on any other day in our nation's history.

Undoubtedly, the millions who prayed on "That Day with God" were turning with a sure human instinct toward the Creator at a moment when their confidence in the stability of earthly things was shattered. Human explanations at this hour helped not at all; human comforts gave no consolation, so men turned to the one Power over which evil and violence could make no conquest—they sought for peace in God.

President Kennedy would have understood all of this, for he was a man of deep faith who knew how to pray. In a short life where crisis and anxiety, pain and illness, tragedy and death were already woven into the fabric, Jack Kennedy had never failed to put his final confidence out beyond the world in the hands of the Unchanging God. His heart must have rejoiced in Heaven to see men and women—and especially the young—in every part of this nation, and in most parts of the world itself, offer their prayers for him and the ideals for which he had lived and labored.

The tributes in these pages touch movingly on many points and serve to recall the days which only the passing of time makes comprehensible. It is good for us to have this permanent memorial of that greatness which we all admired, which was so shortly with us and so swiftly taken away.

Let it remind us to think of the late President, to pray for his repose, and to make endure in our world all those things for which he stood and for which, finally, he gave his life.

RICHARD CARDINAL CUSHING
ARCHBISHOP OF BOSTON

September 1964

TO PEOPLE

May they care

May they share

May they be touched by Him more often

CONTENTS

All sin was of my sinning, all

Atoning mine, and mine the gall

Of all regret. Mine was the weight

Of every brooded wrong, the hate

That stood behind each envious thrust,

Mine every greed, mine every lust. . . .

Edna St. Vincent Millay

PREFACE

In awesome moments man turns toward God.

On August 6, 1945, over Hiroshima, Japan, a bomb was dropped from a United States plane bearing the name "Enola Gay." The bomb drop was at 9:15 A.M. In the co-pilot's log for that day, the only entry was: "My God."

On November 22, 1963, at 2:08 Eastern Standard Time, on an Eastern Airlines plane flying from Miami to New York, the pilot dropped a verbal bomb with the announcement that John F. Kennedy, President of the United States, had died in Dallas, Texas. A man doodling with a pencil in the seat next to mine wrote, perhaps unconsciously, "My God."

It was at that precise moment, I think, that I began to wonder how God and His ministers would interpret this fearful act to the world.

For the assassin's bullet did more than kill President Kennedy—it struck us all, shattering our composure as a people and numbing our senses.

Running through the mountains of words of tribute, praise and explanation that followed President Kennedy's assassination, was the growing humiliation that as a nation we were made to look uncivilized, rebellious against the law of the land and the faith that guides our future.

Many years ago, Walter Lippmann, with a prophetic sense of the future, said, "The decay of decency in the modern age—the treatment of human beings as things, as mere instruments of power and ambition, is without doubt the consequence of the decay of the belief in man as something more than an animal, animated by highly conditioned reflexes and chemical reactions.

"For, unless man is something more than that, he has no rights that anyone is bound to respect, and there is no limitation upon his conduct which he is bound to obey. This is the forgotten foundation of democracy in the only sense in which democracy is valid, and of liberty in the only sense in which it can hope to endure. These liberties we talk about defending today were established by men who took their conception of man from the great central religious tradition of Western civilization, and the liberties we inherit can almost certainly not survive the abandonment of that tradition."

Minutes after the assassination, man began to pray and to appeal to Him for understanding. Earle L. Cadell, Mayor of Dallas, said, "I call upon the churches and synagogues for such devotion to our faith that they speak to us with utmost candor, both of ideals of faith and the shortcomings of our community, so that we may be guided into the path of right."

Churches around the world shared his thought: services, prayers and religious statements rang out with the clarity of a church bell "That Day" and the awesome days that followed. All the sermons relate to the loss of the young, vigorous, world leader—to the loss of a man endowed with so many of the positive qualities of mankind. It was said about John Kennedy, as it was said about a great man from Illinois one hundred years ago, "a tree is best measured when it is down." Kennedy, in his death, endowed the world with a keener appreciation of the things he stood for. His life ran a short course but his effect on the world will fill the long years.

This collection of sermons and expressions approaches the complex problems that confront us today with the quiet kind of wisdom that one rarely finds in professional or political circles. These men remind us to look for more truth in our lives—and to find it through faith and love. Whether the sermon was delivered in St. Bartholomew's, New York; or in St. Paul's, London; or in St. Luke's, Darien, Connecticut—or Whichford, England, with a population of 175—it tells us to stop hating and to start believing in more than man-made inventions to save the peace of the world.

It was obvious as I started my collection of sermons that the peak of religious expression was reached in places like Dallas, Washington, New York, and London, but I have tried to offer other representative areas of this country and the world not in order of their importance—nor by singling out one faith over another—but to reflect the widest possible reaction. Further, I have edited this collection of sermons on the premise that the words expressed have a divine quality that speaks not to a single faith but to all the people of the world.

At one time this sermon collection numbered well over three hundred. Cutting it down to a prescribed length was a difficult task. No doubt I have deleted sermons that were as good as the ones I have included. I hope the generous clergymen whom I have had to omit because of repetition of theme and space limitations will understand.

Most of the sermons in this volume were delivered on November 24, 1963, and these carry no date in their heading. The others were delivered between Friday night, November 22, and Thanksgiving Day, November 28, and are dated for accuracy.

When we look back over the fateful moments in

history, starting with the Cross on Calvary, and moving down through the wars and tribulations of Western civilization to the bleakness of November 22, 1963, we consistently find a man of God speaking to the times, prescribing that we "go forward trusting in Thee."

In the selections on the following pages, religious leaders of the world entrust you with that same hope.

WILLIAM M. FINE

New Canaan, Connecticut
September, 1964

That Day with God

From: HIGHLAND PARK METHODIST CHURCH
DALLAS, TEXAS

Sermon preached by the Reverend Dr. William H. Dickinson

LIVING OUT OUR FAITH

Those of us who were at the Trade Mart Friday at noon waiting to greet and honor the President of the United States found it hard to believe the first report that the President and the Governor had been shot. The news was incongruous. At the very moment when the people of our city had their best foot forward and when we were trying to make amends for the horrible image created a few weeks ago at the time of Adlai Stevenson's visit, tragedy struck and we were left helpless, completely unprepared to know what to say, what to do, or how to act. At the very moment of apparent triumph our world crumbled around us, and we became very conscious of our complete inadequacy to face the cold, hard facts in which we are involved.

If there had been a riot or if the thousands of people along the parade route had been hysterical or hostile, we could have believed the reports of what had happened. But there was no riot. Every detail of the President's visit and itinerary had been perfectly executed. At the moment there was no sign of hostility or hysteria. Instead there was a dignified and sincere expression of honor for John Kennedy and his wife, and a genuine expression of appreciation for the President's visit to our city. What we were told was simply beyond our capacity to understand. It could not be true. Such things happen in story books and fiction, in other countries, but it was too unreal, too fantastic to happen here. And when the cold, hard facts seeped slowly into our consciousness, we were left desolate. There was nothing we could do but pray. The question was *how* to pray? Pray for what?

The facts creating the need for prayer were relatively simple. A man had been killed. He was riding down the street with his wife. He was a husband, a father, a son. He was also the President of a great and powerful nation, and thus it was more than a person that had been destroyed.

John F. Kennedy was a symbol. There are many symbols of our national life, rich and full of meaning: the flag, the national anthem, the Grave of the Unknown Soldier, the memorials of Washington and Jefferson and Lincoln, but none of these even approach the meaning and significance of the symbol of the office of the President. Here is centered our belief in representative government, our belief in the right of the people to choose leaders who are entrusted with awesome responsibilities, our belief in the ordered foundations of freedom and of a society governed by law and order, and our belief in the very concept of democracy as a way of life.

Death always leaves us with a sense of loss, a sense of fear and uncertainty. But Friday at noon in the death of our President, we were robbed of something more than a friend or loved one. Indeed, to many he was thought of as neither friend nor loved one. And yet, because he was a symbol of the most cherished portions of our life, something of us died with him, and we were suddenly haunted by the words of another President who, just a hundred years ago, asked in the face of a national crisis "whether our nation so conceived and so dedicated could long endure."

Why, we ask, has this thing been done? Why would someone, why would anyone, aim a high-powered rifle at us and at our way of life and pull the trigger? To assume that whoever did it was insane or psychotic lends little comfort. There was, no doubt, present in the assassin the stimulant of hate and fear. There are always people in our society lingering on the fringe of violence, motivated by uncontrolled emotions, waiting in animal fashion to strike out at any force which seems to threaten them. One of the great challenges to any society is the way the people seek to heal this kind of mental illness, or the way they seek to isolate it when there is no cure, or the way they seek to so order the life of society that within the bounds of law and order no person can be incited to irresponsible actions. But in the face of this tragic event, the greatest challenge to our society today is to make the orderly processes of a free nation so responsive to all human needs that no man will turn to anarchy, even when he loses faith in the democratic process.

There is in custody today a suspect* for this crime, although we do not yet know who did it or why. We can only await the verdict of the courts regarding the guilt of the suspect in hand. The only thing of which we can be sure today is that it happened and that it happened in our city and in our nation and in our world.

The question, then, we face today is, what does a Christian do? What does a Christian do today in Dallas? What can we do who stood this morning to declare our faith in one God, Maker and Ruler of all things, Father of all men, the source of all goodness and beauty, all truth and love? Such faith cannot be main-

* At this moment in the sermon the suspect referred to was shot to death.

tained in a vacuum. We either have faith *and* God, we either have faith *in* God in our world, or we have no God at all.

In the Gospel of John, Jesus prayed for the church and said to the Father, "As Thou did send me into the world, so have I sent them into the world." And the Master was talking about us, you and me. This is the reason that somehow I cannot find within my heart this morning a willingness to place the blame for the tragedy of this hour solely upon the man who pulled the trigger, for as a Christian I have been sent into this world as a child of God. I am therefore responsible to live in keeping with His law, though this I have not always done. Inasmuch as the world of business and politics, of social relationships and government, is the real world in which I live, here it is that faith must find expression. Consider, if you will, at least four implications in the expression of our faith within the world:

First, this is God's world, not mine nor yours, but God's creation. And being free to make it what God wills it to be, we are thus called to live together, even in our disagreements. We are called to so order our society that our business and our government and our personal relationships in God's world will move toward more justice and compassion, more responsible citizenship, and more awareness of our personal guilt in this less than godly life which our humanity imposes on us.

In the second place, this concept of a world as the only place in which our faith can be lived calls for a new dedication at this very moment in history to law and order. Do not underestimate the essential nature of this problem, for in times of stress and strain, fear and bitterness, the only way our freedom can be maintained at all is by the diligent acceptance of the limitations of some particular freedom imposed by law and order for the sake of the larger good. There can, in fact, be no freedom apart from discipline and law.

This leads to the third implication, which is the fact that our faith must be lived in the world. When I speak of law and order, I do not mean the mere paying of taxes or going to the polls or providing adequate police protection or convening courts for the administration of justice. I mean the subtler support of our orderly society, maintained by deliberately refraining from irresponsible talk and excitement. Many of us are shocked or shamed when we remember conversations in which fine, respectable, highly educated business and professional people have glibly expressed *hate* for the President of the United States and have "wished someone would take a pot shot at him." Less than a month ago an honored and respected doctor in Dallas, a member of a church, could not carry on an intelligent telephone conversation with one of his patients without making abusive and damaging remarks about the United States Ambassador to the United Nations who was, at that time, a visitor in Dallas.

Such irresponsible conversation, even when intended as facetious or humorous, has no place in the life of a Christian. Every Christian citizen in Dallas today may well join with the Mayor of our city, who on Friday evening stated that we must all search our souls for anything we might have said.

There are among us today too many purveyors of hate, people who speak of intelligent, sincere holders of public office as traitors—people who fill our cars with leaflets bearing printed lies and calling our public officials disloyal—people who fill our mail with emotional, bitter harangues and accusations, who make harassing telephone calls to our honest and sincere citizens at all hours of the night. And then there are those who give subtler approval to such extremists through either indifference or through financial support.

Hate, not only in our city but throughout the nation, has become big business and is supported by large contributions and exceedingly competent leadership. And we in Dallas, it seems to me, have more than our share of these extremists. It is not a pretty picture, into which an assassin found his place.

Isn't it ironic that the suspect for the attack on President Kennedy and Governor Connally is a pro-Communist, an extreme leftist, when only recently our city made the headlines with the activities of the extremists from the far right at the time of Stevenson's visit? But if the fact is ironic, it is also prophetic. Hate knows no political loyalty. It is as deadly and as vicious in the hearts and minds of extremists on the right as it is in extremists on the left.

This leads me, then, to the fourth implication of living out our faith in the world to which Jesus sends us as Christians. There can be but one faithful motive for conduct in our world. Civic pride is not enough. Protection of our economic interest is not enough. The maintenance of our political prestige or getting our share is not enough. Recognition of God's law and the response to His love is the only motive by which our actions can be justified.

Every city guards with jealous pride its reputation and its image. The city of Little Rock was chagrined and shamed in becoming known the world over as a symbol of racial violence. But its inner character would have been calloused, indeed, had not thousands of its citizens and its courageous press felt a deeper guilt over the violence against human beings during those troublesome months. For us, there is today new sympathy for Little Rock.

Surely there are those who fear for Dallas' good name. There are those who worked so hard for a safe, sane, courteous Presidential reception. I want to pay tribute this morning to the leadership of our city. Following the Stevenson incident, these men gave careful leadership in the interest of sanity and civilized conduct. They are justifiably in great sorrow today over the damage that has been done to our city's good name, but our sorrow must go far beyond this. It is not only that our city has been betrayed by an assassin's bullet; it is that our God has been betrayed, not only in Dallas, but throughout our nation and around the world by irresponsible and indifferent and selfish men.

Today our intellectual and moral fiber is being tried as never before, and by its trial will be revealed our true dependence upon the God whose world we either honor or destroy.

Here the Christian puts his faith to the supreme test, not in the comfort of his living room nor in isolation with friends who think as he does, but out in the world of conflict and tension, trouble and sorrow. It is not an easy test. It is a test that, as of today, we have all failed. But in our failure we hear again the words of Jesus saying "O Jerusalem, Jerusalem, how often would I have gathered your children together as a hen gathers her brood under her wings, and you would not." Nevertheless, the Master is patient for our response, for He has sent us into the world even as God sent Him into the world.

How, then, do we pray today? For what do we pray? We pray to a God who is still at work in His world. We pray with a faith that calls us to new dedication to law and order. We pray for the ability to be responsible citizens, characterized by orderliness, restraint, and courage. And we pray for a world where our human, selfish motivations will be brought under the judgment of God and our concerns broadened far beyond our city to all mankind.

Finally, we pray knowing that to do what we want to do or to be what we want to be is impossible with men, but we pray with the assurance that it *is* possible with God.

From: SACRED HEART CATHEDRAL
DALLAS, TEXAS

Sermon preached by the Right Reverend William F. O'Brien

November 25, 1963

One of Abraham Lincoln's biographers tells us that on the Sunday following the Great Emancipator's death, American churches were thronged with people who were eager to hear some reassuring word that somewhere still he lived.

Even those with uncertain faith could not believe that he who with sincerity of purpose led a divided nation through the crucible of a terrible war to the very brink of reconciliation and peace should find in that land of mystery beyond the grave no path for his weary feet or crown for his noble head.

President John F. Kennedy, during his campaign in 1960, more than once expressed his consuming passion to serve his country with the same spirit as Lincoln. Cynics accused him of being brash and presumptuous to set his aim so high. But if one has followed the events which have transpired since last Friday, if you have listened to the words of people around the world of high and low estate, if you have witnessed that endless procession of mourners at our National Capitol, estimated at half a million, if you attended by television this morning the ceremonies in Washington at St. Matthew Cathedral and Arlington, if you observed the greatest convocation of government dignitaries ever assembled in our nation, then I believe you would never dispute again that the death of John Fitzgerald Kennedy, nearly one hundred years after that of Lincoln, is history repeating itself.

Just who was this man of destiny, John Fitzgerald Kennedy? After listening for three days to accolades from people great and small around the world, it is difficult for me to conceive an original tribute. In all the testimonials of praise which we have heard I believe that none has more dramatic impact and meaning than the message of Charles de Gaulle, President of France, given before his departure for the funeral which he attended this morning with some sixty other heads of state.

General de Gaulle had this to say of his fallen comrade, a man nearly thirty years younger than himself and who had at times held different political opinions: "President Kennedy died like a soldier, under fire, for duty, and in the service of his country."

Among free people political differences are the very foundations of good government. The best thoughts of all citizens of good faith are weighed and measured and, after due consideration and proper procedures, are merged by a majority into law which is beneficial for all.

Our leaders are chosen by proper voting processes and, when duly elected, even if not entirely pleasing to all, the dignity of their office and their person is respected. It is only in Communist states that there is but one ticket and the people have no choice.

From time to time evangels of hate have crept from beneath their rocks and slithered among us. When I was a young priest in the early twenties, an organization in masks and hoods threatened the unity and peace of America. They draped themselves in flags, called themselves one-hundred-per-cent Americans and barred from membership Jews, Negroes, and Catholics. You could not belong, nor could John Kennedy. Scandals tore them asunder. They hissed and went back beneath the rocks from which they came.

In our day other hate movements such as that of the twenties have come out of hibernation and threaten again the unity of the American people. By the same methods, with the flag and the clarion cry of defenders, they have smeared our leaders, and by spoken and printed word they have given peace and comfort to our country's most deadly foes by striving to divide our own people. President Kennedy, as attested over and over again during the past few days by those better informed than I am, was their victim. Sad to say, but true, Catholics can now have membership and unfortunately are too often found in their ranks. The rifle which assassinated our beloved President and seriously threatened the life of our distinguished Governor was triggered not only by the hand of a poor distorted, frustrated maniac but by everyone who subscribes to a godless gospel of hate.

"If you would judge a man," says an old Indian proverb, "you must walk in his moccasins for twelve moons." Had we done this, we would have seen a man representative of young America at its best, dedicated to the service of his country, conscious of his human frailties, but fearless unto death.

Beautiful experiences have been involved in President Kennedy's death which have reduced its tragic aspects. Our Father Huber here was there to administer the last rites of the Church, and to comfort Mrs. Kennedy. After having done what he could, he said, "It was a very, very long ride back." Young Dr. Perry at Parkland said: "I had never seen the President before. He was much bigger than I thought. He was a big man."

Now twilight is past. Evening has come. Reflection has been good, for President Kennedy has not died in vain. The day of his death will be a day of victory.

From: TEMPLE EMANU-EL BROTHERHOOD
DALLAS, TEXAS

Sermon preached by
Rabbi Levi A. Olan

WHAT SHOULD DALLAS DO NOW?

Jerusalem in the year 520 B.C. was a city despised and scorned by the surrounding nations. She had been decimated by enemies, and those who had returned to her from exile were weak and fearful.

As is so often the case in the Bible, it is at this point that a prophet appears to console the people and challenge them to new greatness. Zechariah, a prophet of visions, speaks to Jerusalem in her hour of dismay. So the angel that spoke with me said unto me: "Proclaim thou saying: 'Thus saith the Lord of Hosts: I am jealous for Jerusalem and for Zion with a great jealousy.' She is not forsaken of God who loves her and will guard her."

This is the text to be spoken to Dallas, who today sits solitary and confused. Reproach is aimed at her from far and near. The people are ashamed, resentful, and distraught. The glamor of "Big D" is tarnished. In the confusion of tongues which followed upon the hour when tragedy struck, the Mayor of Dallas spoke to the citizens in the language of the Bible. "It has occurred to me," he said, "these past few days that perhaps we have spoken too proudly of ourselves. If our deeds are deeds of true accomplishment, we will have so served our nation and our world that we will not need to call attention to our works. I call upon the churches and synagogues for such devotion to our faith that they will speak to us with utmost candor, both of ideals of truth and of the shortcomings of our community, so that we may be guided into the paths of right. . . . I call upon the people to bear every means of strengthening our moral fiber and to make ours a community of tolerance and understanding." This is a call in the prophetic style, and this sermon is a response. The text for us is a paraphrase of Zechariah: "I am jealous for Dallas with a great jealousy."

The first question which must be resolved is psychological. Is Dallas guilty of anything because the President of our country was assassinated on her streets? In the beginning there was a strong current of guilt which the Mayor's prophetic call expressed in noble terms. Many people felt that there was something frightfully wrong with the city and some wanted to face the truth. This mood is passing and now there is a growing resentment of all criticism from without and within the gates. The present tone is that of rejecting all responsibility and disclaiming all guilt. Dallas, it is said, is no different than other cities, and better than many. The assassin was not one of our citizens; he could have chosen any other city to commit his terrible crime. The people want desperately to forget the tragedy and go on with the business of living as though nothing had happened here.

There is just enough truth in what is being said now in Dallas to lead the city astray and into a serious psychological danger. The people of this city did not pull the trigger and they are certainly not assassins. In many other cities in the nation there are irrational and irresponsible citizens for whom a whole community cannot be blamed. This is so obviously true that it blinds us to the distinctive character of Dallas, which makes a vital difference. Before the President came to our city we were apprehensive. The law-enforcing officers were pleading with the citizens on radio, television, and in the newspapers to behave decently, to discourage anyone who could cause an incident. The reception prepared by the leaders of the community was almost tinged with guilt. It looked as though we were protesting our love a little too much. The atmosphere was prepared by the best techniques of modern public relations. Yet the unexpressed mood was quietly spoken by one of the leading citizens: "I wish he were here and gone already; I would feel better." We were all afraid of an incident—never dreaming, of course, that it would take the tragically irrational form of assassination by a Marxist lunatic.

Behind our apprehension lay the fact that we had become the number-one spot in the nation for intolerance. We had been put to shame several times by rudeness, crude manners, and even violence. It is not uncommon for the President of the United States to visit communities hostile politically to him. But, we were afraid of an *incident,* the word which was first used in the announcement of the assassination to the audience waiting eagerly for the President to arrive. The fact is that we are like all other cities—with this difference, however: we were troubled and anxious lest something should happen.

There is a psychological axiom which holds that when a disturbed patient accepts responsibility and blame for his behavior and attempts to do something about it, the prognosis is good. When, however, a patient tends to rationalize away his behavior and justify it, the prognosis appears to be poor. The present mood of Dallas which is one of rejecting responsibility and blame is essentially the greatest psychological danger confronting the city. Time is an important factor here, and the longer the delay in assuming responsibility the worse the prognosis. William James, years ago, wrote that if something is not done very quickly for harnessing an aroused emotion for action, the emotion gets dulled and dissipated and nothing comes of it.

The critical error of the moment is the substitution of a partial truth for the whole. The nation as a whole is frustrated in many areas of its life. The increasing manufacture of atom bombs all over the world has reduced us to impotence in the world. We have been made powerless because we just cannot make war any more. Furthermore, this is a time of change and violent revolutions. The have-nots all over the world are inspired with rising expectations. The old values of religion, family, and society are in radical transition. Power structures are in rapid transformation. Capital in corporate form is confronted by labor in equal corporate power. The government is playing a more prominent role as against the lessened opportunity of the individual. Civil rights are dynamically on the move, introducing social patterns totally new. Many people all over the country fear and resent it all. Some are so shaken that they assume an extreme position. The majority are very anxious and want to stop the rapid process of change. Thus there is tension in many places and on many fronts.

Dallas partakes in this national feeling of anxiety and uncertainty. It is like the rest of the nation in this regard. There is, however, one difference. It is more so! Why this is so is not too clear. Why we have become a haven for the extreme expression of the mood of anxiety has not been carefully studied. It is true that there is a great concentration of fabulous wealth in the hands of a few. But this is surely an inadequate explanation. Why is the possibility of an incident more characteristic of us than of other cities? Unless we face up to the whole truth our prognosis, psychologically, is poor.

The second question—after the psychological—which the city must answer is the ethical. What is now evident is that the value system by which Dallas lives is open to criticism. There are, generally, four categories of ethical codes of behavior. The first and perhaps the highest is the humanistic, in which the individual identifies himself with the highest social good. He sees the larger purposes of life, beyond his own desires, and devotes himself to their fulfillment. He lives by humanitarian goals because they are the reason for his existence as a human creature. The second category is the religious code of values, expressed for us in the Judeo-Christian heritage of ideals. The third is the legal system of values, which in our country is expressed by laws which are the result of legislation with the Supreme Court as the final arbiter of constitutionality. The fourth, and certainly the lowest, ethical code is the personal. This is the value system where a person does that which benefits him personally. It is in almost all of its expressions self-aggrandizing. The fourth category—the personal—is probably the most popular of our time. Many people determine their behavior in answer to the question "What is there in it for me?"

Here again Dallas is like the rest of the nation, only more so. The integration of the schools was achieved not because the law of the land required it, not because God is the Father of all children without distinction of color, and not because brotherhood is a noble value. Token integration was accepted because it paid off in dollars and cents. The examples of Little Rock and New Orleans were not lost upon the practical-minded of the city. We chose the fourth and lowest of the ethical codes as our guide. Consider our city, which boasts of great wealth, high fashion, fabulous bank buildings, and luxurious palatial homes—yet one fifth of the residential area is a slum and has been officially condemned as unfit for decent human habitation. In this "Big D" the local paper recently reported that many children do not go to school because they cannot afford to bring a lunch or buy one. The writer for the Dallas *Morning News* reports that Texas is the lowest of all the states in its aid to dependent children. The national average is $2.81. In Texas it is forty-one cents.

In a city not afraid to boast of its high place in finance and business, the people accept a public school system which is certainly not competing for top position in the nation. The dropout percentage of Dallas is one which ought to frighten any responsible community. Thirty per cent of the white students and over 50 per cent of the colored drop out of high school after they enter. The university in our city, which has celebrated a half-century of service, is starved for funds and neglected by the community when it cries for a chance to meet the urgent needs of modern education. In an attempt to maintain even a modest level of artistic enterprise an art fund was created. It failed miserably in its drive for support.

This failure to accept responsibility for the good city is not unique with Dallas. Many cities are in the same class. What is different and appalling is that we accept a lower level of ethics on a platform of high idealism. The child who cannot have a lunch could be provided for if we accepted the national program of aid for these children. But on high principles we reject government aid and praise individual initiative. The child, to our shame, has been left without a lunch and we are left with our so-called high principles. We voted down public housing to help resolve one of the most pitiful and shameful conditions anywhere in the country. We did that also on high principles, refusing all government aid. We gloried in private initiative. But we ourselves go on living in air-conditioned, luxurious apartments, some of which have piped-in champagne, while ten minutes away are shacks without indoor plumbing, to say nothing of heating or air conditioning.

What is crucial in all of this is the painful truth that we are not motivated by humanistic, religious, or even legal values of ethics. We have accepted the fourth category—the personal—the one which begins by asking "What is in it for me?" So we do not help the dependent child adequately, we do not feed the hungry child, and we do not care about slums, dropouts, second-class culture. These do not fit our self-interest code of values. One of the leading psychologists in America, in a personal letter, writes, "There are, undoubtedly, places that are worse than Dallas. But then, Dallas was our hope in Texas—the only place where we saw the beginning of a development of some culture." Was this, we are asking ourselves, only a front for the fourth category of values?

What should Dallas do now? For its psychological

well-being it ought to accept blame and responsibility for its behavior and act upon that now. It is getting later all the time. Its moral climate needs some lifting up so that it can rise above the fourth level of values which determines all things by "What is there in it for me?"

Church and synagogue are charged with the responsibility of making their people aware of a "sense of values" that comes from a heart fed with truth—a heart that has reached out and touched another heart.

In this city perhaps the time has come to paraphrase the late President—"Ask not what Dallas can do for me, but what I can do for Dallas."

From: FIRST METHODIST CHURCH
HOUSTON, TEXAS

Sermon preached by the Reverend Dr. Charles L. Allen

Because it was in his heart. I Kings 8:18

In a telegram to Mrs. John F. Kennedy, General Douglas MacArthur said, "His death kills something in me." He was expressing what the overwhelming majority of Americans felt when we heard the tragic news of the death of our President. When that news came, many emotions swept over us—disbelief—shock—outrage—indignation—shame—uncertainty—but most of all, sorrow.

We first thought of his own family—his wife and his two children, Caroline and John. We thought of his brothers and his sisters and how they loved each other. We thought of his father and his mother. Theirs was a son in whom they had been well pleased. We thought of the sorrow that his father and mother had borne—two sons and a daughter to die. Another daughter who will never be well.

Thinking of the Kennedy family, one is reminded that no family is protected from sorrow. In spite of wealth—fame—position, sorrow came to their home. It comes to every family. Much of the life of a minister is spent ministering to the sorrowing. What is the explanation? Time and again there just is not any explanation.

After the funeral service for a young girl, her mother said to me, "How long will it take me to get over this?" I asked her, "Do you want to get over it?" She thought for a time and then replied simply, "No." One never gets over a sorrow. Sorrows become precious possessions of our hearts and lives.

In the shock of this news, a second thought came to mind. We were made to realize the uncertainty of life. One is reminded that we can never be sure what may happen. The very night before it happened, I had the privilege of sitting with President Kennedy at dinner. He was young—healthy—in good spirits. His handclasp was firm, his voice was clear, his words were confident. As we sat together I thought of his future. Even after serving the constitutional limit as President, he would still only be in the middle age of life. No man on earth had greater prestige and power than did he; he had a brilliant mind, great wealth. Then suddenly the very next morning—only as long as it takes a bullet to travel a hundred yards—he was gone from this life. The fact is pressed upon us: There is no assurance of tomorrow. We can only live each day as it is given us.

A third thought pressed upon some of us. He did live

a long life, after all. At first there was deep disappointment that so young a man had to die. Then we realized that life is not measured by years. As I contemplated the death of Mr. Kennedy, there came to my mind a young man I had known during World War II. At the age of twenty-two he was a captain in the United States Army. During a very heavy battle, the men under him were ordered to take a certain hill. He got out in front and led his men toward the top of that hill. About halfway up a bullet hit him and he was killed. They sent his body back home for burial. At the cemetery when we had concluded the service, his mother and I stood by the side of his grave talking about him. She was expressing her disappointment over the fact he did not have a chance to live his life. A thought occurred to me which I expressed to this dear mother: During just the thirty minutes he was going up that hill, he lived more than some people live in seventy years. Indeed, it seems that some people never really live.

Think of Methuselah, who lived for 969 years. Jesus Christ lived thirty-three years. Yet as you compare the lives of those two, you would conclude that Jesus Christ lived far the longest. In fact, as far as the record goes, Methuselah merely passed the years. President Kennedy truly lived. He lived as a defender of his country in time of war—as a statesman—as a good man—as a faithful servant of God. He was President of his country for a thousand days and he will be remembered as long as there is a United States. No man can ever say John Kennedy did not live.

Who pulled the trigger of that high-powered rifle? Was it just the finger of one man? In a sense, yes, because every man is responsible for his own actions. In a larger sense, the trigger of that gun was pulled by a spirit of hate and destruction. Though only one man aimed the gun and fired the bullet, many have shared some of the wrong thoughts which were in his mind.

President Kennedy's death shows us what a horrible thing it is to hate. In recent years our beloved land has been blighted by a lack of love in the hearts of people toward each other. Some of the loudest voices in America are the merchants of hate. The highest office our people can bestow deserves more respect than some have given it. Many of our people have gone too far in their criticisms of those who hold public office. Now is a time to cancel our own wrong feelings.

The assassin's wife is a Russian girl. She has not been in our country very long. She has two children, I believe. Doubtless she is without funds, very frightened and bewildered. I think it would be an act of Christian love to send her a gift of money to help her. If you would like to share in this, put something on the altar as you leave the church or send it to me in the mail.*

During these past two days, we not only have felt sorrow—realized the uncertainty of life—thought of how that life is measured by quality instead of quantity—and realize what an ugly thing is hate. We also realized that life must go on. The familiar words come to mind—"God buries his workmen, but he carries on his work." At this time we do pray for President Lyndon B. Johnson. We are thankful for the training and experience he has had which will help him at this time. For many years he has demonstrated his abilities in the affairs of government. He is now our President. We pray for him.

Just three weeks ago Mr. Johnson was interviewed for television by Mr. Ray Miller of Houston. During that

* This offering at First Methodist Church in Houston amounted to $2500.

interview he made this wonderful statement: "I am not afraid and I am not one who hates." We are glad to hear it from Mr. Johnson's lips.

Finally, we are reminded of the experience of David. God said to David, "Whereas it was in thine heart to build a house unto My name, thou didst well that it was in thine heart" (I Kings 8 : 18). David wanted to build the greatest temple the world had ever seen. He planned for it. He selected a site. He purchased many of the materials. This was to be his crowning achievement. He never saw his temple built. He died and his son Solomon built the temple.

In God's sight, however, David did build the temple. The world measures by results—God measures by the heart. I do not believe I misjudge President Kennedy when I say there were two temples in his heart to which he had dedicated himself to the building on this earth. One of those was peace throughout the whole world. The other temple was the dignity of all men.

Let us remember that physical bodies can be killed, but great ideas and ideals never die. One thinks of Abraham Lincoln, who was killed a hundred years ago. One thinks of Jesus Christ, who was killed two thousand years ago. One thinks of John F. Kennedy, who was killed two days ago.

From: UNIVERSITY OF HOUSTON
HOUSTON, TEXAS

Address delivered by Dr. Winfred E. Garrison *

November 26, 1963

The first response to such an event as this is one of sorrow and sympathy, mingled with indignation toward the perpetrator of the crime. It is profoundly shocking that a President of the United States should be the victim of an irresponsible assassin. Sorrow at the country's loss of its President and sympathy with those who had the closest personal ties with the man John F. Kennedy take precedence over all other emotions.

There is a special poignancy about the untimely death of such a man because of the appealing quality of his personality. His co-partisans felt it and loved him for it. His political opponents felt it too, and sometimes resented it, but could scarcely avoid admiring it and wishing they had it on their side, and even secretly loving him for it.

Part of it was that he was a scholar and a gentleman. Part of it was his youth, which was, in fact, more apparent than real. Many a man in his mid-forties gives the impression of being in middle age, as indeed he is. John

* Dr. Winfred Garrison, professor emeritus of philosophy, University of Houston, was ninety years old October 1, 1964. This was his second memorial address for an assassinated President. He delivered one after the death of President McKinley in 1901 at the Central Christian Church in Saint Louis, Missouri.

Kennedy radiated youth. After fourteen years in the United States Congress, one is no adolescent.

He was a seasoned politician and a statesman of experience and finesse. Yet the glow of youth was on him. The young could feel that he was their contemporary, and those who were older fell easily under the charm that always emanates from a young hero. A young prince has often commanded more affection than an old king.

That such a one should be cut off with so much of life ahead of him seems doubly tragic. "Oh, the deep damnation of his taking off." Yet one must realize how fully he lived while he lived. In his short life he had lived more abundantly and more rewardingly than most men do in twice the time.

A mood of national sorrow at such a time as this is fitting and inevitable. It is also appropriate from time to time to call the nation to penitence for the shortcomings of our society. These two are not necessarily related. I do not see in the sad event that now fills our minds any ground for national humiliation. If our society were perfect and if all the people in it were perfect there would be no crimes. That is a distant goal toward which we press, as the sailor may steer toward a star without expecting to reach it. But we cannot honestly claim to be penitent because we have not attained perfection.

A dastardly deed like that we are now mourning does not prove that our society is decadent. It proves that within our society there are some irresponsible persons who are not fit to enjoy the liberties we prize, and that we have not yet learned how to transform them into good citizens or how to identify and isolate them before they do the damage of which they are capable. There are many things we need to learn, but one man's catastrophic crime does not prove that our society is basically unsound.

The possibility of such a crime is part of the price society pays for a concentration of political importance in the person of one trusted and able leader and a concentration of potentially destructive power in such a small package that one man can use it recklessly.

The first of these, strong leadership, furnishes the shining mark, but is essential to an ordered society. The second, power so harnessed that one man can direct it, furnishes the weapon, but is essential to an economy above the primitive stage. It takes only one finger to press an electric button and activate an explosion for a constructive or destructive purpose. It takes only one finger to pull the trigger of a high-powered rifle. *Security* measures can only approximate security. There remains a fatal margin of possibility.

That possibility of a murderous attack upon our political chief, in spite of all reasonable precautions, is also the price we pay for the free and democratic way of life which we rightly prize. We do not want our President to be so isolated from the people that no one can come within shooting distance of him. We want him in some fashion to mingle with the people, to let them see him face to face, even to shake hands with as many as possible. Perhaps we shall have to learn to accept some restrictions upon these practices, and also upon the freedom with which anyone can buy high-powered weapons capable of inflicting death at long distance.

What must we do in such a time of sorrow and stress? Three things: First, we must feel it, deeply and poignantly, and feel it sympathetically with those who suffer most. Otherwise we are less than human, for emotional sensitivity is an essenial part of our humanity.

Second, we must take it, with fortitude and stamina, without letting sorrow prevail over courage and stability. Otherwise we do not mature. Of such fortitude we have lately had an inspiring example where weakening would have been most forgivable.

Third, we must go on, undismayed and unafraid, with renewed commitment to our country's cause and unshaken faith in its future. Otherwise we are not being worthy of our heritage or playing our part in the great drama of life, which has its tragic elements but is not all tragedy.

If winter comes, can spring be far behind?

From: THE ARCHDIOCESAN TELEVISION CENTER, BOSTON, MASSACHUSETTS

Eulogy delivered by His Eminence Richard Cardinal Cushing

In the name of the Father and of the Son and of the Holy Ghost. AMEN.

My dearly beloved, friends in Christ, and guests:

A shocked and stricken world stands helpless before the fact of death, that death brought to us through a tragically successful assault upon the life of the President of the United States.

Our earliest disbelief has slowly given way to unprecedented sorrow as millions all over the earth join us in lamenting a silence that can never again be broken and the absence of a smile that can never again be seen.

For those of us who knew the President as friend as well as statesman, words mock our attempts to express the anguish of our hearts.

It was my privilege to have been associated with John

F. Kennedy from the earliest days of his public life, and even prior to that time, my privilege to have watched him mature with ever-expanding responsibility, to have known some of the warmth of his hearty friendship, to see tested under pain and loss the steely strength of his character.

I have been with him in joy and in sorrow, in decision and in crisis, among friends and with strangers, and I know of no one who has combined in more noble perfection the qualities of greatness that marked his cool, calculating intelligence and his big, brave, bountiful heart.

Now all of a sudden he has been taken from us and I daresay we shall never see his like again.

Many there are who will appropriately pay tribute to the President as a world figure, a tribute due him for his skill in political life and his devotion to public service.

Many others will measure the wide interests of his mind, the swiftness of his resolution, the power of his persuasion, the efficiency of his action, and the courage of his conviction.

For me, however, it is more fitting and proper to recall him during these days of mourning as husband and father, surrounded by his young and beloved family.

Although the demands of his exalted position carried him often on long journeys and filled even his days at home with endless labors, how often he would make time to share with his little son and sweet daughter whatever time would be his own.

What a precious treasure it is now and will be forever in the memories of two fatherless children! Who among us can forget those childish ways which from time to time enhanced the elegance of the Executive Mansion with the touching scenes of a happy family life?

Charming Caroline stealing the publicity, jovial

John-John on all fours ascending the stairs of an airplane to greet his daddy, and a loving mother like all mothers joyfully watching the two children of her flesh and blood, mindful always of three others in the nurseries of the Kingdom of Heaven.

At the side of the President in understanding devotion and affection behold his gracious and beautiful Jacqueline. True always to the obligations of her role as mother, she has been given new dimensions to the trying demands of being America's First Lady.

The pride in her husband which he so eminently justified was plainly reciprocated in his pride of her. The bonds of love that made them one in marriage became like hoops of steel binding them together.

From wherever men may look out from eternity to see the workings of our world, Jack Kennedy must beam with new pride in that valiant woman who shared his life, especially to the moment of its early and bitter end.

It will never be forgotten by her, for her clothes are now stained with the blood of her assassinated husband.

These days of sorrow must be difficult for her—more difficult than for any others. A Divine Providence has blessed her as few such women in history by allowing her hero husband to have the dying comfort of her arms.

When men speak of this sad hour in times to come, they will ever recall how well her frail beauty matched in courage the stalwart warrior who was her husband. We who had so many reasons for holding her person in a most profound respect must now find an even wider claim for the nobility of her spirit.

One cannot think, my dearly beloved, especially one such as myself, of the late President without thinking also of the legacy of public service which was bequeathed to him by his name and his family.

For several generations in a variety of tasks, this republic on one level or another has been enriched by the blood that was so wantonly shed on Friday last. Jack Kennedy fulfilled in the highest office available to him the long dedication of his family.

It is a consolation for us all to know that his tragic death does not spell the end of this public service, but commits to new responsibilities the energies and the abilities of one of the truly great families of America.

What comfort can I extend to their heavy hearts today—mother, father, sisters, brothers—what beyond the knowledge that they have given history a youthful Lincoln, who in his time and in his sacrifice had made more sturdy the hope of this nation and its people.

The late President was even in death a young man—and he was proud of his youth. We can never forget the words with which he began his short term as President of the United States:

Let the word go forth from this time and place, to friend and foe alike, that the torch has been passed to a new generation of Americans—born in this century, tempered by war, disciplined by a hard and bitter peace, proud of our ancient heritage....

No words could describe better the man himself who spoke, one whose youth supplied an almost boundless energy, despite illness and physical handicap, whose record in war touched heroic proportions, whose service in Congress was positive and progressive.

It was against this personal background that he continued by saying:

Let every nation know ... that we shall pay any price, bear any burden, meet any hardship, support any friend, oppose any foe to assure the survival and success of liberty. This much we pledge and more.

All that the young President promised in these words he delivered before his assassination. He has written in unforgettable language his own epitaph.

Two days ago he was the leader of the free world, full of youth, vigor, and promise; his was a role of action, full of conflict, excitement, pressure, and change; his was a fully human life, one in which he lived, felt dawn, saw sunset glow, loved and was loved.

Now in the inscrutable ways of God, he has been summoned to an eternal life beyond all striving, where everywhere is peace.

All of us who knew personally and loved Jack Kennedy—his youth, his drive, his ideals, his heart, generosity and his hopes—mourn now more for ourselves and each other than for him.

We will miss him; he only waits for us in another place. He speaks to us today from there in the words of Paul to Timothy:

"As for me, my blood has already flown in sacrifice. I have fought the good fight; I redeemed the pledge; I look forward to the prize that awaits me, the prize I have earned. The Lord whose award never goes amiss will grant it to me—to me, yes, and to all those who have learned to welcome His coming."

John F. Kennedy, thirty-fifth President of the United States of America, has fought the good fight for the God-given rights of his fellow man and for a world where peace and freedom shall prevail.

He has finished the race at home and in foreign lands, alerting all men to the dangers and the hopes of the future, pledging aid in every form to those who attempted to misinterpret his words, to misunderstand his country, to become discouraged and to abandon themselves to false prophets.

He has fulfilled unto death a privilege he made on the

day of his inauguration—a privilege in the form of a pledge: I shall not shrink from my responsibilities.

Far more would he have accomplished for America and the world if it were not for the assassination here in the land that he loved and for which he dedicated and gave his life.

May his noble soul rest in peace. May his memory be perpetuated in our hearts as a symbol of love for God, country, and all mankind, the foundation upon which a new world must be built if our civilization is to survive.

Eternal peace grant unto him, O Lord, and let perpetual light shine upon him.

In the name of the Father and the Son
and the Holy Ghost. AMEN.

From: HARVARD DIVINITY SCHOOL
CAMBRIDGE, MASSACHUSETTS

Prayer by the Reverend Dr. Samuel H. Miller, Dean

November 23, 1963

Eternal God our Father, through this hour run the ageless mysteries of mortal life, love and death and tears, turning our hearts toward thy mercy.

Our tongues are stunned by a violence we cannot believe; our prayers stumble in the darkness of our shame; we see through a glass darkly, while the shadows shift and fade into the long, long tragedy of hate and fear that seemingly never ends. For him who gave answer to this bewildering world's need with his life, without reservation or restraint, we bow our hearts in silence, knowing no word to speak our debt. Our hearts stand on holy ground and the unutterable burden of their sorrow will be seen of thee, O God our Father and Lord.

Lay thy hands upon our eyes, O God, and make plain the labor of thy servant, John Kennedy. Thou whose hands now hold his soul in peace, keep us in mind of the burdens he gladly and bravely bore; his passion of concern for his beloved country, his swift courage and firm conviction in trying times; his patient but moving pressure for justice and dignity of all men; his earnest effort to enhance democracy with a high concern for intelligence and art; the cost he paid for bearing the guilt of us all; and the sacrifice of life itself in the longest of all wars—the everlasting struggle to keep the world a home for humanity.

In thine infinite mercy, O God, let thy holy love attend his young family, of mother and little children, that in the midst of sorrow they may find a peace that passes all understanding, a peace deeper than terror, stronger than night, more abiding than fame.

For the new President, upon whose shoulders must fall the ponderous burdens of a far-flung government, we pray the sustaining presence of thy holy spirit and divine wisdom. Steady him to walk wisely in the vast web of international complications, that peace may be increased; gird him with unusual insight that justice purchased by pain and heartbreak may at last prevail in our own land; give him an access of power to grasp the duties and dangers of his office; and in all things keep him in thy strong care.

For ourselves and the people of our country, O God, we pray earnestly and with fervent longing. Steady us in this turbulent sea of noisy voices to keep our poise and to think sanely; strengthen us with an awakened judgment lest this death be lost in a welter of aimless sentiment and maudlin curiosity; move our conscience with a new boldness and clarity lest we fall back into a safe cowardice and a prudent timidity; awaken the minds and hearts of us all to the painful cost of freedom and of faith in a world of terror and force.

Dedicate us, both in spirit and in act, to live beyond the limit of our ease; that we may once again redeem the destiny of this nation and its high dreams from petty bickering and primitive prejudice.

Unite us, O God, by thine own spirit that we may lay our lives again in high resolve upon the altar of a noble purpose that we may be a people under God, a blessing to the nations and to humanity of which we are a part.

"Fix thou our steps, O Lord, that we stagger not at the uneven motions of the world, but go steadily on our way, neither censuring our journey by the weather we meet, nor turning aside from anything that may befall us." AMEN.

From: SOUTH CONGREGATIONAL CHURCH
SPRINGFIELD, MASSACHUSETTS

Sermon preached by the Reverend Dr. Frederick Field Driftmier

---

Today we mourn the loss of a great American.

John F. Kennedy was a man with a mission to perform.

It was his destiny as the President of the United States to lead the free world in some of its greatest efforts for peace, and with his allegiance to high ideals of human decency he set new milestones of progress for the cause of human freedom.

Whether or not one always agreed with him politically, all people of good will respected him for two outstanding qualities. His life was a profile of courage. In war and in peace he placed others before self. Never one to permit his wealth to protect him from the hard things of life, he dared to do what many men feared, and he died as he lived, true to his ideals of vigorous manhood.

Whether or not one shared his church background, all God-loving people respected his religious convictions. His life was a profile of faith. His was not a religion of superpatriotism or a religion of nationalism; it was the humble faith of a man who learned to love his God and his church at his mother's knees. His was the faith of a man who trusted God to direct the path of his destiny, and all of us had more confidence in him because of that trust.

Many years ago Ralph Waldo Emerson wrote a poem entitled "A Nation's Strength." There are three verses of that poem most suitable for us to hear right now:

What makes a nation's pillars high
And its foundation strong?
What makes it mighty to defy
The foes that round it throng?

Not gold, but only men can make
A people great and strong;
Men who for truth and honor's sake
Stand fast and suffer long.

Brave men who work while others sleep,
Who dare while others fly—
They build a nation's pillars deep
And lift them to the sky.

Shortly after the first news of the President's death on Friday afternoon, I received a phone call from a tearful lady who asked: "What can we find in the Bible that will tell our nation what to do now? Where can I find God's help for this crisis?" At the time I was so stunned by the news that I could not think of an answer, but since Friday afternoon I have thought of several things I could have said to her, and I hope she is here this morning.

Actually, there is nothing in our religion that provides us with a rule or a law that is applicable to all the crises of life that arise out of situations of tragic death. The genius of our faith is that we are guided by a spirit much more than we are guided by any printed word, secular or religious. We depend for our strength and for our guidance on that which St. Paul called "the spirit of life in Christ."

In the present crisis, or in any of many other crises of life, we as Christian individuals and we as a nation need to remember three things.

In the first place, we need to remember that it is our faith—given to us by Jesus and handed down to us by the saints—that God will never let His children face any hour of life alone. Whatever the difficult situation that confronts us, it is the Christian faith that God is in the situation somewhere, however bad, however tragic the situation may be. In every crisis of life—our own or the nation's—God is there waiting for us to comprehend what it is that He wants us to do. Whatever tragic thing life makes us face, God is facing it with us. However troubled our future, we never walk alone. Our sorrow is God's sorrow, and our heartache is His heartache.

Down through centuries of time, the human race has confronted tragedy and sorrow in a variety of ways. Every age and every people has had some kind of a philosophy of life to guide it in time of suffering and loss, but no people and no age ever has had a philosophy more simple, more direct—and, we believe, more comforting—than the one given us by the Man of Galilee, whose spirit would lead us to write upon our hearts the lovely words of that old hymn: "Count your blessings; name them one by one. Count your blessings; see what God has done."

The second thing we should remember in time of crisis is the fact that God's help comes to those in whose hearts there is the spirit of Christ. I do not mean that His help is limited to Christians, for that is obviously not the case. What I do mean is that God's help comes to one whose heart and soul is what we of the Christian faith believe a person's heart and soul should be, by whatever name such heart and spirit may be called in another religion. There is no religion in the world that can provide a sacred book of divine instructions for the meeting of every crisis, but the followers of every religion can find their way to God's help through the same kind of patience, courage, and hope that blessed the heart of Jesus.

The testimony of the ages is that God's will never is made known to us through bitterness, nor through resentment, nor through cursings and ravings, but rather we learn His will through patience, courage, and hope. Millions of people could testify to the almost unbelievable peace that has come to their hearts when in faith they have trusted God to give them the wisdom they needed for some terrible hour of crisis.

When we remain calm, and when we refuse to lose our faith in God, we discover that avenues of action and highways of thought that never before seemed possible just have a way of opening up for us. When, in the darkest night of life, one can trust and reach out for the guiding hand of God, then one is able to say with the poet Ingersoll "In the night of death, hope sees a star, and listening love can hear the rustle of a wing."

The third factor to keep in mind in time of crisis is that there is something of God in us that no tragedy can destroy—something of God that makes us equal to every challenge and strong for every fight. At those points in life where mountains of sorrow stand squarely before us, too steep to climb yet demanding our ascent, we must remember God's power to make of us just what He wants.

The example that Mrs. John F. Kennedy set for us on Friday afternoon is evidence for the whole world to see and understand. In a magnificent way she has shown us that lurking in the unconscious depths of each human heart there are great hidden powers which begin to function when we are put under pressure. The people who make history, the people who manage to rise above everything that would pull them down, are those who, in the words of Dr. Fritz Kunkel, "consciously or unconsciously turn the switch on the inner switchboards of human character."

In a moment of crisis we see people like Mrs. Kennedy who manage to meet the very worst that life can bring with tremendous presence of mind because in the mind there is a power greater than one's own. We see such people and look in amazement as we observe how they stand up to tragedy and continue to do what is far more than could be expected of them. We see how they become in an hour of shattering disaster the strong nails that hold things together, and then we realize how with God's help we too could join their ranks.

We all need to understand that what God gave to Christ He gives to us all if only we have the faith to accept it. With faith we can sing with the Psalmist of old "Why art thou cast down, O my soul? And why art thou disquieted within me? Hope thou in God." AMEN.

From: THE MORMON TABERNACLE CHOIR
CBS BROADCAST
SALT LAKE CITY, UTAH

"The Spoken Word"
Richard L. Evans

With a sorrowing America, we join this day in mourning the passing of the President. John Fitzgerald Kennedy is mourned by unnumbered multitudes, not only here, but wherever there are knowing human hearts. In a short lifetime he realized an almost incredible accomplishment, and will be remembered unpredictably far into the future.

But our thoughts today are more for those who mourn him in the close relationship of life—his loved ones. The official loss does not make less their personal loss. May the peace and comfort and understanding of the Father of us all be with them in these anguished hours, and in all yet future difficult days—with faith in eternal continuance—faith in His eternal plan and purpose. "There is a future, O thank God!"—a future where our loved ones wait.

And now our fellow Americans, may we turn our thoughts a moment to some words from the past that have much meaning for the present: "It is a time . . . for searching of the conscience, for humility of spirit, for the heartfelt prayer of the whole people for light, for guidance, for strength, for sanity, for that passion for righteousness which consumes all pride, scorn, arrogance, and trust in the things that perish. . . . Therefore let the Nation search itself. . . . And thus let us plead and pray: Almighty God, who in former time leddest our fathers forth . . . give Thy grace . . . to us their children, that we may always . . . do Thy will. Bless our land with honorable industry, sound learning, and pure manners. Defend our liberties; preserve our unity. Save us from violence, discord, and confusion . . . and from every evil way."

From a century past we add to this these lines from Abraham Lincoln: "It behooves us then, to humble ourselves . . . and to pray for clemency and forgiveness. . . . All this being done in sincerity and truth . . . that the united cry of the nation will be heard on high. . . ."

Our Fathers' God, to thee,
Author of liberty,
To thee we sing.
Long may our land be bright
With freedom's holy light.
Protect us by thy might,
Great God, our King!

From: KAWAIAHAO CHURCH
HONOLULU, HAWAII

Sermon preached by the Reverend Abraham K. Akaka

Not only all of us in Hawaii, but the whole world is in tears of grief and mourning today. Much Aloha has already been expressed about our beloved President. Beautiful and moving tributes have been and are being made all over the world.

John Fitzgerald Kennedy gave his life not only for his country, but primarily and rightly for God and all mankind. If he were here now, I think he would say that the most important and significant time in his life has been the past two years, ten months, and twenty-two days of his Presidency. For in this period (as we know) he gave unsparingly of himself in the holy cause of world peace and national security.

I can see him now as he looked just a few months ago among us—graciously accepting your Aloha and mine. But through our tears we oftentimes see more clearly. His death makes more clear the fact that his service to God and country gave him his deepest joy, and that being engaged in a noble work that was bigger than himself was his deepest peace.

This is what comes through to us from his eloquent words and great deeds. And I cannot but thank God for the life of this great President—by whom all people, creative ideas, and the cause of Peace among the nations were combined in the finest purpose to which his life could be used.

Of course he gave his life for you and me and our country. But there is a deeper meaning to his life than that. What we should not miss is his own personal example and lesson to us: *His life had the dimension of eternity in it—the sense of the eternal!*

It is easy to lose heart in such a time as this. But John Fitzgerald Kennedy has set a great example to us of courage. He was no moral pessimist, and therefore no encourager of totalitarian regimes. People invite totalitarian regimes when they lose heart and enter into dark despair. Moral pessimism or failure personally to choose between good and evil encourages the idea that conflicting and competing interests can be harnessed only by absolute human authority. This sort of dark thought has crossed many minds today. But let us replace it with the thought that there is the law of God—built into your heart and mine and in the universe by our Creator.

Unless we remember God's moral law and obey it, we and our nation and world can find no happiness and peace. We must never join the ranks of those who break that law of God, built into your heart and mine and in the Universe by our Creator.

Unless we remember God's moral law and obey it, we and our nation and world can find no happiness and peace. We must never join the ranks of those who break that law. For by obedience to God comes integrity within ourselves, our nation, and the nations. By faithfulness to God comes the sense of respect for self and love for our neighbor that is the foundation of world peace.

Now with deepest Aloha we commit the life and soul of John Fitzgerald Kennedy unto Almighty God who gave him to us. May "angel choirs sing him safely to his rest"—to his place among all those who through the ages have been faithful to God.

And let us now face forward—taking the hand of God into the unknown future—knowing that by His hand the future of our nation and world is secure.

From: WESTMINSTER ABBEY*
LONDON, ENGLAND

Sermon preached by The Reverend Canon Edward F. Carpenter, Archdeacon of Westminster

---

For he looked for a city which hath foundations, whose builder and maker is God. Hebrews 11:10

There is a story, told I think of Edmund Burke, that he was fighting a violent election campaign in Bristol. In the heat of the battle, and indeed while he was addressing a public meeting, a man threaded his way through the noisy crowd and handed him a paper. It told him that his opponent had suddenly died. Burke tore up the fragmentary notes of his speech and there was silence. Turning to his audience he said quietly:

"Gentlemen, what shadows we are and what shadows we pursue."

But was Edmund Burke right? And do we meet in

* When 10:30 on Sunday morning arrived, more than 3000 people had assembled; they were standing all round the Abbey nave and overflowed into the cloisters. The American Ambassador and Mrs. Bruce and their son; the Prime Minister and Lady Douglas-Home; the Leader of Her Majesty's Opposition, Mr. Harold Wilson, and Mrs. Wilson, were present.

such a mood today? Is this the final assessment that we ought to make of our human affairs? Is the life of man but vanity and vexation, and he himself a passing shadow with no continuing stay? Christian faith affirms, calling upon an experience which reflects a providential order, that this is not so: that man's labor is not in vain: that he can build a city that has firm foundations.

No person—and in a measure we all felt that we knew him—could ever dare to say of President John Kennedy (to quote Shelley's words) that he was matched with phantoms and keeping an unprofitable strife. Even while we are still numbed with horror at the suddenness and manner of his passing, we yet recognize and salute in him a rounded and a whole man.

For myself, I must confess that I found his vital energy and sheer zest for living an exhilaration and a perpetual challenge. Its pace, tempo, and sparkle were all so delightfully American. His high intelligence, applied with almost clinical precision to social and political problems, his anxiety to surround himself with experts in every field—these have indeed brought a veritable breath of fresh air into areas of human life too often a sitting target for the stuffy, the amateur, and the inexpert. The White House, under the President and his gracious wife, became a center of cultivation as if the arts were an integral part of civilized living.

And then with intelligence, he had passion—a rare combination—and it is passion which moves the world, excites and galvanizes ordinary men into purposeful action. I think of him in his courageous stand for civil rights; in his conviction that the resources of modern technology could and must be used to feed the hungry—and millions today are still desperately hungry. I think of him in his deep concern to find a homeland for the refugee; to banish illiteracy; and to secure for every man, irrespective of race, creed, or color, the respect and the dignity which his common manhood rightly demands.

Yet in all this high endeavor, John Kennedy was no Utopian dreamer but a supremely contemporary figure, cut and trimmed to measure up to the requirements of our modern age. Uncontaminated by the cynicism all too common around us, he was not ashamed to challenge his own generation with a high and compelling idealism, affirming by so doing that if an ideal is noble and costly enough people will respond. It is the occupational disease of the politician to offer bread and circuses while men, waiting to be reborn, have a hunger beyond these commodities. John Kennedy's was the voice of the young in heart who never abandon the undying hope that the world's great age will return anew; and that the flux and change of history can be directed toward a kingdom.

But there are many, of course, who see visions and dream dreams. Many who glimpse a life for man more chaste, more ordered, more loving. Too often, alas, such men affect to despise the arts necessary to acquire power and prefer to live in their ivory towers, unspotted from the world and, as they say with nauseating self-righteousness, keeping their hands clean. We may be grateful that President Kennedy was not precious in this way. He was prepared at least to try to incarnate his vision, to make it concrete, to bring it down to earth. For this purpose he was not afraid or too scrupulous to seek power; to involve himself up to the neck in the resistant and confused life of men in society; to seek to channel the flow of history; to take, as we crudely say, a practical line.

He well knew the dangers inherent in such an involvement, for power can all too easily corrupt the man who wields it; and I suppose it is commonplace to say of President Kennedy that he had at his disposal more power than has been committed to any other human being in the lifespan of mankind. It would have been tragically easy, in the day-to-day judgments and consequential estimates which politics demand, to lose sight of the end in the often ambiguous means to it, to be preoccupied with the strategy rather than with the object of the exercise. But this did not happen, and it is a tribute to his greatness and essential humility that he did not give way to this most subtle and most insidious of all temptations. Thus, though no man was more astute, in some respects more tough, he yet worked, in season and out of season, for a United Nations which would become an effective instrument for establishing the peace of justice and the rule of law—while he never forgot the ultimate hope that justice would pass over into charity and equal rights into the brotherhood of man.

So the seeming impossible was brought about. John Kennedy, statesman par excellence, a man who saw in politics the art of the possible though lesser men set their sights far too low, John Kennedy became an image for free men, a symbol of hope, a rallying cry to the more timid, reminding them of what they might be and still may become. He thought of men highly and, by thinking this way, helped to make the vision come true.

And now he has gone in the full flood of his powers—a victim of that very violence and irrationality which he sought to curb and restrain. No one can deny that he has fired the imagination of men in a way that will not soon be forgotten; and we can safely leave it to posterity to pay tribute to this tremendous achievement. But it would be naïvely foolish not to recognize here in his untimely death a great tragedy, an expression of that contingency, that ambiguity in human affairs, which rebukes our pride, makes nonsense of our too-tidy systems, and reminds us once again that we see through a glass darkly. Surely Thou art a God that hidest Thyself! He died with his work incomplete and so much that he himself would have wished, and others expected him, to do, still waiting to be done.

How does Christian faith address itself to the mood of frustration which such somber reflections provoke?

The Christian, in spite of much mystery and the seeming obscurity which he sees around him, affirms that it is within time and in this workaday world that God is working His purpose out and moving men through grace to build His Kingdom—that Kingdom which is to be an order of fulfilled persons, in which man confronts man in deep respect for mutual integrity, and a broken humanity becomes one family, where there is neither Jew nor Gentile, Greek nor barbarian, bond nor free. In this respect, John Kennedy was abundantly right to take a high and vocational view of the science of politics and to see it as directing men toward the good life. To strive to build such a kingdom, to be passionately concerned about it, to live sacrificially to bring it to birth—this is never labor in vain. Even though the ideal of a world which is truly one may elude us, and violent men corrode it with their aggression and lust for power, still the thrust of the good man toward it is of infinite worth. Indeed, if the whole universe were to crumble into nothingness this very night, it would still have been good and noble that some men expended themselves in the pursuit of this goodness and that nobility.

But the Christian is not content to leave it here—that is, with the stoical dedication of the virtuous man to that which is most fair and lovely, praiseworthy though this devotion must always be. The Christian believes, and it is basic to his faith, that the city which men painfully build here and now, and the vision of which gives them light often in surrounding darkness, this city is rooted in the eternity of God. Though the movement toward it in time is often a travail of the spirit, the path to it rough and uneven, the cost in sacrifice high, yet all that men do in this cause is never lost but is sustained and cherished in the safe hands of God. These men, dedicated to a Kingdom, thrust a knife through the rib of time into eternity.

So it is within this double dimension, this seeming tension, that the Christian builder lives his life and seeks to incarnate his hope. The city which he fights for in time exists entire in the heavens, and it is the vision of this final reality, and the quickening experience of contemplating it here and now, which encourage and sustain him in his present labor. Even his agony God will use where dedication refines it. It is not therefore length of days which constitutes the measuring rod of human achievement, but the direction toward which a man moves, the loyalties that he cultivates. If the city that has the foundations is guarded by God, then we can, in sure confidence and undismayed, step out boldly toward it.

It was, I believe, such a deep Christian conviction—though he seldom spoke of it publicly—which gave to John Kennedy a perseverence, a realism which was hopeful and optimistic and a determination to build well. I think of him now as in that final Kingdom of persons over which God in His eternity reigns, and in which the human family is to find its home. At a time like this a Christian minister is bold to say "The souls of the righteous are in the Hand of God and there shall no torment touch them." We are right to conceive of him as still serving that Kingdom; and the respectful gratitude that we feel for a life so well lived will be measured by our own passionate and sacrificial self-giving to the same cause. The struggle is still on and must engage us.

For he looked for a city which hath foundations, whose builder and maker is God. Hebrews 11:10.

From: ST. PAUL'S
LONDON, ENGLAND

*Sermon * preached by the Most Reverend and Right Honorable Michael Ramsey, Archbishop of Canterbury*

December 1, 1963

A faithful Creator. (I Peter 4:19)

I speak to each one of you who is sharing in this service here in St. Paul's or in your home in this country or in America or anywhere in the world. Your heart at this time is in its sorrow nearer to the hearts of thousands all over the world than it can have been for a very long time. Why is this? It is because President Kennedy was one who touched something universal in the human heart. Thinking of him we all see so vividly what we admire in a human life, and what are the great causes we care about. The man: brave to the point of heroism as his actions in wartime showed, youthful beyond the

* Delivered in the presence of H.R.H. Prince Philip and other members of the Royal Family.

age when youthfulness always lasts, tenacious when there could be no compromise, infinitely patient when the human touch could win conciliation, and all the time with a lovely home and family around him. There was the man.

And the causes—how they too touch the mind and conscience as well as the heart: peace, freedom, the service of prosperous nations where there is poverty and hunger, the partnership of every race in civil rights.

There was the man, and there the causes: and in a moment of madness the man was done to death, and the causes lose a champion just coming to the prime of his powers. To what purpose is this waste? Men of faith, of every faith, and of none find that question piercing them like a knife.

"A faithful Creator." Here in God's presence we Christian people stammer out those words, *a faithful Creator, a faithful Creator*. We repeat the words not as hiding like ostriches from the sight of evil and sorrow. No, rather seeing evil and sorrow fully in the face we believe that a good Creator holds our little world in his hands, hands of infinite love and power. Evil there is, and evil destroys and divides; call it crime or call it madness, it does its worst. But without turning away from evil we see beyond it God's own answer to it in the Cross of Christ on Calvary and the Resurrection on Easter morning—for there it is apparent how God can turn suffering into a triumph of love and sacrifice, and how God shows the gate to an everlasting life before which the life we know is but a little prelude. Such is our Christian faith. It is a faith costly and glorious—costly, for it is no escapism, no hiding from facts, with sacrifice at its heart—glorious, because it sees man's destiny reaching beyond the miseries of the moment. And in the light of Calvary and Easter, just when our faith seemed to be shattered, we found the words returning: *a faithful Creator*. Yes, "a faithful Creator."

What then follows, for President Kennedy, for the world, for us? He is now committed into his own Creator's hands; surrounded and followed by the prayers of so many: no end, but rather a beginning as he goes nearer to the love, the wisdom, the beauty of the God he has always worshiped: "Let light perpetual shine upon him." And here on earth his service to the world, to humanity, is not ended. The shock of his loss brings home to you his example, his ideals, his character: in our loss we realize him with a new vividness, and this more vivid impact of him after tragedy is very real. The impact of his example will help and inspire men and women for time yet to come. So too the causes which he cared for so greatly will be served, must be served, with new determination. Peace was one. Freedom was another. Yet another was the cause of hungry peoples, a cause for which he pleaded not just because it was expedient but because it was right. And so too the cause of racial brotherhood. His leadership is no more. His example stays for us to follow.

A faithful Creator. In His good and loving hands is the man whom we mourn today. In His hands too is the world we live in, the causes we must serve. But it is in the heart and the conscience of each man and woman that the issue lies. For a faithful Creator made not just the world in a lump but every one of us His human creatures, each of us with a mind to know Him, a heart to love Him, a will to serve Him. "I come from God, I belong to God, I go to God." That is the reason, the meaning of each of us.

There is an old English prayer the words of which tell of what a Christian will at this moment want to say, and as I read it you will find it to be your own.

Thanks be to thee, O Lord Jesus Christ, for all the benefits thou hast won for me, for all the pain and insults thou hast borne for me. O merciful redeemer, friend and brother, may I know thee more clearly, love thee more dearly, and follow thee more nearly.

From: CHRIST CHURCH CATHEDRAL
OXFORD, ENGLAND

Sermon preached by the Right Reverend Stephen F. Bayne, Jr.

I want to say, first of all, what I am sure everyone feels about Mr. Kennedy's assassination. Our hearts are filled with sorrow for Mrs. Kennedy and the children and his family, and we pray for God's deepest love for them. And we pray for President Johnson and his family and colleagues, laden with this immense burden with such terrible suddenness.

I would add my prayers for my own American people, in the grip of the most shocking thing that can happen in a nation's life. Assassination is the ultimate violation of every human grace and truth. Respect, dignity, reason—all these fall to the ground, and nothing is left but the blind power to destroy. It is the final darkness of the human spirit.

Assassination breeds division and violence. Suddenly every man looks at his neighbor with suspicion and terror. Suddenly no one believes in common manhood; no one obeys it; there is nothing left on which trust can be built.

Assassination is born of division and violence. When men can no longer endure the strain of division, violence is, for many, the only remaining way for fury to speak. In the bitterness of the divided American society, the impulse to violence is strong and there are many who share the responsibility for it. Indeed there are not many innocent ones.

Because these things are so, it is true to see this assassination as a kind of martyrdom—the cost of a witness to justice and reason in a tumultuous society where these things are not always held sacred. What is more important, this martyrdom is part of the price we now pay for the sins of men long dead. Abraham Lincoln said, hardly a month before his own assassination: "Fondly do we hope, fervently do we pray, that this mighty scourge of war may speedily pass away. Yet, if God wills that it continue until all the wealth piled by the bondsman's two hundred and fifty years of unrequited toil shall be sunk, and until every drop of blood drawn with the lash shall be paid by another drawn with the sword, as was said three thousand years ago, so still it must be said, 'The judgments of the Lord are true, and righteous altogether.'

"With malice toward none, with charity for all, with firmness in the right as God gives us to see the right, let us strive on to finish the work we are in . . . to do all which may achieve and cherish a just and lasting peace among ourselves and with all the nations."

This is a prayer for America at this time. Behind it lies one of the deepest insights of man into his own nature, that he is inescapably part of the whole of mankind, that he is what his brother is, that there is no escape from the one history in which everyone and every generation shares. Man's inhumanity to man in one time leads straight to another inhumanity at another time. We bear the cost of others' sins. There is one humanity from which we cannot free ourselves. We can only accept it, and bear our witness within it. So Mr. Kennedy believed and lived and died.

So with absolute finality Jesus believed and lived and died and rose again. Indeed this is the entire secret of the Church, which is His Body, and which is thereby the body of our humanity seen from the other side. We are caught and held together in the net of our sins. But this lamentable unity is also, on the far side of the Cross, a glorious unity of healed and completed humanity, of which the Church is the statement.

From: WESTMINSTER ABBEY
LONDON, ENGLAND

The Commemoration of the Departed spoken by The Very Reverend Eric Symes Abbott, M. A., D.D. (1959)

Evensong

I bid you to remember before
Almighty God
John Fitzgerald Kennedy
by sudden death taken from his family, from his fellow countrymen and from the whole world of men and nations, taken from us in the
fullness of his fame.

For that fame we thank God
the giver of all good gifts,
recalling with gratitude
the greatness of his statesmanship,
the firmness but patience of his diplomacy,
the courage he showed as each new trial of strength was presented to him,
his wielding of political power with personal sincerity,
his zeal for peace,
his care for the poorer nations,
his stand on civil rights,
his vision and wisdom,
his faith in God.

And from our hearts we are not afraid to say what our hearts have told us, that in him greatness was combined with humanity, and that we are mourning not only the President of the most powerful nation in the world, but the man of forty-six, boyish in looks, young in heart, eager and vigorous in spirit, the fine flower of the post-war generation who spoke to youth, the devoted husband, the loving father of two small children, serene in the turmoil of public affairs in the happiness of his family life.

Therefore

with a great multitude of men of good will in every part of the world we join in commending into the hands of God, as into the hands of a faithful Creator and most merciful Saviour

John Fitzgerald Kennedy.

Rest eternal grant unto him, O Lord, and let light perpetual shine upon him.

Let silence now be kept for a space while we hold him in our minds and hearts before the God and Father of us all.

The souls of the righteous are in the hands of God.

We pray for Mrs. Kennedy and the children and for their family.

Almighty God, Father of all mercies and giver of all comfort; deal graciously, we pray thee, with those who mourn, that casting every care on thee, they may know the consolation of thy love: through Jesus Christ our Lord. AMEN.

Finally,
let us hear the words of the Apostle Paul:

Therefore, my beloved brethren, be ye stedfast, unmoveable, always abounding in the work of the Lord, forasmuch as ye know that your labor is not in vain in the Lord. I Corinthians 15:58.

May the souls of the faithful,
through the mercy of God,
rest in peace. AMEN.

From: BIRMINGHAM CATHEDRAL
BIRMINGHAM, ENGLAND

Sermon preached by the Right Reverend John Leonard Wilson

November 27, 1963

I have the privilege of speaking this morning on behalf of the people of the Diocese of Birmingham, which includes so many other boroughs of this great industrial Midlands, and whose representatives are here to share this tribute to John Fitzgerald Kennedy and to express their sympathies to the peoples of the United States through their representative the American Consul here.

My first word must be one of sympathy for Mrs. Kennedy in her great sorrow, combined with sincere gratitude for her shining example of noble dignity in her grief and her bereavement. In the days and years ahead we will continue to remember her.

And let us not underestimate the inarticulate grief of little children, especially those who loved their father so much.

And we extend our sympathy to the government and peoples of the United States who are shocked and bewildered by the violent and sudden death of an honored leader greatly beloved. There are those of us who would wish to give a special word of consolation to those Americans who in this country or elsewhere are absent from their mother country on this occasion of her great sorrow. One can understand how much they long to be with their friends in their own country at such a time as this.

A true appraisal of their great and generous-hearted President must await some later occasion, but we pay our tribute to him for his fearless leadership in the West in the realm of peace, justice, and freedom, which has touched the hearts of all humanity—of friend and foe alike.

John Kennedy was the supreme example of a realist combined with a practical idealist. He had already shown in the years which had tested him a statesmanship beyond his years, and many people all over the world were looking to him for even greater statesmanship. Why then was his work cut short?

I cannot answer this question wholly; I can only suggest one or two lines of thought.

Christ lived for thirty-three years at the most, possibly less. Can anyone say that the life of Jesus was a complete waste of time? So it is with all heroes who have taken their lives in their hands. They reached positions of importance where they suffered greater dangers than other people, and they deliberately took that risk in order to serve their country and humanity.

Instead of a long life they have been given a place in the splendor of history which will thrill other generations to the end of time. They are the glorious tradition that will always be handed down, and to keep this will be the chief ambition of the Western world, and probably in time of the whole world. They are part of the tale that will be told to each new generation of young people, and these new hearts will catch fire, and these new eyes will light up, as they come to see how brave and chivalrous a life can be and how valorously it can be used. They are part of those immortal dead who live again.

In minds made better by their presence live
in pulses stirred to generosity,
In deeds of daring rectitude, in scorn
For miserable alms that end with self.

My firm unshakeable belief is that they live on as individual personalities. But however controversial that idea may be, none can deny that they live in our memories and in the most hallowed tradition of humanity. There is no sense then to talk about a waste! To what Jesus called the greatest they attained: "Greater love hath no man than this, that a man lay down his life for his friends."

The only real, the only fitting remembrance is that we should go and do likewise. We may not have the gift of wisdom, but we can offer ourselves for the service of mankind—in our thought, in our home life, in our business, in our politics, and in our handling of social problems. We can use and hand on the blazing torch that they in falling threw to us.

It is for us, the living, to dedicate ourselves to the unfinished work that John Fitzgerald Kennedy has thus far so nobly advanced.

The soul of this great and righteous man is in the hands of God, in whom he believed and whom he served on earth. He serves still in the Eternal Kingdom, and he serves on earth still, by the example he has left.

From: BRISTOL CATHEDRAL
BRISTOL, ENGLAND

Sermon preached by the Right Reverend Dr. Oliver S. Tomkins

November 25, 1963

We are gathered here because this is one of those moments when believing people can only turn to God in the face of the mystery of evil. The death of John Kennedy is one of those senseless tragedies which mock belief in a rational world. No words are adequate to the stunned grief which has hit the world. Yet I must try to say some words in the face of this tragedy, which is at the same time personal, national, and international.

Our first thoughts as men and women naturally turn to that lovely young widow. We echo her incredulous and horrified "Oh no!" The sympathy of all mankind has gone out to her and her two small children in the shattering of a home life which had so triumphantly survived the strains of high office. Part of the appeal of John Kennedy was that, like our own Royal Family, there we saw one, carrying an unbearable weight of public responsibility, happy in the simplicities of his home. Our thoughts turn too to the numbed and bewildered American people and to the man who suddenly must shoulder a weight greater than any human being should be asked to bear. Because, in our divided world, such immense responsibility lies upon the American nation and upon its President, the whole world mourns, spontaneously and sincerely, united for a moment in a simple grief.

And now, as the shock is slowly absorbed, our resolution must be to dedicate ourselves afresh to the goals for which John Kennedy lived and died. He was a young man but an amazingly mature one. Three things at least stand out in my mind as part of what he stood for and as part, therefore, of the memorial which we would raise to him.

First, he showed a singular gift for putting the good of the whole above the parts. He died in that southern part of the subcontinent of which he was the leader, in which he was struggling to get his conception of the civil rights of all men fully recognized throughout the whole of the U.S. He had to contend, as every politician must, with the balancing of one set of interests within the community against another; for politics is at all times the art of the possible. But throughout the labyrinth of American domestic politics he kept steadily before him the good of the community as a whole. We can only hope and pray that the very circumstances of his death will not now be exploited by one section of the community against the rest. We can all of us take courage and fresh inspiration from his example as we see how readily he gave himself to the uttermost in putting the good of the whole above the parts. In him the difficult and dangerous art of politics had been lifted to a level above mere partisanship; and that is an example which every country in the world can gladly accept as part of the memory he leaves behind.

Secondly, he showed a respect for facts as the servants of vision. We live in an intensely complicated world in which the hardest responsibility of those who care for the life of the community as a whole is to reconcile their dreams with the harsh facts of existence. John Kennedy did not for one moment despise the necessity for becoming acquainted with the complexity of modern life. And yet he never allowed the details to obscure the vision. He worked hard, prodigiously hard. But through it all there shone that kind of vitality and spontaneity which a man can only keep alive through all the hard grind of life if he is sustained by the vision of something great that lies beyond the small things.

Thirdly, he was a man of the present moment. There was something so refreshing about his youth, far the youngest of the responsible statesmen in the international scene; he was one who saw that the present gets its significance from being the basis of the future. He had a fine sense of history and of the destiny which history had thrust upon his own people. But he always saw the present moment as the moment in which the future is being built. It is natural that a sense of weariness should descend upon us all as we realize that that vital and forward-looking figure is no longer exercising the tremendous power which he held. We in this country face our problems, too, created by history which has brought us to the present moment. Let us hope that the memory of John Kennedy will strengthen us all in our readiness to see the present moment as the basis of the future, able to live vividly in the present because we are inspired by its possibilities.

These are some of the characteristics which made him a great leader and a great politician. But beneath them is the greater fact that he was first of all a true man. And he was a true man because he had a living faith in God. We share sympathetically the grief of those who belong to the great Christian communion of which he was a member. We share too with the Roman Catholic Church that fundamental faith in the God who is made known in Jesus Christ. As Christians we know that this world can be a hard and cruel place. When God Himself became a man in our world, He was murdered. But we know too that was not the end of the story. We too follow One who said, "In the world you shall have tribulation. But be of good cheer; I have overcome the world."

Christian faith, however strong, staggers under the senseless cruelty of such a happening. But we know that that is not the end. We know that to be given to love and compassion and justice is to be given to something stronger than the tragic and the cruel and the senseless. We meet here in God's house to offer Him our grief. We meet also to give thanks to God for a great and good man, who by his own faith strengthens ours. By the mercy of the Crucified and risen Christ, this sudden death, which remains a grim outrage, may yet be turned to God's glory if here and in his own country, and throughout the world, the faithfulness of John Kennedy kindles fresh faith. John Kennedy lived to serve justice and peace. Let us pray and resolve that they may be served also by his death.

From: WHICHFORD CHURCH*
WHICHFORD, ENGLAND

Sermon preached by the Reverend E. J. Rainsberry

I returned, and saw under the sun, that the race is not to the swift, nor the battle to the strong, neither yet bread to the wise, nor yet riches to men of understanding, nor yet favor to men of skill; but time and chance happeneth to them all. For man also knoweth not his time: as the fishes that are taken in an evil net, and as the birds that are caught in a snare; so are the sons of men snared in an evil time, when it falleth suddenly upon them. Ecclesiastes 9:11–12.

On Friday night I was preparing this sermon. I was in the study at the vicarage, the children were in bed, and my wife had gone down to the village to a sale of work at the local chapel.

I switched on the BBC. A news flash interrupted the program. It was the news that we all now know. President Kennedy had been shot in Dallas, Texas. He was being rushed to the hospital. I felt, as we all did, that this must not be true. It must be a nightmare. We shared the words of Mrs. Kennedy, who was by her husband's side—"Oh, no!" How many times did men and women and children around the world echo these words that night?

* Whichford is situated twelve miles from Stratford-on-Avon in Coventry Diocese. Its parish church is Norman, with a list of rectors going back to 1275.

The full measure of this terrible tragedy cannot yet be realized. We feel only that the powers of darkness have reached out and, by an assassin's bullet, struck down the leader of the free world. President Kennedy was the acknowledged leader of the Western world. We felt that in many ways he was a European. Coming as he did from New England, he and his wife had a sympathy and love for the riches of Western culture, both in the arts and sciences.

Now John Fitzgerald Kennedy is dead, his wife a widow and his children orphans. We all feel that we are bereaved, that we have lost one of our own. In the short space of three years since he became President, by his gaiety, frankness, and friendship he has won the admiration of millions, not only in America but in the streets of Paris, Berlin, London, and Dublin.

When he came back to Ireland last summer to visit his relatives, what a welcome he received in Dublin and in Wexford! Ireland had not much to give him except a warm welcome, and Ireland was proud that he found time amid all the other cares with which the President of the United States is burdened to visit the old country.

A career full of promise has now been cut short when it had hardly begun.

Today we must remember in our prayers the members of his family, the American people, those statesmen who now must lead the Western world, and all the peoples of the world who love peace, justice, and freedom.

We may ask, with the writer of Ecclesiastes who wrote two hundred years before Christ, "Is there any reason, any meaning in the tragedies of life?" The Preacher wanted to find some meaning in life, a meaning in all the struggles of humanity. He wanted to discover some moral order on which one could rely in order to plan for the future, to advance the cause of human life and happiness. He wanted to abolish injustice, corruption, and oppression that none of the children of men should be lonely, without significance, comfort, and hope. He could find no plan. He could find no meaning. It is because he is baffled by life that he is beaten, broken-hearted, and in despair. "Vanity of vanities," saith the Preacher, "all is vanity." The shadow of his disappointment hangs over his whole book. It is because he loves life and mankind that his heart is broken by the "tears of things." The wise men of Proverbs believed in the retribution dogma—that the good and wise are rewarded in life, and the foolish and evil punished. Ecclesiastes is a criticism of this facile dogma, as is the Book of Job.

This is the last Sunday of the Christian year; it is fitting that the lesson should be from a book written perhaps two hundred years before Christ. The Advent season which begins next Sunday reminds us of the coming of God into the world in the person of Jesus Christ. The people that walked in darkness have seen a great light; they that dwell in the land of the shadow of death, upon them hath the light shined. When God lived on this earth among men, He also found disappointment and betrayal. In the end He died with a broken heart and body on the Cross. We, as we look at the mystery of the Cross of Christ, see that it has been transformed into a sign of triumph and salvation. The Cross is not just a pious symbol on our altars and church towers; it is a basic fact of our experience, as we realize today. The Cross of Jesus was not a defeat but a victory.

God knows the secret of bringing good out of evil. "To every thing there is a season, and a time to every purpose under the Heaven. A time to weep, and a time to laugh; a time to mourn, and a time to dance."

Today is a day of mourning. If we weep, we must not lose hope because—unlike the writer of our text—we are Christians.

"For man also knoweth not his time. As the fishes that are taken in an evil net, and as the birds that are caught in the snare, so are the sons of men snared in an evil time, when it falleth suddenly upon them."

From: "THE TIMES"*
LONDON, ENGLAND

A Poem by John Masefield

JOHN FITZGERALD KENNEDY

All generous hearts lament the leader killed,
The young chief with the smile, the radiant face,
The winning way that turned a wondrous race
Into sublimer pathways, leading on.

Grant to us Life that though the man be gone
The promise of his spirit be fulfilled.

* This poem is reprinted by permission from *The Times,* November 25, 1963.

From: THE VATICAN, VATICAN CITY, ITALY

Statement by His Eminence, Pope Paul VI

November 23, 1963

We are highly touched by the tragedy and sad news of the loss of the President of the United States, and the grave accident of Governor Connally; we are profoundly saddened by this senseless murder; for the mourning it has brought to Mrs. Kennedy, their children, and his whole family.

We deplore with all our hearts this happening. We mourn the great loss of so popular an American; we pray God that this sacrifice of John Kennedy will be an example to keep peace and liberty throughout the world.

He was the first Catholic President of the United States. We remember that we had the honor of one of his visits and of knowing his great wisdom [*sagezza*] and his good intentions for all humanity. We offer the Holy Mass tomorrow for the peace of his soul and for those who mourn his death.

[Noontime, November 23, from the Pontiff's studio window:]

We wish this manifesto to be of public expression (1) We deplore the criminal act, (2) We have admiration for this man of state, (3) And we pray for his eternal peace and rest and for the world that knew him as a great leader, (4) And finally we pray that his death does not retard the cause of peace and that this sacrifice be an example for the love of all humanity.

From: CASA DELLO SCUGNIZZO
(HOUSE OF URCHINS) NAPLES, ITALY

Eulogy by Padre Mario Borrelli

He who searches the history of Scotland will encounter a John Kennedy, fourth Baron of Cassilis, who roasted the Abbot of Crossraguel on a spit at Dunure in Ayrshire.

The tricks of history! That one Kennedy should be an executioner and, centuries later, another should be a victim!

It is certain that men, wherever born, have never been victorious simply because they have resorted to violence.

It is equally certain that he who is killed violently while defending an ideal for the good of humanity does not truly die.

Time comes to a standstill for the victims of violence.

Violence has the power to make those it intended to destroy more alive in death than they were in life.

A pistol shot is intended as judgment of a person. But he who passes judgment without regard to the right of defense and appeal is a judge too insecure in his motives to justify his right to condemn.

Violence is therefore the action of one who is powerless and ineffectual.

We Christians, as children of a good school, behave differently. The history of Christianity is a story of violence that was never victorious, but never subdued. To the hand which strikes we know no better than to return the gifts of a smile and a loving hand of forgiveness. In this lies the secret of an age-old victory.

From: MARBLE COLLEGIATE CHURCH
NEW YORK, NEW YORK

Sermon preached by the Reverend Dr. Norman Vincent Peale

The famous words which we find in the fifteenth chapter of St. John's Gospel, the thirteenth verse, seem to apply on this occasion: "Greater love hath no man than this, that a man lay down his life for his friends."

Of all the fine things that have been said regarding our departed President one seemed to me extraordinarily meaningful. It was a statement by Richard M. Nixon. Referring to a book in which Mr. Kennedy described men in American history who were immortal by reason of their courageous action, Mr. Nixon said, "President Kennedy yesterday wrote the finest and greatest chapter in his *Profiles in Courage*. The greatest tribute we can pay is to reduce the hatred which drives men to do such deeds." And this I believe to be true, for he literally died for his country, and he was courageous.

Many years ago when Woodrow Wilson died, I attended a memorial service to him in Boston. It was held in the old church of Phillips Brooks on Copley Square. The preacher was the late George A. Gordon, a Scotsman who was the pastor of the Old South Congregational Church. He was a very impressive man both in body and in speech. On this sad day he stood before a great throng of people in the church and there was a deep silence. Standing in the lofty pulpit, he raised his hand and said, "There are some heights to which no dust ever comes." He was referring, of course, to the partisan conflict of which Wilson had been a part, to the clamor of his day. He was referring to the critics and to the enemies of the dead President. But he was also calling to the attention of the American people that there is a lofty height, the height of death, where no dust ever comes.

Thus today we think of the goodness and the dedication and the fairness and the earnestness of this young man who had such a meteoric career, rising to be the youngest man who ever held the office of President of the United States. Thus today all dust is settled, as we think of the fact that riding the crest of the wave, full of vitality and energy, in one instant he was struck down and he took his place in the history of the Presidency. We honor him today and revere his memory.

One thought his passing leaves in our minds is that we have witnessed the rising tide of violence in this country which at last has reached its apex in striking down in a diabolical manner the man who had been elected to uphold the laws of this country. Lawlessness struck him down and destroyed him. For many years now this lawlessness has been developing among us, this violence.

Political discussion which was once a science has become a personal smear. There was a time in this country when every citizen was a political philosopher. Men sitting around the cracker barrels in the old country stores were readers of the great political documents upon which this country was established and they fought the battles of politics on the basis of issues. But of late years, with the introduction of the smear technique, the battles have shifted from principles to personalities, and hatred emerging from this type of soil struck down the man who was the symbol of the Constitution of the United States, of law and order.

There has been a pampering of the juvenile delinquent. We've gone easy on the criminals. The law has been designed, apparently, so that the criminal is overly protected. I rode down a street in this city this morning looking at the signs on the marquees of the theatres. Every single one of them implied that the picture they advertised was either one of sex or violence. And if a nation becomes conditioned to violence they need not be surprised when some one man or a group of men take the law into their hands and destroy the man who has been elected by the sovereign people to enforce the laws of this land. Certainly we can learn from this tragic circumstance that there must be a new emphasis in this country on respect for our leaders and for our laws. Naturally, at such a time as this we are shocked. Let us be shocked into a new appreciation of the fact that we must insist that this become a nation of reason and law.

Our nation has been wounded and the American people need to find comfort. This is especially true of the family of the President and of those most closely associated with him. "Comfort ye, comfort ye my people"— this is the message of the Church of Almighty God to the people on this day. Those whom we've lost are still with us. We long for the touch of a vanished hand and the sound of a voice that is stilled; but those whom we've loved and lost a while are still with us. These men who die in the faith of the Lord Jesus Christ live on, and they shall be met again by their loved ones who mourn them. I often think of those wonderful words of Whittier:

Yet Love will dream, and Faith will trust,
(Since He who knows our need is just,)
That somehow, somewhere, meet we must.
Alas for him who never sees
The stars shine through his cypress-trees!
Who, hopeless, lays his dead away,
Nor looks to see the breaking day
Across the mournful marbles play!
Who hath not learned in hours of faith,
  The truth to flesh and sense unknown,
That Life is ever lord of Death
  And Love can never lose its own!

We mourn for the passing of the President but we rejoice, as would he also, in the stability of the United States of America. There are nations where such a crisis as this would rock the government on its foundations. But not the kind of government the forefathers of this country established. They must have been a very remarkable breed of men to foresee the long future and to provide against the shocks that could upset a weaker nation.

When Lincoln died on that tragic night at the end of the Civil War, the mobs were surging through the streets. Anarchy and revolution were in the air. The country seemed leaderless when, it is said, there came out on a balcony a General of the Army who was himself to become President later on, and he held up his hand. People began to call out, "It's Garfield. It's Garfield." And finally he got attention and then his voice rang out over the throngs. "God reigns, and the government at Washington still lives!"

God gave birth to this country and those who made it made it good. It is a nation of law and rises above man. Men come, have their little day, and pass away.

But the great nation lives on. The last thoughts of one of our greatest men were for our country. In the well-known book *The Adams Family,* Jane Truslow Adams gives us a picture of John Adams' last hours: "Mrs. Clark, his daughter-in-law, said to him that it was the Fourth of July, the fiftieth anniversary of independence. He answered, 'It is a great day; it is a good day.' About one in the afternoon he said, 'Thomas Jefferson survives.'" But by some strange Divine coincidence that very day at Monticello Thomas Jefferson—he of the golden pen who wrote those immortal documents—was himself dying. So the two colossal figures passed away. But the nation still lived.

And the reason this nation still lives is that this is a spiritual country, the only such that was ever established on a definitely religious basis. This country was formed by two streams. One stream took its rise in the thinking of classical antiquity: Socrates, Aristotle, Plato. These men lived in a society where the individual was of no account, yet they conceived a great and immortal idea that the human mind is sacred and ought to be forever free. They said that no man shall ever make a slave of the mind of a free man. Freedom at that time was only in the higher classes, but it permeated down to the very bottom.

This stream flowed across history until finally a man named Dr. Small set up a school in Virginia where he taught such men as Randolph and Jefferson. He poured into their minds this philosophy of the sacredness of the human mind. That was one great stream that washed the American continent.

The other great stream took its rise when a man named Moses went out into the wilderness and struck the shackles from a nation of slaves and said they were children of God and must forever be free. Then there came walking into history the greatest figure of them all, sun-crowned both in His intellect and in His soul. And He said, "Ye shall know the truth, and the truth shall make you free." Men put Bibles under their arms and they sailed across the sea and landed on the American continent and the second great stream washed these shores.

At the confluence of these two streams was established an island where grew principles unshakeable because they are of God.

And the greatest man ever to rise among us, Abraham Lincoln, said that this is the last best hope of earth. Never let anybody take it away from you. Our leaders come. We follow them, and they go. And the nation lives. And they want the nation to live. Therefore, it is our duty to pray for the leaders in this land and to see to it that "this nation, under God, shall have a new birth of freedom."

I went back into one of my old schoolbooks last night and copied off a poem called "The Building of the Ship" by Henry W. Longfellow:

> Thou, too, sail, O Ship of State!
> Sail on, O Union, strong and great!
> Humanity with all its fears,
> With all the hopes of future years,
> Is hanging breathless on thy fate!
> We know what Master laid thy keel,
> What Workmen wrought thy ribs of steel,
> Who made each mast, and sail, and rope,
> What anvils rang, what hammers beat,
> In what a forge and what a heat
> Were shaped the anchors of thy hope!
> Fear not each sudden sound and shock,
> 'Tis of the wave and not the rock;

'Tis but a flapping of the sail,
And not a rent made by the gale!
In spite of rock and tempest's roar,
In spite of false lights on the shore,
Sail on, nor fear to breast the sea!
Our hearts, our hopes, are all with thee,
Our hearts, our hopes, our prayers, our tears,
Our faith triumphant o'er our fears,
Are all with thee,—are all with thee!

Let us pray:

Our Heavenly Father, we thank Thee for the life and the dedicated service of Thy servant, our fallen President. To him we extend honor and gratitude. We ask Thy blessing upon Thy servant who has been called so suddenly to assume these great responsibilities, Lyndon B. Johnson. Give him guidance and give him strength and wisdom. And we thank Thee for our beloved nation which has stood always for freedom, for equality of all men, and for Almighty God as the directing force of our lives. Dedicate us, Thy children, to the service of God and country. Through Jesus Christ our Lord. AMEN.

From: TEMPLE RODEPH SHOLOM
NEW YORK, NEW YORK

Tribute by Rabbi Louis I. Newman

In the funeral services in tribute to President Kennedy, a "Riderless Horse" participated—a symbol of the loss of a beloved chieftain in the midst of the battle. Perhaps the following verses can speak more effectively for the sorrow in our hearts than any formal eulogy:

A horse dark of hue wears a blanket of black;
Its saddle is empty; its guiding reins slack;
Its footsteps move sidewise; the touch at its head
Is strange to a creature so lovingly bred.

A sword in a scabbard is strapped to its side,
A sign its commander has made his last ride;
His stirrups and boots are turned backward, to tell
A soldier has fallen. Brave martyr, sleep well!

A horse walks along, 'mid the music of grief,
Bewailing the loss of a gallant young chief,
Shot down in the battle, his arrows unsped,
His mission unfinished, his message unsaid.

Oh, mourn for the leader so heartlessly slain,
Whose voice could command, yet so wisely restrain!
Oh, mourn for the steed, of its master bereft,
That looks for its friend to the right and the left.

Our nation stands trembling, a riderless steed,
That yearns for a hand that can halt and can lead.
Oh symbol of majesty, honor and pride,
How long shall we weep, now our chieftain has died?

Alas for the warrior who lies in his tomb,
Alas for the horse in its vestment of gloom!
But hail to the horseman who mounts to his place,
The saddle refilled for the challenging race!

And when this great charger is freed from its bonds,
Behold how it leaps and with ardor responds!
Oh, thus may our country, still bowed under pain,
Courageously take up its burden again.

From: ST. PAUL'S CHAPEL
NEW YORK, NEW YORK

Memorial delivered by Dr. Grayson Kirk President, Columbia University

November 25, 1963

On this sad day unnumbered millions of men and women have gathered together as we have done to pay a last word of respect and tribute to the memory of a great man. The earth that this afternoon receives the shattered body of John Fitzgerald Kennedy is wet with the unashamed tears of an outraged mankind. The world has been stunned by the effect of a single senseless and brutal act committed by a creature who at that moment forfeited his right to membership in the human race.

No greater blow can be dealt a nation than to strike down a chosen leader who had amply demonstrated a capacity for leadership rare among men of any generation. The entire nation grieves, not merely out of a decent sympathy for a bereaved family and close personal friends, but because it knows that it too has suffered a crippling loss; that it too has been impoverished; that it too has been shamed before the world. And as our people bow their heads in their grief, they bow them also in shame that such a thing could have happened in our land and in our time.

The poignancy of our grief is all the more intense because we do not need to wait to be told by future historians that this was no mere and ordinary man thrust into high office by the chance results of democratic political process. We know in our hearts, and we know with deep abiding conviction, that this was a man who possessed in abundance those special and unusual qualities of which our people at this time in their history stood in great need, from which they derived deep and lasting benefit, and without which they must look into a bleak and troubled future.

And on this afternoon of national mourning, it is fitting that we recall, for the benefit of all our citizens, some of the reasons why our loss is a national disaster, the like of which few generations have had to endure. So doing, we take some small measure of comfort in remembering what we have had; so doing, we set up in ourselves criteria by which we may measure those who would follow our President in this, the highest of all our offices.

We honor the memory of John Kennedy because he was a man of courage. He knew instinctively the importance of this quality among leaders. He wrote discerningly about it, in order that we might all be more aware of our national need for men who possessed it. In his youth he demonstrated that, in his own character, it was stronger than even the primal instinct for self-preservation. In his maturity he did not flinch from decisions that he knew would evoke hostility and abuse from men whose vision of the nation's welfare was narrow, selfish, and distorted. First among all leaders he faced the terrible risk of nuclear war in order to protect the basic national interests of the people whom he had sworn to protect and defend.

But his was not the blind courage in face of danger which, happily, comes to many men in time of crisis. His was the courage derived from the intelligent evaluation of all facets of a complex and perilous situation and fortified by the strength of basic convictions. His was the courage of intelligence, the courage that goes beyond that of many intelligent men who, faced with a grave and unpleasant problem, lapse into the agony of indecision and the error of impulsive judgment.

Though as a young man he offered his life for his country, his final gift of this, the most precious of man's possessions, was more than a supreme sacrifice just in defense of his country. He wanted his country to become a land in which our democratic ideals would be more fully realized, a land in which we and our children could take ever greater pride, a land in which the old dreams of mankind might at last be realized. And he gave up his life because despicable and selfish men, hating this prospect, so filled the atmosphere with their venom that one mean creature became their tool and their agent. Now that the deed is done, and our President is gone, their protestations of innocence and even of grief ring hollowly upon our ears. John Kennedy died because he wanted a better America. Consciously, he strove for policies that would inflame his opponents. Consciously he fought them, knowing—as he must have—what the risks were. Bravely he died, not so much for the America of today as for the America of the future.

John Kennedy had more than courage and intelligence. He had compassion. Born to wealth and, had he so chosen, a life of ease and indolence, he elected a career of public service, one in which he could put his talents to work for his fellow men. Just as he was proud of the great qualities and achievements of his country, he was deeply troubled by the inequities and inequalities which still persisted in a society ostensibly dedicated to their elimination. He was troubled, too, by the new injustices, the new hazards of life, that grew out of social and technological change.

He saw a society in which men of one color were being denied that equality of opportunity which is the foundation-stone of America. He saw a society in which the benefits of modern medical progress were on occasion denied to men and women because they lacked the means to pay for their needs. He saw a society in which aged men and women of limited resources were being ruthlessly pushed aside and allowed to live out their final years in that quiet helpless desperation that only poverty without hope can breed.

And because he was a man of compassion, he grieved over these cancers in the body politic. And because he was a man of action, he strove to excise them and to heal their wounds. And because he was a determined man, not content to allow an affluent society to be so afflicted, he died.

Today as we reflect with gratitude upon those great qualities, this constructively directed energy, this vision of what our country might be and must become, we must ask ourselves what good, what possible benefit, we as a people can derive from this man's life, what lessons we may take to our hearts from this crushing tragedy. Our grief must be tempered with the resolution that the sacrifice was not vainly made, that out of our national sorrow there may come some good, that from the shrine of this bloodstained soil in Arlington there may come a chastened and better America. In no other way can we justify to him what he did for us.

First and foremost, we must resolve to be more responsible in our thoughts and actions. This land of ours is plagued by men of small minds, men of vicious and uncontrolled emotions, men for whom hatred is greater than love, men whose concern for their fellow men is lost in insensate bigotry, men who in their hearts despise all that this nation stands for, men who do not deserve the land in which they live. It does not matter whether they are of the reactionary right or the radical left, the menace which they present to this country is equally ominous because they would—in order to bring back a world that never was or one that betrays the cause of human freedom—destroy all our effort.

Since we are obliged by the imperatives of that freedom to permit such men to carry on, to a reasonable extent, their destructive activities, it is the obligation of those of us who really love our country to be more energetic, more alert to the danger, more willing to remind our citizens about the dangers implicit in the ravings of the extremists. When we are silent in the face of this danger, when we deride our chosen leaders or sit quietly by when others do so, when we allow ourselves to become irrational in our partisanship, when we allow others to sneer at our principles, we are unconscious accomplices in the sabotage of our country. Apathy in these circumstances is cowardice. If this experience through which we have passed does not chasten our hearts, and does not steel our determination to combat these forces of destruction about us, then may God help us, because we will not help ourselves.

It has been the historic pride of this country for the past century that our excesses of political partisanship have never reached the point when the conflict on either side jeopardized loyalty to our Constitution and our democracy. This is still true of the overwhelming majority of Americans, but we face today, in this respect, greater dangers than at any time since the Civil War. Respect for law is lost in the selfishness of men who try to cheat and evade its commands. Respect for law is lost in the organized resistance of men to the application of the Constitution under which they live. Respect for law is dead when our highest officers are physically assaulted, when their lives are threatened, and when such threats become grim reality. To these dangers we must become more alert. Against them we must devise countermeasures. From them we must learn and practice that self-discipline which has never been congenial to our people but upon which the future of our country depends. In this respect, we hang our heads in shame over the spectacle which we present to the world, a spectacle which ill accords with our boasting.

More energy against the extremists and their poison, more self-discipline—even these are not enough if we are to justify by the future health and progress of our society the sacrifice John Kennedy made for his country. Each segment of our society must re-examine its responsibilities. The press, radio, and television, through their emphasis upon the reporting of violence, often go beyond their basic need to keep us informed; by these emphases they may condone and inflame still further violence, and they cannot escape social responsibility by saying that they are merely giving the public what it wants. In the home, the extreme permissiveness of our modern parents breeds in their children contempt for all authority, a contempt that takes its toll in broken youthful lives and bewildered parents who try to evade responsibility for their own failures by casting the blame on others. And, of course, our schools, our colleges, and our universities need to re-examine their functions and to try to discover how, along with their traditional duties, they can impart to their students a greater sense of social responsibility. The death of our beloved President carries a lesson to every part of our society and to every institution. In his memory we must heed it.

Thus today, in our grief and our remorse, we look

sadly but with new resolve to the future. We are determined to create in this land the democracy in which he believed, one which applies the ancient principles of human dignity, equality and opportunity to the conditions and necessities of modern life. As we do this, and as we bring nearer to reality the dreams of men like the man we mourn today, we make out of his gallant life and its tragic ending a national treasure for the future. We can do no more, and we can do no less. His soul is in the hands of God, his heritage in the hearts of our people.

From: ST. GEORGE'S EPISCOPAL CHURCH
NEW YORK, NEW YORK

Tribute by the Reverend Dr. Reinhold Niebuhr

The untimely death of President Kennedy by an assassin's bullet aroused a depth and breadth of grief in the nation and in the world which historians of the future may well regard as unprecedented. The dimension and universality of the sorrow may be due to three reasons.

First, the assassination cut short the life of a promising career. Kennedy possessed a unique combination of gifts. He had a quick and searching intelligence which was combined with a rare degree of political shrewdness and personal and political courage.

Other Presidents have died in office, and three before him were assassinated. But most of them died when their essential work was done. This applies even to Lincoln, who led the nation through a crucial period of our national history. Kennedy was the youngest of our Presidents and he was seemingly destined to lead our nation for eight years. But he was cut down after only two years of a promising political career.

The second reason for the dimension of grief was the promising but unfinished character of his political leadership. He proved his mettle in forming policy by having the courage on the one hand to confront the Russians in the Cuban incident when a nuclear war was threatened—and averted by a combination of boldness and prudence. And, on the other hand, he was more dedicated to the tremendous task of avoiding a nuclear catastrophe than any other contemporary leader. He courageously articulated the limited test ban agreement which may well go down in history as the beginning of a new era in the Cold War.

In domestic policy, perhaps his greatest but alas unfinished task was to lead the nation in what seemed to be a final chapter in solving "the American dilemma"—that is, the failure of the nation to grant its Negro citizens equal justice and respect for their human dignity.

President Kennedy did not initiate the Negro revolution. Perhaps it was initiated by the Supreme Court decision of a decade ago. Perhaps it was a spontaneous combustion of century-old resentments of citizens who had been defrauded of freedom and justice supposedly inherent in the American dream. But the young President, confronted with the revolt, did not vacillate or temporize. He gave the Negro citizen the full support of the federal power and summoned the nation to solve what indeed was a great moral crisis.

If his name will be associated with various creative endeavors, his stand on civil rights will certainly lead the list. Incidentally, it is too early to say whether his untimely death will arrest the movement toward racial justice or whether his death may be proved more important than his life in completing the unfinished task of restoring the moral integrity of our nation.

The third reason for the immensity of the grief beyond our national borders is that the creative thrust into world affairs by a gifted President was combined with the increasing world prestige and power of the American Presidency, derived from the growing prestige of our nation as a leader of the non-Communist world. This concentration of power and prestige is so great that we must view President Kennedy's death with mingled gratitude for the providential selection of so gifted a leader to exercise that power and with an anxious and prayerful attitude about our American world responsibilities in the future.

From: TEMPLE EMANU-EL
NEW YORK, NEW YORK

A Tribute by Dr. Julius Mark, Senior Rabbi of the Congregation

---

Monday, November 25, 1963

I cannot say, and I will not say, that he is dead;
He is just away.

With a cheery smile and a wave of the hand,
He has wandered into an unknown land

And left us dreaming how very fair it needs must be,
Since he lingers there.

And for us who the wildest yearn
For the old time step and the glad return,

Let us think of him as still the same, I say.
He is not dead; he is just away.

James Whitcomb Riley

Spiritually, John Fitzgerald Kennedy is very much alive, but we know that physically he is no more. His tragic death was the direct result of the dark hatreds and insane hostilities which poison the hearts of otherwise decent and respectable citizens of our country. These hatreds, so vicious and so depraved, were transferred to the twisted mind of the maniac who, in murdering the youthful, brilliant, and brave President of the United States, sought to destroy the loftiest symbol of the American way of life. And now, the infamy has been further compounded when another psychopath, taking the law in his hands, shot down the suspected assassin, who may well have been the guilty man but—not having had his day in court—is innocent in the sight of American law.

The people of our country experienced three reactions when the incredible news of the President's violent death reached them. The first was one of shock. It was beyond belief that such an outrageous crime could be committed in broad daylight in one of America's great cities. We were stunned and literally speechless.

The feeling of shock was followed by that of grief—grief over the untimely death of a man so young and wise and vibrant and intrepid, Chief Executive of our nation and leader of the free world, a man who hated violence and constantly appealed for the establishment through law and mutual respect of justice and peace in the relations between man and man, race and race, religion and religion, nation and nation. There was and is grief in our hearts, too, for a young widow and two orphaned children, for the bereft parents and other members of America's most distinguished family.

The third reaction is now gripping our hearts—that life must go on, though our souls are hurt to the quick. We are grateful that our Constitution provides for immediate and peaceful succession to the Presidency when that awesome office becomes vacant. We thank God that the new President, Lyndon B. Johnson, possesses the ability, the experience, the ideals as well as the determination and courage to carry on in the glorious tradition of his fallen predecessor. God bless the President of the United States with good health and strength, with wisdom, valor, and vision, as he assumes the heavy burdens of his office.

John F. Kennedy was President of the United States for a period of less than three years, and was cruelly cut down at the age of forty-six. He accomplished much during his brief career and will not have died in vain if we, the citizens of the United States, of all races, colors, parties, religions, dedicate ourselves to the sacred task of rooting out every vestige of hatred, prejudice, and bigotry from our hearts and do what in us lies to make strong the foundations of a land and a world wherein every man shall live in peace under his own vine and fig tree, and with none to make him afraid.

Our beloved and ever to be cherished President of the United States, John Fitzgerald Kennedy, has entered into the peace of life eternal. He still lives on earth in the acts of goodness he performed, and in the hearts of those who will ever cherish his memory. May the beauty of his life abide among us as a loving benediction. May the Father of peace send peace to all who mourn, and all of us are indeed mourning, and comfort the bereaved among us here and wherever they may be. AMEN.

From: ST. BARTHOLOMEW'S CHURCH
NEW YORK, NEW YORK

Sermon preached by the Reverend Dr. Terence J. Finlay

God is our refuge and strength, a very present help in trouble. (Psalm 46:1)

In the midst of life we are in death; of whom may we seek for succour, but of thee, O Lord, who for our sins art justly displeased. (From the Burial Office)

Those of you who have read the papers or listened to television or radio know that messages of condolence and sympathy have come pouring in from all over the world, even from those we have considered hostile to us. We know that on Monday delegations from many countries will join with the leaders of this country in paying their last respects to the thirty-fifth President of the United States.

What can one say? First of all the things that must be said is that we are grateful for what has been accomplished during his Presidency. We thank God for the leadership of John Fitzgerald Kennedy, and there have been dark and difficult days during his tenure of office—days when he felt that world peace, our safety or destruction, hung by a thread. In that crisis we looked for and found leadership. I believe that we may look forward, under God, to the same type of leadership, because it is under God that we seek our guidance.

Certainly I would be less than realistic if I did not

know, as you well know, that this man had his critics, and this is right in a democracy, else we cease to be democratic, using that term in its fullest meaning. We do not live under a dictator; we have no use for tyrants; and if we do not like what our leaders do, we feel that we have the right to criticize, but surely not to destroy with a bullet the life of the man who is the head of the country. What does such an assassin think that he may accomplish? He removes one life, but the country goes on under a new President.

Secondly, there is the sense of mourning—not mourning for ourselves, but sorrow in our hearts, first of all, for the immediate family. Any woman in this congregation can barely guess what the feeling of the wife of the President must have been as his body fell across her in that automobile, and she watched the blood streaming from his head and neck as he was rushed to the hospital. Our sympathies go out to all the family; we think of those two little children, who loved their father —to them he was not the President of the United States: he was their father. We think of his mother and father, his brothers and sisters. Mourning for the family, and mourning for the type of mentality that can pull the trigger of an assassin's weapon!

Is this a symptom of our day? If it is, we need to mourn not only for the family of the President; we need to mourn for our sins. "In the midst of life we are in death; of whom may we seek for succor, but of thee, O Lord, who for our sins art justly displeased." There is a sin in the hearts of men everywhere, not only in this country but throughout the world. It is the sin of prejudice which, if nourished either by propaganda or by brooding solitude, may develop into the cancer of hate; and hate can destroy, as it has destroyed the life of the man whom we are remembering today.

Yes, we need to mourn for the sins that we have in this country—the prejudices which we have allowed to grow into hate in our hearts. If we have come to church today simply to pay a sentimental tribute to the thirty-fifth President of the United States, while it may be good, it is not enough. Every man and woman in this congregation should search his or her heart to see if it harbors this prejudice of race, of color, of class, of nationality, because it will produce in us, perhaps not the disastrous consequences which happened in the city of Dallas, but a cancer which will affect the people with whom we come in contact. One of the great boasts of this country is that it has brought together a multitude of peoples from all over the world and welded them into one nation under God. Are these just sentiments, or will they become truths? If we let our mourning become something practical in our lives, so that it produces better and more Christlike living, then we shall have mourned the President in the way I am sure he would wish to be mourned.

Some time ago I read the story of a woman in the South whose son, her only support, entered the armed forces during the second world war to fight for the freedom of his country and for all freedom-loving people throughout the world. Later, word came back to that little village in the South that this young man had been killed in action in Normandy; so the neighbors went to sympathize with the mother. When they arrived at the little house which stood at the center of a poor farm, they found the house empty, but away on a sandy knoll was the mother, working. They could hardly believe their eyes. They trudged through the sand up to the top of the knoll and tried to convey their sympathy to her. They suggested that it was not quite fitting that she should be out working when this news of her son had just arrived. She looked up at them and said, "Thank you. I know you mean well, but you see this land. It is my son's land. Every time I put the hoe through the earth, I can feel his hands alongside of mine, and I can hear him saying to me, 'That is good, mother, that is good. Keep working our land.' So, if you don't mind," she continued, "I'll do my grieving in my own way."

Let us go forth with the determination that we will live so that we may be worthy in some small way of the price that has been paid, not only by John Fitzgerald Kennedy, but by all those who have given their lives for our country's freedom *under God.*

From: YALE UNIVERSITY
NEW HAVEN, CONNECTICUT

Sermon preached by the Reverend William Sloane Coffin, Jr.

So I exhort the elders among you, as a fellow elder and a witness of the sufferings of Christ as well as a partaker in the glory that is to be revealed. Tend the flock of God that is your charge, not by constraint but willingly, not for shameful gain but eagerly; not as domineering over those in your charge but being examples to the flock.

Humble yourselves therefore under the mighty hand of God, that in due time He may exalt you. Cast all your anxieties on Him, for He cares about you. Be sober, be watchful. Your adversary the devil prowls

around like a roaring lion, seeking some one to devour. Resist him, firm in your faith, knowing that the same experience of suffering is required of your brotherhood throughout the world.

And after you have suffered a little while, the God of all grace, who has called you to his eternal glory in Christ, will Himself restore, establish, and strengthen you. To Him be the dominion for ever and ever. AMEN.

I Peter 5:1–3, 6–11

America has grown a lot older in the last forty-eight hours. Many more of us have learned—and this learning comes hard to Americans—that as a child is more secure in his small world than is a grown man in his wider one, so a nation in its hour of greatest strength is less able to work its will than it was in the days of its infancy. We could not even keep our President alive. We have learned then that the maturity of individuals and nations alike consists less in the expansion of their freedom, more in the recognition of their limits.

This is wisdom, for as a river can never flow deeply until its banks are defined, so we until we find our limits have little chance of becoming profound. This is a painful process. Few are naturally profound. Most of us have to be forced down. And this is not an automatic process; we can easily have the experience and miss the meaning.

The words read from I Peter were written for early Christians hard up against the limits of life. As I hear these words they are tough, yet tender with a tenderness that only the strong can show; full of sorrow, but of a marvelously refined order; strangely powerful hopeful words. And their central thought is the thought central to all Christians in both the dust and divinity of life: "Cast all your anxieties on Him, for He cares about you."

However true, this thought should never be expressed

to a widow such as Mrs. Kennedy in the first or second day of her bereavement. For every such person should first go through a time of "My God, my God, my God, why hast Thou forsaken me—"; and anyone who says prematurely "God has not forsaken you," no matter how true this may be, sounds always as if he is refusing to go with the other to the depths of sorrow, is trying to pretty up the situation before accepting it. This is always experienced by the other as the worst kind of rejection.

But perhaps in our grief, a grief which is not as personally acute as that of Mrs. Kennedy, the thought that God cares is a good one for us today. I am eager to think so, for with many another pastor I have been struck at how few people on their deathbed or beside the deathbed of their beloved—even professed Christians—see at that moment much relation between their faith and their predicament. Christianity is just so much more professed than respected in our country. It is tragic how little faith there is in the churches.

God cares. The Bible maintains on almost every page that God not only cares for but suffers with His people, and no matter how wayward.

> *How can I give thee up, O Ephraim?*
> *How can I give thee up, O Israel?*

The best-known Psalm begins with this thought:

The Lord is my shepherd; I shall not want.
He maketh me to lie down in green pastures: he leadeth me beside the still waters.
He restoreth my soul. . . .

David, notice, is talking of God in the third person, but in order the more poignantly, passionately to portray his conviction of God's concern, when he comes to faith's most trying time he suddenly switches persons:

Yea, though I walk through the valley of the shadow of death, I will fear no evil: for thou art with me; thy rod and thy staff they comfort me.

Almost equally moving is the 121st Psalm. In a story called "The Cockpit," a Jewish poet makes the Queen comment scornfully on the New Testament phrase *the peace of God:* "As I lie sleepless I think of the eternal insomnia of God." When her attendant protests, she goes on, "I only quote the Bible. 'He that keepeth Israel shall neither slumber nor sleep.' Ah, it is the pain of God, not His peace, that passes understanding."

The same admonition permeates the whole New Testament. Jesus said, "Are not five sparrows sold for two pennies? And not one of them is forgotten before God." He is referring to the practice of the poor who, unable to afford calves and bullocks for sacrifice, bought sparrows instead. Sparrows went two for a penny, and for two pennies' worth a fifth was thrown in. God cares for that fifth sparrow! And Jesus goes on: "Fear not; you are of more value than many sparrows," and dies to prove it. Is not the whole New Testament the story of God's pain incarnate, God suffering not only with but for His people.

Why is it so hard to believe that God cares? More and more I think anthropomorphism is indeed our stumblingblock . . . only not Biblical anthropomorphism, that is, ascribing to God human traits, for this is dangerous only to the literalist. What is far more dangerous is our anthropomorphism, the way we project onto the world and God our own anthropomorphic expectations. Academics expect the world to be rational, but whoever said it was? Haven't we learned over the last two days that life is felt and borne as much as thought? And don't all of us expect God to care for us only as we want Him to, which usually means tampering with the laws of nature or with man's freedom in order to clean up man's mess?

A time of crisis is a time not for words that are pleasing but for words that are true. (God I am sure would like to please us, but would rather save us.) So isn't it true that we find it hard to believe God cares because we ourselves care so little, and we generally doubt most what we lack most?

But God is caring for us right now in all the forms of love that have manifested themselves in this country over the last forty-eight hours. The truth has come home to us that our lives are limited, fraught with tragedy. But as always, hasn't the security of love made bearable the insecurity of truth? And God is caring for all of us in the tears that have been shed, for tears themselves are signs of caring and are God-given to wash clean the heart of all bitterness. By talking about a loss that seems unbearable we are learning that it is bearable. By being driven to our knees out of a sense of no other place to go we are opening ourselves to the help God so wishes to give. Ask God only for a thimbleful of help and you will receive an oceanful in return. For God does care.

"Tend the flock of God that is in your charge, not by constraint but willingly, not for shameful gain but eagerly, not as domineering over those in your charge but being examples to the flock."

President Kennedy tended his flock as a human being, a compound of strength and weakness. But, according to the tributes flooding the capital, at his best he exemplified freedom both at home and abroad. Who can forget his words at the Berlin Wall? President Kennedy also exemplified courage which in his well-known book he defined in Hemingway's words, "grace under pressure."

If we would be true to the best memory of this man we might now on his behalf with a little more reliance on grace and with a little less regard for pressure take up the unfinished business of freedom. America is not free, not in terms of the Fourteenth nor even of the First Amendment—our press is private but far from free; many of our citizens are free only to sleep in the cold-water tenement of their choice; and none of us are free of the greed, trivia, and superficiality that mark so much of our national life. As Christians let us be honest; if Christ is repugnant to the Soviet Union, He is embarrassing to the United States.

Death is a mystery not to be dissolved. And suffering is always a tragic limitation of life. But death and suffering by limiting our power on one level point us to a greater power on another. And death and suffering are never unavailing if by God's grace they send us back to bless the living.

"The Lord gave and the Lord has taken away. Blessed be the name of the Lord."

From: CATHEDRAL OF ST. JOSEPH
HARTFORD, CONNECTICUT

Sermon preached by the Right Reverend John S. Kennedy

On Friday last, man brought the touch of death to the thirty-fifth President of the United States. John Fitzgerald Kennedy was committed to Christ, who is the way and the life, forty-six years ago, when the enlivening waters of Baptism were poured upon him. He was committed as well to the cause of life in his personal conviction and in his public service.

It was in the cause of life that he strove for peace in the world. In the cause of life, he sought and suffered for justice and freedom for all Americans without distinction or exception. In the cause of life, he aimed at extension and improvement of education, the quickening of the life of the mind, our intellectual advance as a people. In the cause of life, he advocated banishment of the fear and the want which shadow and shrink the existence of the needy and the aged. In the cause of life, he labored for reconciliation of the classes, and a common, fraternal endeavor within our society. In the cause of life, he looked to, and beckoned all of us on to, a new day of concord and cooperation for the whole human family. He represented life, personified life, its promise and opportunity for millions within our borders; he represented life, personified life, its forces of faith and of hope for millions who endure a miserable existence in the stifling grasp of tyranny.

But the touch of death is still in the world, like the shark lurking in the sunlit sea. And although we call America God's country, and flatter ourselves as being superior if not sinless, America is not clean of the hatred which is both the spawn and the seed of death. Hatred for fellow men because of the color of the skin given them by the God we profess to worship and obey, hatred because these would claim the dignity and the rights which God gave to them no less than to us—that hatred burns in bitterness and has set off violence and has brought death to many. Hatred for our fellow men because their religion is different from ours—this is a poison ever stealing through the populace and periodically flooding forth to drown and to destroy. Hatred sprung of greed or of envy. Hatred fed by social philosophies and political programs which are extremist, intolerant, fanatical. Hatred of objective principles and standards, of moral demands and decencies, of sensible restraints and of due respect for legitimate authority, of reasonable stability or of reasonable change—hatred of these and all who embody or champion them. There is a sickness of hatred in this country today; there is disorder in the private heart and in the public community because of it.

What is in the heart can carry away the head. The head of our nation was carried away in death a few days ago because of what has been in the hearts of all too many of us. His death should sober those drunk on hatred of whatever sort and from whatever source. They should—we should, for which of us is without some guilt?—look upon the horrid yield of hatred, death to the bravest and the brightest and the best, and cast off addiction to this murderous vice. It has brought death to our thirty-fifth President; it can bring death to our society and our nation.

Another man whose name was John, Pope John XXIII, and who left us but a few months ago, said, "Any day is a good day to die." For death, though men may inflict it in malice or madness and intend it as obliteration, is still in God's hands, and, like everything in and from His hands, can lead only to good for those who love and look to Him. May the Son of God, who touches men with the life of grace and with life everlasting, say to John Fitzgerald Kennedy, "Young man, I say to you, 'Arise!'" May he say it no less effectually, if in another sense, to us: "Arise from rancorousness, spite, prejudice, anger, hatred. Arise to sanity, charity, brotherhood in me and under God."

From: IMMANUEL CONGREGATIONAL CHURCH
HARTFORD, CONNECTICUT

Sermon preached by the Reverend Robert L. Edwards

In all our history there has been only one Sunday quite like this one. That was nearly a hundred years ago. It is true that other Presidents have died of murderous gunshot more recently than that. President Garfield did. But Garfield lingered a long, hot, painful summer, and there was time to adjust to the danger he might die. President McKinley fell before an assassin. But McKinley lived for more than a week, so there was time for the public to get ready. What happened day before yesterday, however, happened with stunning suddenness and finality. In the space of half an hour a young and vigorous President, in the prime of life and power, was utterly gone.

Surely the press and the broadcasters have been right in comparing the assassination of Kennedy with the assassination of Lincoln, ninety-nine years ago next spring. Then, too, the whole drastic tragedy was over quickly. That, too, happened on a Friday. Then, too, many a church service had to be revised on very short notice. Then, too, far more than in the cases of Garfield and McKinley, the country was in the midst of tense times.

In the face of this kind of sudden shock one thinks again of the line in the beautiful and well-known prayer "Lord, we know not what a day may bring forth." When it brings forth a nightmare such as we now have, we are all of us thrown back on more than our own resources.

It is from that standpoint that we speak now. So much has been said in the last forty-eight hours, one almost questions whether anything more can be said, or whether it needs to be said. Yet we are here in a particular setting—in a church, and not in the political arena. We are here as a believing company, looking at Christ Jesus, and not simply part of the crowd looking everywhere in general. In this setting we may not say anything very new. But it may be possible to say a few familiar things with an emphasis that is different.

In a rather special way, to start with, we may be able to appreciate the man who has been shot down, and the size of the loss we have suffered. You can travel to some quarters of the globe where death is largely good fortune. Human grief is there, but life is considered illusion, and to escape it by dying is in a real sense the height of success. You can travel to other parts of the earth where human life is priced cheaply. If a man dies it is nothing much. Hundreds more are being born every hour. In the Christian faith, however, loss even of a single life is a momentous affair. Every person, be he famous or obscure, has been fashioned by the hand of God. Every life is a new creation. There never has been one just like it before, nor ever can be again. Each life at its best is needed by all the rest of us. When it goes, there is a vacancy no one else can fill. And the more the life is torn away ahead of its time, the more empty the vacancy seems to be.

So it is with this singular life. It does not matter what political views you may hold. It is nonpartisan knowledge that John F. Kennedy was the youngest candidate ever elected to the Presidency. As so young a man, he had to rise to its enormous responsibilities with a minimum of experience, especially executive experience. When Premier Khrushchev heard of his election he is reported to have said in puzzled mood, "How can someone who has never even been part of an administration suddenly become the head of one?" Even those of us who had voted for him may have wondered whether this "boy" leader could make it. But he did make it. He made it without appearing to become drawn or flustered. He stayed young, even under the heavy load. Whatever it was about him that produced that stamina and confidence, that is a large loss from our American family.

Friday showed us afresh the discouraging power of evil. When have we seen it in worse guise? One tragically twisted life, a life for which we can only feel the deepest pity, inflicting immeasurable tragedy on everybody else. We would like to feel this could not happen here. But it did happen. We would like to feel this could not happen now, with all our advanced knowledge and techniques. Yet now we know that it can happen, even today. In our country, which is in so many ways prosperous and progressive, we have often grown optimistic about the negative elements of existence. It may be they have come to seem like vestiges of the caveman that modern man is rapidly leaving behind.

After Friday we must take another look. One of the things about the day that hurts most is the irony of it. To all outward appearances everything was under the firm control of good. The forces of law and order were deployed everywhere. The car in which the President was riding was supposed to be a miracle of up-to-date security. Skies were sunny and the crowds were somewhat unexpectedly in a festive and friendly mood. Mr.

Kennedy was happy to have his wife with him again on a trip for the first time since her long convalescence, and, despite problems, he was himself still enjoying wide prestige. Everything seemed bright and right. Then the hand of evil cut through this impressive array, and in an instant turned it all to tears. The figure of that Secret Service man nearest the President, grasping the car and struggling to do something, and yet knowing that for all his weapons and all his skill and all his aching heart there was nothing he could do against this wrong—that seemed to sum it all up.

It seemed to sum up something about our own condition as well. Thank heaven, we do not have to live in crisis all the time. Nor is it so that we are helpless in everything. But when it comes to the ultimate things we are bewilderingly helpless on our own. We labor as best we may against greed and prejudice and disease and death and doubt and fear. Days come when it would appear we are managing to get the better of them. But no sooner have we begun to block them on one front than they break out again on another, just as malignant as before.

If we were using a formal text this morning, this is where it would come in. It would be the words of Jesus in the Gospel of John: "In the world you have tribulation." The New Testament often has understood the real force of evil better than we have. It was strong in the long-ago days of Caesar. "In the world you have tribulation." After twenty centuries of the noblest advances humankind has been able to make, it is still strong. "In the world you have tribulation."

But if the Gospel has often been clearer on this than we have been, so also it has often been more magnificent in its answer than we have seen. The rest of the text would be the other half of the saying: "Be of good cheer. I have overcome the world." So the New Testament announces that there is God. That He has this problem of evil in hand. That He has each of us in hand. This is the heartening answer faith has to give. This is the news from Calvary and the Empty Tomb: "Be of good cheer! Evil may win a battle. It cannot win the war."

The point for today is this: How can a man live without this assurance? How can we hope to do good apart from the encouragement it gives? This is what Christianity is for. We need it to guide our steps. But far more than that, we need it to ground our hopes and strengthen our hands. By ourselves we are simply not adequate, whether in private heart or on public scene.

> Stand up, stand up, for Jesus,
> Stand in His strength alone,
> The arm of flesh will fail you,
> You dare not trust your own.

Underneath all the detail and dismay, last Friday seemed to say this to us as Christians. It said it so plainly that we could hardly fail to understand. It said it so tragically that it hardly seems possible we could ever forget.

Then, finally, look at Friday as a Christian, and perhaps we can realize more surely that for all the shock and loss, life does go on, and life must go on. Consider the future of President Kennedy himself. He was a head of state. But he was also a man, and increasingly a maturing Christian man. Perhaps, then, we ought not to say, "The President is dead" . . . but rather, "The President is alive."

Perhaps both are right. He is dead. Death is a fact of every life. Friday it came to him. Yet every deep Christian conviction we own persuades us that, beyond death, this young President is alive.

When Lincoln died, it was only a day until Easter. It was a golden opportunity to stress the message of eternal life. More than one church used the chance and used it well. But Easter is not just for a day or a season. In our Christian experience together, every day is Easter, and every Sunday is a celebration of Easter. So it is appropriate that we mark this tremendous truth again now. John F. Kennedy has left the honors of earth for a fullness of life that passes all imagination. This is our comfort and his joy. His life goes on.

And so must ours. We have work to do. Remember the disciples after the Crucifixion. In their loss they felt there was nothing more they could do. Down the Emmaus Road two of them went, walking away from it all. Then Jesus met them, and sent them back to Jerusalem to work His work. Remember that later time when messengers stood by those same men after they had lost the Master from sight. "Why do you stand looking into heaven?" they asked. And back to the workaday world He sent them.

The call to go back is the call we have now. The sense of loss is keen, and it will last—who knows how long. All the same, we have work to do.

We have work to do restoring the picture of democracy in the eyes of the world. One reason we have all felt such shock is that Friday's attack was more than an attack on a man. It was an assault on our most distinguished office. It was even more. To a disturbing degree it left a stain on democracy and our whole enterprise of free and peaceable government. There will be some repairing to be done. The outpouring of a nation's heart in indignation and sympathy must already have done some of the work. The rest can be done if we are as nearly one in work as we have been in grief.

We have work to do in extending what Kennedy began. This, too, is a nonpartisan summons. Regardless of what party he may represent, a President's task is to work with us, and to help lead us among the problems and opportunities of liberty. It fell to this President to take some new steps toward peace. But even he could take only a few. There are many left for us to take. He helped us work our way a little further through the tangles of our ever more complex technology. He did the same for civil rights, and for public education and for care of the aged, and for new recognition of the arts, and for the adventure into space. But even as a President, he could move only a little way in the time he had. There is still nearly everything to be done. Whatever party may be in power, the work he was in needs to be pressed. We cannot afford to linger too long, even after a heavy loss like this.

We have work to do in giving support to the new President. Now he takes up the office which is almost more than a man can fill. He has asked God's help. Publicly he has also asked our help. So it is not for us to stand back and wonder whether he is adequate. Our job is to come to his support, and to do all we can at every level to help make him adequate. A letter would help. Prayer will help. Attention to the integrity of our own citizenship will help. He will need all the backing we can give if he is to do what we expect him to do.

So we pass roughly and suddenly from one chapter of our history to another. The transition brings to mind the custom begun by the French in the late Middle Ages. "The King is dead," they said. Then with equal emphasis they also cried out "Long live the King!"

Now it is for us to take up a like refrain. "The President is dead." For the moment, no doubt for months to come, this is what will seem most real. Yet more and more, even in the midst of sorrow, we must raise another voice: "Long live the President! And long live this nation, and this country among the nations, and under God!"

PRAYER

Father of us all, source of life and deliverer from death: hear these words and thoughts wrought from our dismay and our Christian hope. Use them to fashion and refashion our own lives for the days ahead, as only Thy Spirit can do. Be new grace to him who sets out in these shaken days to lead us. And as we say farewell to one who has bravely served our people, give us all the purpose and endurance we need to run with patience the race that is set before us, steadily looking to Jesus as the author and the finisher of our faith and of our lives. AMEN.

From: SAINT LUKE'S PARISH
DARIEN, CONNECTICUT

Sermon preached by the Reverend Robert Nelson Back

In the Burial Office, when all are assembled at the grave and "while the Body is made ready to be laid into the earth," a rubric instructs the minister to say or sing, "Man, that is born of a woman, hath but a short time to live, and is full of misery. He cometh up, and is cut down, like a flower; he fleeth as it were a shadow, and never continueth in one stay. In the midst of life we are in death; of whom may we seek for succor, but of thee, O Lord, most mighty, O holy and merciful Saviour, deliver us not into the bitter pains of eternal death. Thou knowest, Lord, the secrets of our hearts; shut not thy merciful ears to our prayer; but spare us Lord most holy, O God most mighty, O holy and merciful Saviour, thou most worthy judge eternal, suffer us not, at our last hour, for any pains of death, to fall from thee."

The first two sentences are from the Book of Job and the remainder is a medieval German antiphon used as an army battle song and at times of deep mourning. The antiphon is supposed to have been written by a monk named Notker in the ninth century in the Abbey of St. Gall in Switzerland, and Martin Luther made a metrical version of it. The modern American resists these hard words and even more the thought behind them. He is not willing to accept the "sense of awe and dread in the presence of death, acknowledged as a judgment upon our sins."

In a Latin class in Darien High School at 2:20 P.M. on Friday, twenty-two healthy and lively juniors were translating Caesar. The principal's voice over the intercom broke into their study, "I am sorry to inform you that the President of the United States has been shot." They knew it was no joke; principals don't joke about things like that. In a masterful way Mr. Atkinson informed his students of a most serious and solemn event in the history of this nation and the world. "In the midst of life we are in death."

At 5:45 Friday evening in Darien, Phil Jones had his dancing class as usual. Well, not quite as usual. The same active, rambunctious twelve-year-old boys and girls were there. But they didn't dance. Solemnly they watched television instead; the story of a President in a free land who was cut down in the prime of his manhood. "In the midst of life we are in death."

The assassination of John Fitzgerald Kennedy is, in the words of Winston Churchill, "a monstrous crime." Yet it is the measure of the greatness of this nation that men moved with incredible swiftness to repair the damage of the moment. One hundred and six minutes after the death of the thirty-fifth President of the United States, the thirty-sixth President was sworn into office and was winging his way back to the capital. Planes full of government personnel were rerouted and brought home. Business will go on as usual. Nothing will be disrupted. Already the new President is putting his house in order and with his advisers laying plans for the future. America is bigger than any man, no matter who that man is. The nation will go forward—to use Mr. Kennedy's own favorite words.

But the shock of the assassination goes deeper than any outward event would indicate. On the way to his own death Jesus said to the women of Jerusalem, "Don't weep for me, weep for yourselves." And that is precisely what we are doing, and with every reason for doing it —weeping for ourselves. We have come face to face with reality; we can't push our fears into a dark corner; we can't sweep our insecurity under a carpet. "In the midst of life we are in death." And the undertaker's art won't help us much. Everything in this world is fleeting, ephemeral, and unstable. "Man, that is born of woman, hath but a short time to live. . . . He cometh up, and is cut down, like a flower. . . ." We live in the kind of world where sin and evil are rampant, where death is an ever-present reality, where Presidents of free nations can be assassinated. This knowledge cuts deeply. There is nothing sure and certain and we cry desperately for things sure and certain. Lyndon Johnson is said to be a flexible man; it is important to be flexible in the midst of uncertainty.

The President's death is "a monstrous crime," an ugly bleeding sore. But we live in the kind of world where such things can be expected. It takes a pain almost beyond enduring for us to accept this simple truth. We are bound up inextricably in the President's death, for as the Dean of St. Paul's Cathedral, London, said in a famous sermon in the seventeenth century, "No man is an island, entire of itself; every man is a piece of the continent, a part of the main . . . any man's death diminishes me, because I am involved in mankind; and therefore never sent to know for whom the bell tolls; it tolls for thee." And as the medieval antiphon reminds us, the President's death is a "judgment upon our sins, from whose bitter pains we can only hope to be delivered by the mercy of our Saviour and Judge." It is the genius of the Judeo-Christian tradition to hear the voice of God speaking through national tragedies as well as triumphs. We are chastened. "My dear children ... be not surprised," said Henry Ward Beecher, on another occasion, "certainly not out of your faith. God is not angry with you.... For your good God afflicts you; and he says to you, 'What father is he that chastiseth not his son? If ye endure chastisement you are my sons. Whom the Lord loveth he chasteneth.' O glorious fact! O blessed truth! These are God's love letters, written in dark ink. 'Whom the Lord loveth he chasteneth, and scourgeth every son whom he receiveth.' If ye endure chastening, ye are the sons of God; if not, bastards.

"Grant, O God! that we may be sons. Now speak and

see if thou canst scare us. Now thunder and see if we tremble. Now write and see if we do not press thy message to our heart. Afflict us, only do not forget us. Comfort us, and we will bear to others the comfort wherewith we are comforted." Carry in your hearts and pray, even if it is not your wont to pray, for the family of the President, his widow, his children, all those who are most closely affected. Pray for Lyndon Baines Johnson, President of the United States. Pray for this nation and all the peoples of this nation. Pray for the world—and the peace of the world. For "we can only hope to be delivered by the mercy of our Saviour and Judge."

From: FIRST BAPTIST CHURCH
SIOUX FALLS, SOUTH DAKOTA

Sermon preached by the Reverend Dr. Roger L. Fredrikson

We have come to God's house in this hour a shaken and a different people than we were a week ago. The strange events of history have forced us as a nation to pass through the valley of the shadow. Deep within us are emotions and long thoughts that outrun our words and which move us to tears. We are struck by the peculiar meaning of this single life. And we ask "What good can come of all this?" "Are we called to national repentance?" "Can there come new humility?" "Will men give themselves to greater purposes because of all this?" Yes, we have come to worship this day haunted and shaken.

In the wake of our President's assassination, we are struck by the vast uncertainty of all human life. We sail our little vessels surrounded by a mystery called death which no man can avoid. It can come with a sudden violence or like a creeping paralysis. The plain, unvarnished truth is that all flesh—and this includes the great and the small—is as grass.

We are moved again by the depth of our common humanity. Who of us has not felt the poignancy and the suffering of the young, beautiful widow who now travels alone with her memories and a bloodstained dress? Who of us did not wonder which person would tell the little children that their father would not return? The heartbreak of this is not altered because their father was the President of the United States. Certainly we have wondered if the aged father could survive the shock of losing another son. The same ache and anguish of this family is our common lot whenever death comes. We are bound together in our mortality and pain.

In the midst of this we have sensed America's amazing ties with the world. In spite of our having been analyzed as the "ugly American" and the hostility we have witnessed at times toward the power of America, we have been made aware of great affection expressed toward us throughout the world in unexpected places. Think of those lights burning in West Berlin and that incredible voluntary gathering of forty thousand people standing quietly at the point along the wall where Mr. Kennedy had given his speech of courage. Or think of the bell that has rung now for an American President in England—that bell used only on previous occasions for royalty. And all of us are surprised that Charles de Gaulle of France, often aloof and critical, has announced plans to attend the President's funeral.

And one reporter spoke of the tear that came to Gromyko's eye when he heard the news of Mr. Kennedy's death. And the Japanese people simply stopped in stunned silence through Tokyo. The way America has handled her role of leadership has often been misunderstood. But something of the American dream, the revolutionary spirit that still lives on, is an inspiration to the peoples of the earth. We sense this now in our valley.

Let none of us forget that there is in all of this the darkness of evil. It is easy for us to pick out one man and cry "He did it!" This is to evade the issue. The power of evil is an awesome, demonic reality. It affects us like a disease. In the words of the Apostle Paul, "We wrestle not against flesh and blood but against principalities and powers." The prejudice and hatred of ordinary men can become the twisted mentality of a killer. Carelessness and indifference can breed violence on the streets and death in the highest places of responsibility. We cannot wash our hands of this incident in Dallas. We are our brother's keeper and we are involved.

In the end, Mr. Kennedy fell in the line of duty. On one occasion, Jesus said, "This is my commandment, that you love one another as I have loved you. Greater love has no man than this: that a man lay down his life for his friends." I am not wrong when I tell you our President who died on the streets of his country surrounded by his fellow Americans gave the last full measure.

Now my friends, there is a power and a grace which moves through human affairs both of joy and sorrow. In the final analysis, this gift of the grace of God is our last hope. It summons us to greater tasks. Our late President at the beginning of his administration summed it up when he said, "Now the trumpet summons us again—not as a call to bear arms, though arms we need—not as a call to battle, though embattled we are—but a call to bear the burden of a long twilight struggle year in and year out, rejoicing in hope, patient in tribulation—a struggle against the common enemies of man! Tyranny, poverty, disease, and war itself."

Let this hour of concern and questioning be a time of repentance and renewal, of prayer and a chastened spirit, that God may do His work among us.

From: PILGRIM CONGREGATIONAL CHURCH
SEATTLE, WASHINGTON

Sermon preached by the Reverend Ralph S. Barber

As all of you, I have listened with horror and dismay to the reports of the events taking place within the last forty-eight hours—two days that will live long among the darkest hours of this nation's history. We are stunned and grief-stricken, and ashamed. I am sure that most of us have felt that such a thing as the cold, calculated, brutal murder of an American President just could not happen in this country any more. In recent years we have watched with anxiety while our heads of state toured foreign lands, and heaved sighs of relief when they arrived home again, feeling that once more they were safe from all except some tragic accident or illness. Even now, two days after, it seems so incredibly unreal that one has the feeling it must all be a terrible nightmare.

It is very difficult to be objective at a time like this, yet we must try to stand aside for a few moments and look at what has happened and what is happening. It is a time when there are too many words being spoken. There is not enough silence. Nor enough time to pick up the main threads and see them for what they are. Just now we are shocked and grieved. We are too saddened to think clearly. But the time will soon come when we shall need clear heads. The implications of this crime will be far-reaching. Intemperate words will be uttered. Accusations will be made. Extremists will try to make political capital out of the events. We shall need to be calm and clear-headed. Only by being so will the people of this nation avoid fear, and panic, the consequence of fear, and chaos, the consequence of panic.

The President and the nation have been the victim of an act of insane hatred and violence. In some twisted mind or minds this was a good work. Some will say it is the result of a sinister plot with international implications. Whatever and whoever brought about this terrible thing, we must not allow an act of blind violence to lead to national hysteria, national hatred, or national violence. This great nation, with its roots in the Christian virtues of reason and justice and mercy, may go through some trying times in the not-too-distant future. But, thank God, there are, as there always have been, rational minds and moderate emotions to lead us.

The reader of history must face the truth that since the moment Abel's blood cried out from the ground our history has been one of violence. The history of mankind is murderous. The history of our own land is no exception. Much as we wish it were not so, the undercurrent of violence, which we abhor in other lands, runs through our land also.

[While I was writing this the news came over the radio that Lee Oswald has been shot in the city hall at Dallas.] Now another act of violence has followed hard on the heels of the assassination. I was just about to say: "John Kennedy's is not the only blood spilled in this year of our Lord, 1963, at the hands of violent men." All of us are, in a very large measure, responsible for this atmosphere of violence that has taken lives this year in our land, and now has taken the life of our President. We are a duplicitous people. We pride ourselves that we are a nation of laws and not of men, yet we glorify, in the name of "entertainment," the men of violence who take the law into their own hands. Daily, and almost hourly, violence, lawlessness, and immorality are glamorized on television screens and movie screens; in books, magazines, and so-called comics. It is almost as if we put our real faith in violence and lawlessness, despite our protests to the contrary.

But the Christian believes that the command to love is buried even more deeply in the human heart than the command to hate. The Christian believes that in all the voices of clamor and chaos crying vengeance and hatred, prejudice and intolerance, the voice of God can still be heard, and that when those voices cry the loudest, the voice of God can be heard most clearly summoning men to turn from their vicious ways and serve Him. The voice that echoes most clearly in our ears today and over the centuries is not the voices of vengeance and violence that clamored for the life of Jesus, but his own gentle words speaking for God above the chaos that swirled about his head.

It may well be that the Christians of our land and the Godfearing peoples of all lands need to speak more clearly than ever for God in the days to come, reminding the people of all lands that we are all children of

God. That this great nation in which we live, and which we love, is still a nation under God.

It may well be that we shall have to raise our voices more clearly against the hatred and suspicion, intolerance and injustice, pride and prejudice that set man against his brother, and class against class, these cancerous growths that breed the kind of violence we are witnessing. It was to eradicate these things from the life and body politic of mankind that this nation was founded. So long as we remain true to that purpose God will bless us and strengthen us, and we will succeed, for we will surely be a nation under God.

We have lost a President under circumstances that are shameful and appalling. This morning we have witnessed another act of lawlessness that shames this nation, which has proclaimed itself before the world as a nation of laws and not of men.

May God forgive us.

Now, as we have done in our darkest hours in the past, *but* with an even firmer faith in God than in the past, let us rise up and stand beside the new President, as he has asked us to do, united with him, and with each other, and with God, to face whatever lies before us.

From: GOLER METROPOLITAN A.M.E.
ZION CHURCH
WINSTON-SALEM, NORTH CAROLINA

Sermon preached by the Reverend Dr. John H. Miller, Sr.

Seeing his days are determined, the number of his months are with thee, Thou hast appointed his bounds that he cannot pass. Job 14:5

Every man lives in his own little world in this big world that God has given us. Within it he builds his family, achieves his riches and fame, and falls prey to poverty, sickness, success, and failures. Herein he makes friends and enemies and allies himself with God or "gods."

Some men have long spans of life. Others do not. Years, chronologically, mean very little. It is the quality of one's life that counts, not length. Methuselah lived 969 years and all that could be said of him was "and he begat children." Jesus lived only thirty-three years, yet he made it possible for all peoples to know God and qualify themselves for eternal living. Alexander the Great lived only thirty-three years, and it was said of him that he sat down and cried because there were not other worlds to conquer. John F. Kennedy lived forty-six years, and it was said of him that he was a man who lit the torch of hope and friendship around the world. He brought inspiration to the young of the world, and strove for better relations and understanding among peoples and races of the world. Only three years as President! But look at the frontiers pushed back: frontiers of freedom, peace, academic excellence, civil rights, and the projection of ambassadors of good will.

His life was one of service to a day and age that needed the freshness and youthfulness that his personality gave. Our hope was in him in moments of despair. He was our incentive to carry on when violence raged in the streets. He brought poise to a depressed people when times seemed out of joint—and some men, seemingly, had lost their reason. From this rubble we felt sure a new world would be born. A world, not clashing and fighting—but a world of new ideas and freedom.

One cannot squeeze out extra years beyond those determined by God. Maybe our late President knew this full well. Maybe this is why he was never idle, always moving, challenging, evoking, admonishing, and encouraging the people of the country and world to be strong to meet any challenge, to be ready and willing and able to assume any responsibility; and to lose one's self in an abiding concern for the common good. He gave us this truth: that no experience, no event at any particular moment in time and space, exhausts what life is trying to do. His work will live on. His dreams will be realized. His spirit will know, for the eternal flame will light the course. So, let us emulate our fallen chief. We will become a part of all that we have met, knowing that all experience is as an arch through which gleams that untraveled world whose frontiers fade forever when we move.

We have lost a friend. The world has lost a statesman. His family lost a dearly beloved. The church has offered him to God.

I want the faith
The envies not
The passing of the days;
That sees all times and ways
More endless than the stars;
That looks at life
Not as a little day
Of heat and strife,
But one eternal revel of delight
With God, the Friend, adventurer and light.

From: SAINT PHILIP'S CHURCH
DURHAM, NORTH CAROLINA

Sermon preached by the Reverend L. Bartine Sherman

A MAN IS DEAD

A man is dead.

Men die every day.

Every man dies someday.

This death, as grievous as it is, is of less concern than the manner of his death, and its meaning to our nation.

A man is dead.

In his position, and as a man of strength, he made political enemies. None of these could have wished him personal harm, save for the unbalanced. Men of all nations are united in their grief and shock. Indeed, the whole nation seems to have been suspended in a state of shock.

Out of this shock, one reaction seems to have been common to most of us. As we first heard the news, we immediately assumed that the killer was a member of the extreme right wing. The liberals among us felt that this action discredited the whole movement to the right and were inclined to lay the responsibility for the murder on the leaders of this wing. The conservatives felt that the killing was a tragic reaction to the unwelcome pressure from the left and were willing to ascribe the basic guilt to the leaders of this wing.

I pray that we have now learned our lesson, the danger in an overanxious concern in establishing guilt. Let the man who has been accused of the killing be judged by the court; and let history alone decide if any responsibility is to be placed on any larger movement.

A man is dead.

Whoever is guilty of his death, as Christians we can only pray for that guilty man, for his repentance and God's forgiveness.

But what of our nation? Surely this is, above all, a time for prayer. We need the peace of God, lest the divisions within our nation, evidenced by the opposing reactions to this murder based on our early false assumptions, bring lasting damage to the fabric of our national life. We need the strength of God, to face the stresses produced by this sudden shock to the political, economic, and social structure of our nation. We need the faith of God that our national grief may bring us to a closer realization of our utter dependence on the God of all the nations.

A man is dead.

He was a man of faith in God, a man of God's peace and of God's strength. In sure and certain hope of the resurrection to eternal life, we commit him confidently into God's hands. Some of us loved him, some admired and respected him, some feared him. But none of us can grieve for him; all of us can grieve for his family, for ourselves, and for our country.

Our grief is compounded of our love, our respect, and even our hostility. But we must not, we cannot, allow our grief to distort our behavior as Christian people, those who believe in the resurrection and in the loving mercy of our God.

We mourn his death, indeed. But let not our mourning lead us into extremes of recriminations or of hasty action. The nation has lost one who was committed to the principle of the freedom of man under God. So let our grief over his loss lead us to commit ourselves more firmly to the same principle, to the end that the glorious liberty of the sons of God may be realized in the life of every man, of whatever race or creed or political persuasion.

So now I bid you to prayer as an act of penitence for our national sins, and as a solemn supplication to Almighty God for His gifts of strength and peace and faith for our nation.

From: DUBLIN, IRELAND

Tribute by the Most Reverend Dr. G. O. Simms, Archbishop of Dublin

When the tragic news reached Ireland, inevitably our minds turned back to the memorable visit of last June and President Kennedy's unsparing giving of himself during days packed full of engagements.

Each one of us will have special memories of those hours of swift travel from city to city and the happy, welcoming meetings. In his speeches there was no repetition or formal phrase; each event was given added and unexpected significance because he brought himself into the center of it with the active and particular interest that made the occasions live.

Several scenes stand out in my mind: perhaps they illustrate something of the personality of one whose concern was world peace and international stability as well as the sound leadership of his own country.

His swift adaptability to a fresh situation and a completely new set of circumstances impressed us all greatly. He flew to Ireland from Berlin and spoke to us at the airport; straightway he showed his understanding of our place in the world of nations and at the same time exhibited his eagerness to learn from his visit to the land of his fathers something fresh about our outlook and way of life. Each day, after that first welcome, saw him become increasingly at home among us: he responded in a most engaging way to the genuine and widespread happiness, evident wherever he went.

His speeches, also, were delivered with an individuality that made each utterance distinctive. He avoided the platitude and expressed in very practical terms something picked out in relief that he wanted to say, in the particular scene of his oration, for the mutual benefit of two countries. His asides, his local knowledge, his obvious pride in his Irish origins brought a warmth and intimacy to his approach to public affairs. He brought people we know and places quite familiar to us into his talks and illustrated from these local touches what he was aiming at and what were his ideals in international matters.

At the delightful luncheon party given by him as host at the Embassy in Phoenix Park, he summed up, with humor no less than with genuine emotion, his impressions of the Irish visit. Here he was obviously on very happy terms with our own President and Mrs. De Valera and also with our ministers of state. Details seemed to attract his attention—and a bright question about something that caught his eye, put to the stranger to whom he was introduced, turned the formal handshake into a constructive conversation. We discerned a love of music, a fondness for home life, a delight in children, and a regard for persons: things all too easily forgotten when administration and affairs of state loom large.

Lastly, there was an air of simplicity about his bearing that attracted. The slight young figure and the pleasing expression belied much of the responsibility that weighed upon him and the strain that surrounded his life. His bearing, however, enabled us to see power in his direct approach; to observe the keenness with which he went out to meet people and to learn from them at first hand about human and public problems the things that were not always included in written surveys. This human interest proved to be a very special thing in a person often called away from people to attend to affairs. The spiritual emphasis was quietly present, free from piety of a forced kind, yet maintained with a gentle firmness that could be discerned in speeches, carefully prepared and also less formal.

For these reasons the sense of bereavement felt here at this moment is acute and personal. Our sympathy goes out to his family circle no less than to the people of the country he led with vigor and forthrightness; there is also the conviction here that much of what he did and was will continue to have influence after this shattering day.

From: DOMINICAN CHURCH OF THE HOLY CROSS
SLIGO, IRELAND

Sermon preached by the Reverend Gabriel Bowe, O. P.

Good Night, Sweet Prince . . .

My dear people, this is indeed a sorrowful day—not only for President Kennedy's family, not only for his great nation, not only for Irishmen everywhere, but for all mankind.

Rare in the history of mankind are those occasions when we are made vividly aware of the underlying unity of the human race; when the heart of mankind, as it were, misses a beat, when all the world and all its business stops and looks and gasps. There is the universal experience of a deep emotion, the presence of a sudden tragedy, known almost instinctively to affect profoundly the lives and future of the great nations as well as the small, the great men as well as the humble and unknown, the old and the young alike. This year of 1963 has seen two such moments: one of them the death of a saint, of the late Pope John XXIII. The other has come quickly upon us: the death of a hero, of John Fitzgerald Kennedy. It is a sad comment on the conduct of human affairs that we seem to need occasions of great sorrow and tragedy to draw us together.

Nevertheless we draw strength and hope from the thought, for in the midst of a world fraught with danger for the future of mankind, torn with strife, threatened by despair, such an occasion as this points to the underlying goodness of men, their fundamental sympathy and compassion.

His successor in the Presidency has described him as a man of "wisdom, strength, and peace; he did not shrink from his responsibilities, but welcomed them. . . . He said it himself: 'The energy, the devotion which we bring to this endeavor will light our country and all who serve it—and the glow from that fire can truly light the world.' "

There are many qualities which distinguish him from the general run of political leaders whom we have known: his gaiety, his youthfulness, the freshness and vigor of his approach to the troubles which beset the world. It seems to me, however, that the virtues which he possessed, and to a very high degree, and which have aroused the admiration, and now the sorrow, of mankind, are the virtues of hope, of courage, and, above all, of faith.

In these virtues lay the essence of his answer to the depressed, the dejected, the despairing, the corrosive, and destructive cynicism which eats into and destroys so many of the endeavors undertaken by great men of our time. He was a man of indomitable hope, of incorrigible optimism (we are reminded of the late Pope John's castigation of the "prophets of doom"), and allied to this hope was an equally indomitable courage—the mark of the authentic hero, of the man who is ready to tackle the seemingly impossible situation, to face enormous opposition, to encounter frightening odds, with supreme confidence—not, however, with the mistaken confidence of the foolhardy, but with the steadiness and confidence of the man of true fortitude.

In a remarkable tribute to the late President the British Prime Minister, Sir Alec Douglas-Home, referred to him as "a man of peace, a man of deep religious faith. . . ." Can any of us remember when before in the history of human affairs the leader of one great nation spoke of the leader of another in terms such as these? For my part I cannot. *A man of peace*—yes, many times. But *a man of deep religious faith*—this is something different. This is not the kind of description we expect to find pinned to a great political leader. In this case it is a very accurate description, for it uncovers the spring from which welled up all the sparkling qualities of John Fitzgerald Kennedy. For, above all, this was a man of faith.

His profound conviction that all men are equal in the sight of their Creator, whether they be rich or poor, whether they be white or black, red or yellow, was the motive force behind all his policies. And not only are they born *equal* but they are born *free*. The passion to recognize that equality and to implement that freedom was the dominant passion of his life.

Thus he recognized the need to revise the American immigration laws, and he quoted with evident approval the poet who warned his fellow Americans to "avoid organized charity, scrimped and iced in the name of a cautious and statistical Christ." Like his predecessor George Washington, he wanted the "bosom of America open to receive not only the opulent and respectable stranger, but the poor and persecuted of all nations and religions."

His measures to end racial segregation in his own country were a further recognition of the equality of men, regardless of their color. And so determined was his stand on this issue that when the first news of his assassination was received many thought it must have been done by some racial extremist.

But not only in his public utterances and his political activities was this conviction apparent. His respect for the human individual, the person beloved of God and redeemed by the Blood of Christ, showed itself in his personal life: his refusal to occupy a special pew in his local parish church, his preference to remain with his family in the main body of the church. He acted occasionally as an usher! Here in Ireland we saw it in his readiness to set aside prearranged plans in order to speak to bystanders, to shake the hand of waitresses who served him at state banquets, to take tea in an Irish kitchen, to bow impulsively and kiss the cheek of Mrs. De Valera. Touching gestures, of all these and many more, reflecting the warm humanity that endeared him to millions, but indicating the deeper knowledge that came from his faith, the knowledge that under God all men were his brothers.

His murder is an evil and monstrous act. It is a sin against humanity; for the human race, in its hour of peril, can ill afford to lose a man of this caliber, a leader of this stature. But for all that, each of us this morning must not harbor hatred or thoughts of revenge toward the man who perpetrated this foul crime. For he too is redeemed by the Blood of Christ and is our brother. To hate him for his deed would be to betray the ideals for which President Kennedy gave his life, to multiply the violence which he pledged himself to end. We may hate the sin, but, like our Lord, we must love the sinner. This is the only road to true and lasting peace—to drive out of our hearts the ill-will we may feel toward this man, and indeed the ill-will we may feel toward any man or race of men. Peace is born in the individual soul. This is the real battleground of this world, the place where is fought out the struggle between truth and falsehood, light and darkness, goodness and evil, God and Satan. Here man must by God's grace achieve mastery, and from here that peace will spread to all the world.

No greater tribute could we pay to our late beloved President Kennedy than to resolve that we will carry on the striving for this peace, peace with God and man, the beginning of that eternal peace which we fervently pray he now enjoys in Heaven.

In his address to the Dail in June he closed with these words:

Great powers have their responsibilities and burdens, but the smaller nations of the world must fulfill their obligations as well. A great Irish poet once wrote "I believe profoundly in the future of Ireland, that this is an isle of destiny, that that destiny will be glorious, and that when our hour has come we will have something to give to the world."

My friends, Ireland's hour has come. You have something to give to the world....

Little did he think then—and perhaps it would have

made him more than a little proud—that in such a short time the people of Ireland would justly claim that their hour *had* indeed come, that they *had* given something to the world, and that his name was John Fitzgerald Kennedy.

While we mourn his loss and send our sympathy to his widow and children, to his family, and to his nation, let us remember too to thank God for those three great, glorious, and proud years when one of our race stood at the head of mankind's never-ending search for peace and freedom.

He liked to quote Shakespeare. We might find, in our sorrow, an appropriate text in Hamlet:

. . . the rest is silence.
Now cracks a noble heart;—good night, sweet prince:
And flights of angels sing thee to thy rest.

From: THE CONFERENCE OF AUSTRIAN BISHOPS
LINZ, AUSTRIA

Eulogy by Suffragan Bishop Dr. Jakob Weinbacher of Vienna

Consternation, sorrow, and anxiety are the emotions moving Austria as well as the world. John F. Kennedy represented much more than the head of a friendly government. To our youth he was a symbol, to lovers of peace a hope, to devotees of freedom a guarantor, and to justice, even in his own country, a promise. He did not hesitate to subordinate political tactics to an ethical goal.

He consciously risked his popularity and his chances for success in the question of civil rights for Negroes. He was the first Catholic President of the United States. The new style created by Kennedy in the realm of politics became a style of politics which brought about understanding and a new responsibility for peace and freedom throughout the world.

From: SPASO HOUSE
(AT UNITED STATES EMBASSY),
MOSCOW, RUSSIA

Prayer delivered by the Reverend Donald V. Roberts*

November 25, 1963

I ask that you join with me now in these prayers of eulogy as we give thanks to God for John Fitzgerald Kennedy, thirty-fifth President of the United States of America.

Almighty God, from Whom cometh every good and lovely gift;
For this dear man,
We thank Thee, Our Father.
For his excellent mind, his uncanny ability in comprehending vast, technical problems,
We thank Thee, Our Father.
For his splendid sense of humor which revealed the

* Prayer Session attended by 1000 people, including Soviet officials and Diplomatic Corps.

ambiguities and contradictions of every human situation, assisting him to see more deeply into the real questions of our time,

We thank Thee, Our Father.

For his willingness to lead the people and not be led by them,

We thank Thee, Our Father.

For his *Profiles in Courage* and loyalty to shipmates in war,

We thank Thee, Our Father.

For his growing conviction that racial injustice must be rectified so that all Americans at last be truly free,

We thank Thee, Our Father.

For his abounding concern that young people in America continue to grow in wisdom, in stature, and in favor with God and all men everywhere,

We thank Thee, Our Father.

For his knowledge of history that enabled him to deal constructively with unanticipated events, and rapid social changes,

We thank Thee, Our Father.

For his sense of time, the fitness of things which gave purpose and direction in an age of uncertainty,

We thank Thee, Our Father.

For his insight on human nature that enabled him to approach questions of foreign policy recognizing that every nation has its just claims as well as its peculiar obsessions,

We thank Thee, Our Father.

For his glad, unwearied vision to create new understanding between nations, races, and classes,

We thank Thee, Our Father.

For those qualities of heart and mind that made him dear to his own family,

We thank Thee, Our Father.

For his father's love for his children whom he adored and longed to be with, and who rejoiced to be with him always and always,

We thank Thee, Our Father.

For his love as a husband, cherishing the little sanctities of family life,

We thank Thee, Our Father.

For his faith in Thee, O God, a faith by which he lived and by which he died,

We thank Thee, Our Father.

And in that faith, we tenderly commit him to Thee, this day, Our Father, through Jesus Christ our Lord.

AMEN.

From: ST. OLAV CHURCH
OSLO, NORWAY

Sermon delivered by the Reverend Olaf I. Waring

November 26, 1963

In the twelfth chapter of the Gospel of St. Luke we read these words of the Lord Jesus Christ to His disciples: "I say unto you my friends, Be not afraid of them that kill the body, and after that have no more that they can do. Fear him, which after he hath killed hath power to cast into hell; yea, I say unto you, Fear him."

Certainly John Kennedy was a fearless man in the pursuit of those goals which were for him his destiny, his vocation to achieve. It is said that in times of actual warfare, men often display wonderful courage in the face of great physical danger. John Kennedy showed that kind of courage indeed, as a sailor in war. But later, as President of the United States, his was a courage of perhaps an even greater and more noble kind as he led his country through another type of warfare, more subtle yet potentially far more explosive. At the same time, in keeping with the spirit of the Gospels, he never lost sight of the fact that life itself and all events connected with it is but a means to an end—that end being the ultimate knowledge and possession of the Creator in Whom we shall find all the fullness and completion of our being.

President Kennedy was then a man of faith, a man who possessed a reverential filial fear of God our Father, and who did not hesitate to cast his cares upon the Lord both in his public addresses and, what is even more important, in his personal and private family life.

It is not by accident that so many great statesmen are also God-fearing men. One calls to mind the memory of the late Dag Hammarskjold, a man in whom were marvelously combined the qualities of keen insight into the problems of men and nations and what approaches a true Christian mysticism. In Dag Hammarskjold's recently published diary *Markings** we find the following verse which I believe admirably sums up the outlook, the driving force in President John Kennedy's life. Mr. Hammarskjold wrote:

The road,
You shall follow it.
The fun,
You shall forget it.
The cup,

* From *Markings* by Dag Hammarskjold, translated by Leif Sjoberg and W. H. Auden. Copyright © 1964 by Alfred A. Knopf, Inc., and Faber & Faber, Ltd.

You shall empty it.
The pain,
You shall conceal it.
The truth,
You shall be told it.
The end,
You shall endure it.

And indeed, in very truth, we shall all—we can all—learn the Truth and bear the End.

From: ST. GILES' CATHEDRAL
EDINBURGH, SCOTLAND

Extract from sermon preached by the Reverend Dr. H. C. Whitley

It can be said now and will be said that in a day of racial hatred he dared to proclaim the rights of man. He knew well the dangers of the stand he had taken on behalf of the American Negro. A weaker man would have avoided trouble, but he was a brave and strong man who would not back down from his courageous stand.

It can be said now and will be said that in a day of East-West tension he dared to penetrate iron curtains and proclaim not just a policy of containment, of co-existence, but a policy of cooperation between great power blocs.

From: AMERICAN CATHEDRAL
PARIS

Sermon preached by the Very Reverend Dr. Sturgis Lee Riddle, Dean

Ask not what your country can do for you. Ask what you can do for your country.

He asked it. He answered it—with his life.

The President of France, his fellow leader of the free world, who will be attending his funeral in Washington tomorrow, put it this way:

"President Kennedy died as a soldier, under fire, for his duty and in the service of his country. In the name of the French people, a friend at all times of the American people, I salute his grand example and his grand memory."

We, his countrymen, do likewise.

It is fitting and proper that on this Lord's Day, in the Lord's House, we should commemorate the passing into the Lord's nearer Presence of one of the Lord's most faithful servants. As the trumpets sound for him on the other side, we hear the voice of the Lord: "Well done, good and faithful servant. Enter thou into the joy of thy Lord."

"Greater love hath no man than this, that a man lay down his life for his friends. Ye are my friends, if ye do whatsoever I command you."

On August 2, 1943, in the South Pacific, Lieutenant John F. Kennedy risked his life for his friends. On November 22, 1963, as Commander in Chief, he gave it.

He was his Lord's friend—the friend of all who love the Lord, no matter what they call themselves in church or creed. He tried to do what his Lord commanded him. He gave himself in unselfish devotion to that "service which is perfect freedom" to his country, his world, and his times.

For his country, he worked tirelessly to bring the American dream closer to fulfillment, to forge a more perfect union out of liberty and justice for all. He thought of the aged and infirm, that they should not be forgotten of their fellow men, that none should lack for healing and succor, whatever the state of their riches. He thought of children, that no child's life should be blighted because he didn't have the chance at a decent education. He thought of young people, that they should have healthy minds in healthy bodies, that they should be given outlets, new frontiers, to express the natural idealism and exuberance of youth, to "break their hearts for a laurel wreath." The Peace Corps, the symbol to the world of our country's youthful idealism, was his idea.

But I suspect he will be longest remembered in our country for his will and determination to finish the unfinished business of Thomas Jefferson, Abraham Lincoln, Franklin D. Roosevelt, and so many others who stand in the great succession of American Christian humanists, to see to it that even the least of these our brethren, whatever their color or condition, should have their full rights as full citizens of our brotherhood in fact as well as in name. He tried to finish what the Great Emancipator had begun. He wanted America to be itself.

In the world, John F. Kennedy fought the good fight with all his might. He fought it against forces anywhere who threaten the remaining bastions of man's freedom and dignity as a child of God, made in His image and endowed with his spirit. He fought it successfully. He held the fort, be it in Cuba or Berlin. He honored our commitments to friends and allies. He shared in a common sense of responsibility to the downtrodden and underprivileged of the world. He tried to keep the heart of America warm and charitable, equal to its duties as leader of the free world. Until such time as present tyrannies crumble under the pressure of their own people demanding their rights as human beings, no man could have done more.

Certainly, there were and are and will be differences of opinion about the way he did these things. There always are when it comes to putting principles into practice. But his heart was in the right place. He was on the side of the angels. He "bore not the sword in vain." "His body is buried in peace, but his deeds live forever more."

But we are here to do more than honor the name of John F. Kennedy, to claim for him the eternal promise that he will go "from strength to strength in the life of perfect service in the heavenly kingdom," to grieve that his life was cut down, like his Lord's, in the middle of the way, before his job on earth was fully done, to share with his loved ones and people of good will everywhere our common sorrow.

We are here, just as well, to humble ourselves and our countrymen in deep contrition and repentance, in the presence of the Holy One, for the sins that cut down this faithful servant in the flower of his manhood.

For the dark prejudice that still haunts the hearts of many of our countrymen, have mercy upon us, O Lord. For the ignorance, fear, superstition, egotism, and jealousy that still divide Christian Americans into mutual hostilities of color, race, creed, class, privilege, and underprivilege, have mercy upon us, O Lord. For the murderous insanity that these things foment and express in our society, have mercy upon us, O Lord. For man's inhumanity to man, have mercy upon us, O Lord. For knowing what Thy will is, and not doing it, have mercy upon us, O Lord.

May this innocent blood, may the sorrows of these stricken innocents who are in our prayers today, cleanse and turn our hearts. May our nation and our world be the better for this martyrdom. May there be a new dedication to that freedom, justice, and friendship among the nations for which he gave his last full measure of devotion. He would have wished it. He would have willingly paid this price.

I have seen beauty, rising like a star
Out of the grimness of some ancient wrong;
I have seen honor bursting like a song
From out the jangled clamorings of war.
For evil dies, self-slain with hate and strife
And good springs up from its own seed of life.

From: THE AMERICAN EMBASSY
LAGOS, NIGERIA

Sermon preached by the Reverend Dr. Howard Thurman *

The time and the place of a man's life on the earth is the time and place of his body, but the meaning and sig-

* Dean of Marsh Chapel, Boston University.

nificance of his life is as vast and far-reaching as his gifts, his times, and the passionate commitment of all his powers can make it.

President John F. Kennedy is dead.

It is given but rarely to an individual the privilege of capturing the imagination of his age and thereby becoming a symbol of the hopes, aspirations, and dreams of his fellows, so that often in their enthusiasm and relief they are apt to forget that he was the symbol—that he stood for them, and his strength was their strength, and their strength was his strength, and his courage was the courage he drew in large part from his faith in them and their faith in him.

This, by the grace of God, was John F. Kennedy's privilege.

When he became President of the United States, the youth of the land and the young in spirit were caught up in the sweep of his confidence, his sense of purpose, and his direction. There was an aura of destiny in his assurance. When he said, in essence, "Do not ask what can my country do for me, but rather what can I do for my country," the winds of God blew across the land. When the Peace Corps was announced and it was clear that he was calling upon young and old alike to become apostles of sensitiveness, placing their lives and talents at the disposal of human need anywhere without benefit of anything other than the opportunity to give, the morning stars sang together and the sons of God shouted for joy. They felt that, for yet a little while, life and time were on their side because the future belonged to them.

Again, by the grace of God, it was John F. Kennedy's privilege to become the first Roman Catholic to be elected President of the United States. This marked a turning point in the history of the nation. It was a recognition of one of the basic elements in the genius of the democratic dogma—that a man must be free to worship God after the manner of his own spirit and in accordance with the private promptings of his personal conscience as expressed in a free choice of the faith to which he will give his devotion and his life. As a Protestant clergyman, I rejoice to say that the people as a whole found spiritual strength in his authentic devotion to his own faith. By some instinctual wisdom they sensed that a man must be at home *somewhere* in order to *feel* at home anywhere.

Again, by the grace of God, it was John F. Kennedy's privilege to become the voice of the American conscience in the matter of the civil rights of its citizens, particularly of the twenty million American Negroes and other so-called minorities in the land. Whatever may have been the impatience as to the speed with which his leadership affirmed itself, there was never any doubt that he was acting out of the center of an informed heart and a conviction as to the true spirit and meaning of democracy and the American dream. It was his insistence that the North, the South, the East, the West were held together by a spirit that transcended all sectionalism and that after the laws had spoken and the formal intent of the nation had declared itself in a language all could understand, the ultimate place of refuge for any man was in another man's heart.

What he felt to be true of his own country he dared to project as the creative possibility of all the nations of the earth. The unfinished work, the outlines of which he has vouchsafed to us in his living, may we carry on and may what we leave undone be the sacred work of those who in their turn shall follow us.

The time and the place of a man's life on the earth is the time and place of his body, but the meaning and significance of his life is as vast and far-reaching as his gift, his times, and the passionate commitment of all his powers can make it.

LET US PRAY:

Close present Father, to whom Life and Death are expressions of Thy Wisdom and Thy Love, wilt Thou accept our stricken hearts and unabated grief as but an expression of our frailty and the depth of our dependence upon Thy Grace.

When we are most ourselves we know that there is in Thee strength sufficient for our needs, whatever they may be. May this assurance hold us in the Way lest our feet stray from the places, our God, where we met Thee.

Brood over us with Thy Spirit as we stumble along the Path of our Remembrance:

We remember President Kennedy and say our muted *Amens* to his spirit as he spreads his life before Thee in his sudden homecoming. And we rest in what he reports to Thee concerning us, his people, whom he loved with such abiding affection.

We remember his family, particularly she who called him husband, those who called him father, brother, son, and who cradled him in all the love and tenderness that are within the power of mortal man to share with mortal man. Out of all that Thou hast garnered from all the generations of the suffering of Thy Children, share with them the full measure of Thy Grace in all the levels of their pain.

We remember him upon whom falls the vast responsibility of office at this fateful moment in the history of our world. Be strength to his weakness, steadiness to his faltering steps, courage to his heart, vitality to his body, vigor to his mind, and keep before his eyes the vision without which we shall all stumble in the darkness.

Tutor us in all ways needful to companion him with confidence and help.

We remember all the nations and peoples of the world who hoped with us that together a way may be found to lift the burden of war and the threat of war from the heart, to move the great weight of poverty from the backs of the poor, to bring in a time of tranquility when everywhere, at home and abroad, the barriers that separate shall be no more and men will love and trust each other and nations will dwell together as friendly peoples underneath a friendly sky.

Our words are ended and the rest is silence.

Let the words of our mouths
and the meditation of our hearts
be acceptable in Thy Sight,
O Lord, our strength and our Redeemer.

From: ST. MARY'S CATHEDRAL
PORTLAND, OREGON

Sermon preached by the Reverend Joseph J. Neuville *

November 25, 1963

With the privilege of sharing in the great and tragic moments of history there comes a burden. And in the tragedy that America has suffered, and by way of the awesome means of communications at our hands, we have as a people—a hundred and eighty million—borne

* Principal, Central Catholic High School, Portland, Oregon.

a burden of sorrow with an immediacy and poignancy never known beyond the limits of our personal families. These unprecedented hours of sobriety, silence, and prayer and weeping have been a spiritual retreat on the part of the American nation, following one of its saddest hours.

We gather this morning as citizens who have lost a leader, a leader not lost in an isolation of his own leading, but one tremendously conscious of history, the history of his country. He studied it, he wrote about it—he made it in the war as a Navy lieutenant, in the Congress as a Representative and a Senator, in the White House as President. President Kennedy wrote history, made it, and has become history.

We gather as Christians who have lost "a member of the household of the Faith." In the election of our late President an ugly, unwritten, prejudicial folklore was destroyed. As a Church we thank this man and his family for their image before the nation as individuals and as a family.

This wealthy family, for whom comfort was assured, have seen fit to serve and to work for the nation with courage and dignity and a vitality that has captured the heart of all.

The dignity of this same family in this desperate hour of their history inspires by its handsome silence and propriety. Some of that silence is born of Faith and Hope.

It has been the wont of American Presidents to mingle with the people. President Kennedy was no exception—very much the contrary. We can recall him being discovered among surf-splashers on a California beach; we can see him moving down from a speaker's platform into a crowd of delighted students; we've watched him reach out for the friendly hands in a hundred crowds; we've watched him ride in an open car in city after city, affording us the immediacy of his charm, as well as that of his wife when she accompanied him.

And so it was Friday. And as such, he died, a martyr to the image of fraternity and paternity of the American President.

Had he sped by in bullet-proof Cadillacs and talked to us only from the safety of his offices, we would not have known him so well. Though our sorrow is deeper for the degree we have come to know him, we thank him for the open friendship he gave us and we are sorry that it cost him his life.

On the land from which he has passed we can draw no conclusions in this hour. We can say that any delusions of an evolved national gentility have been brutally shaken through these hours. If reports of increase in crime bored us, if the last battles of the nineteenth-century Civil War in the streets of Birmingham in 1963 left us cold, the anarchy of this November week end has not.

May the evils of these hours awaken a land for which many have worked, and for which many have fought and died. And not among the least of these is John Fitzgerald Kennedy.

May the sacrifice of John, John Fitzgerald Kennedy, "ascend in the sight of Thy Divine Majesty with a sweet savour, for our own salvation and for that of the whole world. Amen."

From: CONGREGATION BETH ISRAEL
PORTLAND, OREGON

Sermon preached by Rabbi Emanuel Rose

November 25, 1963

Our President is dead—his life stolen in ruthless wanton waste. But no human being on earth can destroy the soul of the Presidency of the United States unless it be a citizenry uncaring, indifferent, and—worst of all—silent to the ambusher who lies in wait.

By all that is sacred and holy in our land, we demand of ourselves eternal vigilance lest this day of mourning be itself a mockery. Surely we are here not to mock, but to mourn. And in mourning let us be mindful of the dreams which were his—"we will pay any price . . . to assure the survival of liberty. . . . Here on earth God's work must truly be our own. . . . The right of our cause must always underlie our strength. . . . Ask not what your country can do for you, ask what you can do for your country."

May we be worthy of our nation's ideas and ideals which we claim we cherish, for as our President, in representing us, in carrying out his responsibilities, we placed him in Dallas, Texas, on November 22, 1963.

May God bless his memory and grant eternal rest unto his soul.

May God have mercy upon us.

From: THE UNITARIAN CHURCH
PORTLAND, OREGON

Sermon preached by the Reverend Dr. Richard M. Steiner

DEATH AND TRANSFIGURATION

It is, I think, doubtful that the course of history has been altered in any significant way by the killing of John F. Kennedy. The Ship of State will not alter its course. Resistance to tyranny will continue. The rights of citizenship for all Americans, regardless of their color, will inevitably be realized. The welfare state, in which the government recognizes its responsibility for the aged, the unemployed, the ill, and the indigent will not disappear.

His death has made us think about death and grief. Death and grief were not strangers to his household, nor will death ever be a stranger to any household. To live is to die; to love is to lose. To live is to share in grief; to love is to fear separation. Those who sit in the seats of the mighty are no less able to love and to grieve than the humblest among us. Grief is assuaged by time, for "life is eternal and love is immortal."

The love that he shared with Mrs. Kennedy, the love and the pride that he had in his children and the adoration that they gave to him, have not died with him any more than the hatred and the hostility toward the things for which he stood. The one has the power to create, the other the power to destroy. The love and respect which were given to him by many millions of his fellow citizens have not been diminished by his death. The hostility and the hatred which were felt toward him by others of his countrymen have, at least in part, been buried by shame though the ideas which created them still live.

It is easy to overidealize this man. He was by no means the ideal President; no man ever was or ever will be. The office is too great, the demands too enormous for one man to achieve an invariable excellence, but during his term of office he grew in stature and wisdom, and by his death he gained an immortality of influence vouchsafed to few and envied by many.

It is one of the ironies of history, of life, and of death, that men despised, as he was despised by his assassin, should be transfigured, as he was transfigured.

O Father of all mercies and God of all comfort, we join our prayers this day with the millions of our fellow citizens, beseeching Thy presence in the midst of a stricken nation and a grief-stricken family.

We pray for our country that it be united by love and not divided by hatred. We pray for our President that he be strengthened to bear the burden of his high office, given wisdom to know the right that he may do Thy will.

We pray for ourselves, begging forgiveness if we have in any way by our words and our lives given utterances to hatred, given voice to prejudice, given death to love.

We thank Thee for the life that has ended upon this earth, for all lives great and small who have given of themselves that our freedoms may be preserved, our privileges extended, our hopes realized.

We pray for the man who killed our President. Have mercy on his soul, and the souls of all who sow the bitter seeds of hate and reap the whirlwind of violence and death.

Preserve Thou this nation that it may live as an example to the nations of the earth to find unity in diversity and peace among men. AMEN

From: CHURCH OF THE MASTER
MIAMI, FLORIDA

Sermon preached by the Reverend F. Daniel Sladden, Jr.

We are in the midst today of an experience that may well be the most outstanding in any of our lives. The President of the United States has been cruelly assassinated and we are shocked and confused and cannot comprehend how this deed could have come about in our day and in our country.

We will mourn his death, we will eulogize his life, we will bury his body and honor his memory for as long as we live. Our nation will suffer from the loss of a great and vital President; our world will suffer from the loss of a courageous champion for human rights and freedom. Loving parents will have lost yet another son, a young woman her husband; and little children will not understand why they have no father to love and guide them through life.

A man has been apprehended and it would seem that he will be put on trial for having committed this crime and if proven guilty he will be punished according to the laws of this land and we will still hear echoing again and again within our hearts and minds "How could such a thing be?" "How could this have happened here?"

Murder is a subject which few if any of us understand. We would not take a gun or other deadly weapon and rob a person of his very life. But where do murderers come from? Are they a race, a nation, a class unto themselves? From where do they get their ideas? How are their emotions so aroused that they have the impetus to retaliate in blood?

Murder is the final fruit of a twisted and deadly tree whose seed is hate. To the inexperienced gardener, it is difficult to look at an anonymous seed and realize what its ultimate fruit will be. One can plant and nuture what seems to be a harmless seed only to reap a disastrous harvest. I believe that this act is exactly that—the ghastly and terrifying result of thousands of people who knowingly or unknowingly have planted and nurtured hatred and have so expressed themselves in malice and condemnation that a climate has been established wherein a man could believe that something could be revenged or settled by destroying a man he never even knew.

I have been alarmed for years by the increasing organization of various groups dedicated to malicious hatred and the desire for destruction. There are groups to the far left and to the far right and to the south and to the north and those against certain races and religions and those aimed directly against certain individuals. I have received from various people and their organizations literature of a vile and sordid nature accusing our President, his church, our government, our local authorities, and even our teachers and ministers of the most outrageous of actions and motives. I have heard our former President Eisenhower accused of being a Communist.

This summer I saw a public billboard which appealed to the passerby to impeach our Supreme Court Justice Warren. These things are not a part of decent and acceptable give-and-take competition in political life. These are seeds of hatred, planted by irresponsible people and nurtured both by their fellow workers and by our apathy to denounce them. We tend to write these organizations off as being filled with a "bunch of fanatics"—and no doubt they are, but as we must realize a fanatic can and evidently has taken a gun and in his warped way settled the problems he has come to believe had to be settled in this fashion.

Yes, we are shocked at this despicable act and yet how can we do otherwise than to wonder which of us has not thrown a little soil, a little fertilizer on this innocent-looking plant as it was maturing to produce, if not this particular murderer, then some other. Or if not a murderer of the body then perhaps one of the many killers of a man's hope or reputation or spirit, for all of these are branches of the same tree and born of the same seed. The Bible says "For we know that whosoever hateth his brother is a murderer."

We have come to a time in our lives and in the life of our country when we can no longer afford the emotion and results of hatred. We have come to a time when we must realize that there is a difference in disagreeing with someone's ideas and in nurturing a hatred and resentment for him personally. We have come to a time in our political world when we must realize how naïve and ridiculous it is to heap the blame for our troubles in this world upon the shoulders of certain individuals who undertake the great task of national leadership. The great lack, the great fault in our world does not lie at the top of the government but at the bottom, where each person can and must control and discipline his own motives and emotions and undertake his own responsibilities under God. He must learn to curb the impulse to despise, to blame others, to harbor jealousy and resentment, and he must teach his children to do likewise.

I believe that truly all things work together for good to those who love God and that God can bring forth good even out of such a great tragedy. A man has lost his life, a man who lived a vibrant, constructive, positive life and who contributed all he had to fulfill the ideals he held. It is my sincere hope that even as we mourn his passing we can join together in prayer to God that God forbid that we should ever be found guilty of contributing in any way to that awful conspiracy of hatred which brings forth death and destruction and such deep sorrow. May we at this time look to God and to each other and truly unite our hearts and minds and motives that we might truly be one nation under God with liberty and justice for all.

From: BOSTON AVENUE METHODIST CHURCH
TULSA, OKLAHOMA

Sermon preached by the Reverend Orra G. Compton

Nothing we can say will add to or detract from the stature of President John Fitzgerald Kennedy. His life and service is now a matter of record and only God and history are able to correctly assess his greatness and enshrine his memory.

We have come to mourn. We have been drawn together from our various churches just as a family is drawn together for comfort and strength when it loses the head of the family. We mourn the waste of talent and leadership which has been cut short in midlife. We mourn with the family of President Kennedy just as our Lord stood beside the grave of Lazarus in the company of his good friends, Mary and Martha, and wept.

We have come to confess. To confess that we feel the great shame which has befallen our nation, and we share in the guilt which has allowed the fires of fanaticism to burn until hatred is expressed in destruction and death. We confess that we are one national family and that just as the Kennedys are a part of our family, so are the Oswalds and the Rubys. We are all brothers, but we have not been brotherly and we are ashamed.

We have come to pray. To pray not only for the soul of President Kennedy and for the comfort and solace of his family, but to pray for ourselves and all members of our national family that we may become more nearly one nation under God. A nation of people who will hear and heed the admonition and promise of the Lord God, who said to Solomon "If my people who are called by my name will humble themselves and pray and turn from their wicked ways, then will I hear from heaven and forgive their sin and heal their land."

We have come to give thanks. To give thanks in the name of Him who gave men hope to say "O death, where is thy sting, O grave, where is thy victory"; to thank God that we live in a free and democratic society where political leadership is responsible to the people to survive the loss of any individual. We give thanks that the government of the people, by the people, and for the people shall not perish from the earth.

We have come to worship. To worship the God who

created of one blood all nations and to reaffirm our faith in the sovereignty of God.

We have come to dedicate. To dedicate ourselves in a more meaningful way to fulfilling the will of God in our lives which leads us to a more responsible citizenship. We dedicate ourselves to love God and to love of neighbor, with the confident assurance that love will triumph over hatred and good will overcome evil, and that men will eventually attain the maturity that will allow us to beat our swords into ploughshares and our spears into pruninghooks.

May God bless the memory of John Fitzgerald Kennedy, President of the United States of America, to our hearts and lives, and to the hearts and lives of generations yet unborn. *Amen.*

From: THE CHURCH OF THE REDEEMER
BALTIMORE, MARYLAND

Sermon preached by the Reverend Bennett J. Sims

In grief there is a time for silence, and there is a time for words. Whether it be the one time or the other this Sunday morning, I cannot be sure. But at some point our aching hearts, struck speechless by calamity, must speak.

Though it be a terrible toil to find the words, there is a Christian witness to be made in facing the nation's sorrow.

First we are witness to the preciousness of persons. All that put us on one side of the political fence or the other evaporates in the response we make to our President's dying.

The sniper's gun cut down a living soul, not a Democrat. We did not know how much we valued him as a person until we knew his head had been cradled bleeding in his wife's anguished hands. Here he became a man who loved and was loved, and the sorrow we feel and the outrage is the response of a great and reverent people who hold persons to be sacred. This is a declaration of our fundamental politics, the deep point at which politically we are members of a single party. And this is our creed: Man is made in the image of God. And ours is a personal God, known to us supremely as a Person, by whose name we Christians are known.

Our politics are the most democratic the world has ever known. Rooted as they are in the spirit of a people, they dare to commit government into the hands of the people—and always a people needs a person in whom their common humanity comes to focus. Should that person be torn from the people, they themselves are torn. The assassin's bullet has entered into us all and all bleed. The life that most belonged to us as a nation has been taken from us. We are one in sorrow.

Second, we are witness to the horror of hatred and repudiate it as a gross and festering wickedness. Hatred is a killer because hatred is precisely to will another person out of the way.

This is what slew the President—not opposition, not the contest his leadership aroused, not the conflict his social liberalism provoked. These inevitabilities in a free society did not kill him. What killed him was the tyrant cowardice that refuses to allow opposition—the craven bitterness that refuses to face an honest conflict. Conflict is not our enemy. Christians have always been fighters for justice and the right. Controversy is not evil in itself, but the wrath that seeks or wishes the destruction of the other side.

That is why we are enjoined to love our enemy, lest in giving way to the terrible temptation to have him we become his murderer. Hatred is the essence of sin, for it is essentially a displacement of the will of God by a blind self-will—by an insistence that all things and all persons exist to serve one's own desires. This is sin.

God deliver us from the weakness of character that creates a kind of cult of contempt and sucks us into its bitterness. God deliver us from running with the crowd when it becomes fashionable to hold anyone in contempt. God cleanse us, His people, from the works of darkness that have corrupted men's souls and blackened the pages of history and set a cross against the daybreak.

From: WILSHIRE BOULEVARD TEMPLE
LOS ANGELES, CALIFORNIA

Sermon delivered by Rabbi Edgar F. Magnin

We are here to bring comfort to each other as millions are doing in similar places all over the world.

We are here to pray that God may bring solace to the bereaved family of our beloved President.

One hundred years ago Abraham Lincoln was the martyr. He died but his soul lives on. His sincerity, courage, and love of humanity has endeared him to all people of all nations and will for all time to come.

Neither will John F. Kennedy be forgotten. He will go down in the annals of history and will live in the hearts of all good people everywhere.

Lincoln grew up in poverty, Kennedy in wealth. Lincoln had little formal education, Kennedy was a Harvard graduate. Still both of them had much in common. They drank from the cup of sorrow. They loved people. They were devoted to America and the best that it stands for. They longed for peace here and around the globe.

By their life and tragic death we rededicate ourselves toward creating a better America and a better world . . . a sane, sensible society with freedom and justice for all.

Kennedy was the first Roman Catholic president. Abraham Lincoln was a Protestant. Both of them were religious at heart. Both believed in God and the brotherhood of man. Both were influenced by the Bible. Religion was a great catalyst in their lives and thoughts.

John F. Kennedy's untimely passing has awakened us out of our lethargy.

Because of it the Negro will soon be accorded the rights and liberties which are due him and every other citizen of this country.

Because of this we will be more vigilant in the preservation of our own liberties.

To our great President we say: "Good-by, dear friend, God take your precious soul under the shadow of His wing and give you perfect rest. We who are still among the living will march forward shoulder to shoulder—white . . . colored . . . Jew and Christian—toward creating a kind of America and world for which you lived and died."

From: MISSION DOLORES BASILICA

SAN FRANCISCO, CALIFORNIA

Sermon preached by the Right Reverend Dr. Joseph D. Munier*

November 26, 1963

During these days of historic sadness we have been inspired by the universal testimonials to the excellence of John Kennedy the man, John Kennedy the statesman, John Kennedy the intellectual, John Kennedy the devoted father, but at this moment we pay tribute to John Kennedy the man of religious principle, the President of genuine Christian commitment.

President Kennedy's Christian commitment was sealed on the morning of his inauguration when he humbly knelt at Mass in Holy Trinity Church to identify his thoughts, words, and actions with the work of God.

A few days earlier he had declared: "Humbly I ask His help in this undertaking, but aware that on earth His will is worked by men, I ask for your help and your prayers as I embark on this new and solemn journey."

And in his inaugural address he concluded with these words: "With a good conscience our only sure reward, with history the final judge of our deeds, let us go forth to lead the land we love, asking His blessing and His help, but knowing that here on earth God's work must truly be our own."

* Delivered at the San Francisco Archdiocese Civic Requiem for President Kennedy.

God's work was truly his own. Our Holy Father, Pope Paul VI, during the private audience last July acclaimed the spontaneous harmony between the candid declarations of President Kennedy and those of Pope John XXIII on the dignity of the individual human person. How clearly that fact is reflected in many inspiring messages.

Facing the racial crisis in June of this year he told the nation: "We are confronted primarily with a moral issue. It is as old as the Scriptures and as clear as the American Constitution. The heart of the question is whether all Americans are to be offered equal rights and equal opportunities; whether we are going to treat our fellow Americans as we want to be treated."

In the matter of human rights, President Kennedy was even more pointed when he spoke to the United Nations General Assembly only two months ago. "But man does not live by bread alone, and members of this organization are committed by the Charter to promote and respect human rights. Those rights are not respected when a Buddhist priest is driven from his pagoda, when a Synagogue is shut down, when a Protestant church cannot open a mission, when a Cardinal is forced into hiding, or when a crowded church service is bombed. The United States of America is opposed to discrimination and persecution on grounds of race and religion anywhere in the world, including our own nation. We are working to right the wrongs of our own country . . . to rid our nation of discrimination which has existed too long—in education, in housing, in transportation, in employment, in the Civil Service, in recreation and in places of public accommodation."

Finally, here are the warning words from his commencement address at American University: " 'When a man's ways please the Lord,' the Scriptures tell us, 'he will convert even his enemies to peace,' and is not peace in the last analysis basically a matter of human rights—the right to live out our lives without fear of devastation, the right to breathe air as nature provided it, the right of future generations to a healthy existence?"

Yes, God's work was truly his own as reflected clearly in his realistic regard for the needs of the poor, for the needs of all victims of discrimination, for the needs of the culturally deprived.

John Fitzgerald Kennedy could honestly report to his Judge, "I have truly loved your people." And God certainly turned to him and said, "Come, blessed of my Father, take possession of the Kingdom prepared for you from the foundation of the world; for I was hungry and you gave me to eat . . . naked and you covered me, sick and you cared for me. . . ." (Mt. 25 : 34–36)

Is the supreme sacrifice of John Kennedy in vain?

After the spiritual experiences of this mournful week end, we certainly cannot say that he died in vain.

There has been a remarkable redemptive quality to his martyrdom, *for never in our history have Americans of every creed turned to God and prayed more fervently for any hero or for any bereaved family.*

Did President Kennedy die in vain?

Not if we heed the words of that Dallas speech that he never gave: "In a world of complex and continuing problems, in a world full of frustrations and irritations, America's leadership must be guided by the lights of learning and reason." May those lights go on all over the world!

John Fitzgerald Kennedy, a man of religious principle, a President of Christian commitment, has passed our way. "Blessed are the dead who die in the Lord. . . . Let them rest from their labors, for their works follow them."

From: ENCINO COMMUNITY CHURCH
ENCINO, CALIFORNIA

Sermon preached by the Reverend Dr. Fletcher A. Harding

It is with an inspiring confidence, though heavy heart, you and I have been privileged to witness the torch of leadership taken from one hand and placed in another with swift efficiency, without the interruption of our constitution. This should make each of us feel we are part of a country that, by evidence of its great spirit, has intellectually and morally earned the right to its world leadership.

I think we can all feel more acutely conscious than ever before the pride and privilege of being an American. We will never forget the moment, but we will survive it.

Our new administration inherits a civil war of unprecedented nature, at least in emphasis—the civil war which is evident between the rational and irrational. In the struggle for the preservation of reason, clear logic and sound thinking, we have in too many instances allowed the reckless emotionalism of the fanatical groups to grow up among us.

Every person who has, even in the privacy of his own life, expressed thoughts or words of hate has helped to provide a stage on which a fanatic punk with a mail-order rifle could vent his insanity through this outrageous deed.

Every person who has damned our President has

helped to create a psychic atmosphere in which violence could become a terrible reality.

We are the richest people in the world. We have the highest standard of living of any nation in the world. And yet one of our prominent Senators made this statement: "We have never been so totally without freedom nor have we ever been more lacking in honor." These are harsh words. But he was not talking about freedom as we know it, as an overt fact. We are rich, healthy, and strong in might. But there are among us those who are sick in mind. Unless we are a healthy people at the core of our mental life, we are an enslaved people.

Those who are the messengers of hate must be made to realize that they have contributed to the blackness of this hour in our history. Those who are the ambassadors of love and peace and reason must be even more committed to spreading that gospel throughout the world. A world without love and peace and reason is a world without hope.

Mental health involves one's internal reactions. No marriage was ever broken up solely from outside influences. Inner psychic conflict is the primary ground for estrangement. Individuals seldom become sick because of the effect of outer circumstances. How they react to these circumstances depends on their capability to relate themselves to them.

Nations rarely crumble because of outer circumstances, but because of internal decay. We must become more aware of this principle of mind. I am not afraid of the invasion of communism in this country. It is inconceivable to me that Americans could accommodate, in their thoughts, a totalitarian government because we have drunk too long of the sweet cup of freedom.

But I have an honest concern for the mental health

of our nation because of the extreme rights and extreme lefts, which have been allowed to flourish among us, with our indifference, with our lack of concern.

Any group which persecutes and denies equal rights to another is not dedicated to the Christian principles of our forefathers.

Through the years there has evolved evidence that the circumstance of inner thought is what determines the outer experience of the human race. As a man thinketh in his heart, so is he. As a man soweth, so shall he reap. As we believe, so shall it be established unto us.

We must grow up and learn that these are not platitudes, but by the very nature of law and by the decree of God, they are the governing principles of life.

We cannot hate and experience health. We cannot walk in anger and avoid violence becoming a common ingredient in our everyday life. The world is in need of a better understanding of the principles of mind which Jesus taught; which Isaiah taught, and Jeremiah and Joseph taught. Let us bolster our private devotions in our homes and open our Bibles to read again the wonderful words which the inspired of all ages have taught and which you and I must make live in our community, in our part of the world, and in our individual lives.

The world will never be well until it is well in the hearts of men. And this will only occur as man becomes conscious of the living God in his own heart and the absolute necessity of giving intelligent expression to this communion in his daily life.

We must monitor our words as we monitor our thinking and learn that disagreement does not necessitate violence, but calls for deeper understanding and clearer communication of values.

We pray that the newly established leadership of our nation be mantled with God's understanding heart, strength, and courage of rightful conviction, a vision of commitment to the welfare, freedom, and dignity of all mankind.

So this day we are privileged to advance upon tomorrow with a deeper conviction of the power of God in the life of man, through the medium of mind. We have again been taught the awesome lesson that hate kills. We have the privilege to learn that faith heals. I have faith in our country. I have faith in our new President. I have faith in the power of God to heal the wounds of the savagery that has been recklessly rent upon us.

From: ST. CECILIA'S CATHEDRAL
OMAHA, NEBRASKA

Sermon preached by the Reverend William L. Kelligar

Look well, you that pass by, and say if ever there was grief like this grief of mine.

When God the Father devised His plan to redeem the human race, there were as many courses open to Him as the variety of creation itself embodies. Through the knowledge of Faith we know that He chose a startling course. He sent His Son, Who assumed human flesh and became like unto us in all things, save sin. He chose further to exact of His Own Son in obedience what He had claimed of men in punishment. That Son must die.

The source of the vitality of the mission of Christ derives from His death and subsequent resurrection. There can be no doubt of that. The spread and development of the Christian faith in the generations that followed have been directly the result of the Christian willingness to face death for the Faith and to accept martyrdom. "This is the greatest love that a man can show, that he should lay down his life for his friends." And for his principles.

The human instinct has always grasped this truth, since natural wisdom too draws a parallel between the power of character with its personal spiritual values and a man's willingness to offer his life. As a people, we have just witnessed this truth tested anew. A modern captain has fallen, cold and dead.

The death of every man is important, for it is the definitive event of his lifetime. But there is an added dimension in the assassination of President John F. Kennedy. We have passed through the experience of shock at the suddenness of what has happened. There are several thoughts that we should single out lest we forget the real and permanent contribution this remarkable man has left as his heritage to our national life. As we pray for the repose of his soul there are several titles of mourning worthy of note.

We mourn him as our national leader in the cause of world freedom who successfully confronted the Communist challenge to this hemisphere, who pursued a limitation on nuclear testing with patience, who sent the young men and women of this nation abroad to carry the lamp of learning to emerging peoples and young nations. In the brief two years, ten months, and two days of his Presidential service only the premises of his national service could be laid. He left unfinished work.

Secondly, we mourn him as a Catholic leader who was dedicated to healing the divisions among men, none of them more painful than hatred arising from racial diversity. Surely it is well known that he echoed Pope John's thought that racial discrimination can in no way be justified in theory. He dedicated his efforts to strengthening the United Nations, to aiding underdeveloped nations of the world, to assisting freer movement of minorities through revision of our immigration laws—all themes very prominent in recent papal teaching. Here too he left unfinished work.

When he took office the fear of a Catholic as President was very real in many hearts. This unreasonable fear has now been calmed forever. This myth may still be whispered in darkness, but his example in office is the light that will expose it to honest men. And is it not more than coincidence that our first Catholic President served in a time when the renewal within the Church finds the layman assuming a larger role, contributing more of his talents to the life of the Mystical Body than merely his financial ones?

Finally, we mourn John Fitzgerald Kennedy as a fellow man who enriched our national life. He enriched it with his heroism in war. He enriched it with the clarity of his intellect. He enriched it with the evident warmth and love he offered his family. He enriched it with his vitality and humor. He enriched it with his attention to common folk. Here again, the work he would have performed is left unfinished.

God the Father has taken the life of His adopted son John, as He exacted the life of His Own Son, as He takes the life of every one of His children. Surely the work of the late President was not unfinished in the sight of God. The efforts he began will have even greater chance of success *because* his life was taken suddenly. The spiritual values he relied upon as guiding principles will be diffused more widely *because* his life was taken suddenly. The virtue of faith which infused his work will be all the stronger among men who recall his memory *because* his life was taken suddenly.

This is a time of national grief. In this grief we pray to God for a kind of national forgiveness. In this grief we also pray to God for a kind of national salvation.

From: TEMPLE ISRAEL
OMAHA, NEBRASKA

Sermon delivered by Rabbi Sidney H. Brooks

Friday evening, November 22, 1963

This is a tragic hour of sorrow for the family and loved ones of John F. Kennedy. They have lost a husband and father, brother and son.

This is a tragic hour of mourning for our nation. Our country has lost a man sworn to defend with his life our democracy and the civil liberties which make it meaningful.

This is a tragic hour of shame for all those whose hatred contributed to every act of violence that has injured and hurt and killed from the least to the greatest of our nation's people. These have surrendered even more of self-respect and dignity.

This is a tragic hour of pain for men and women all over our world who would wish to resolve their differences without violence and to live with each other in harmony, who dream of a life secure for all mankind. These have lost yet more of the dream of peace among men.

Our prayers tonight cannot but have deeper significance as in fervent devotion we reflect upon the tender thread that separates us from destruction and the brittle defense that shields us from the insane and violent actions of men.

We turn to our God—a God of love and mercy and justice. We turn to our Jewish tradition, to the source of all goodness, truth, and kindness. From God we beseech a comfort for the family of our President, for our nation, and the world.

Expressions of sorrow, however deep, have little meaning if we cannot at the same time better understand both the good and the evil inherent in tragedy.

At this early hour even before the details can possibly be clear, a great deal is certain. It was not a bullet which felled our President but the irrational hatred of one man who pulled a trigger, exploding the prejudice and insanity of many millions of others.

The inherent evil which killed our President and still endangers our nation and the world is the same evil which has killed and endangered and bombed others, be they children or adults, white or black.

The inherent evil which killed our President is the abuse of power, not just the power of a rifle, but the power of government officials to abuse the rights of office by refusing to abide by the laws of our land and deliberately procrastinating in their duty to give every citizen the rights to which he has always been entitled.

The inherent evil which struck down the life of John F. Kennedy is our stubborn insistence upon the use of strength to solve our differences.

These in all facets comprise the evil which felled our President.

John F. Kennedy is dead. He lies in death with the men of all ages, men of humble station and men of greatness, even with little children who, in our land too, have been laid as sacrifices upon the altar of freedom.

But no great and good idea can be killed. What John F. Kennedy stood for above partisan politics in his defense of civil rights and his championship of equality for all people of our land will not die. Others may yet have to pay the price of their life for the final winning of those rights.

We, together with all of our fellow Americans, pay tribute to our President. We pay our tribute in sorrow and in sadness, with the honor and dignity the heritage of the United States demands of us.

But we pay tribute also in our own conscience. For whenever we put our hands to violence or our hearts to deceit, whenever we destroy the rights of others which we demand for ourselves we, too, assassinate goodness and dignity and our self-pride and honor.

Death shall not end what our President has said or done that contributed to the welfare of our nation or the freedom of anyone anywhere. Great thoughts live forever, as indeed they shall in the memory of mankind and in the name of John F. Kennedy.

May the memory of John F. Kennedy be a blessing. And may his death even more than his life shock us to our senses, urge us to goodness, lead us to honesty in our dealings with each other.

May God enfold the soul of John F. Kennedy in His mercy and may He bless with His wisdom and strength the leadership of Lyndon B. Johnson upon whose shoulders falls the mantle of leadership as President of the United States. AMEN.

From: SECOND BAPTIST CHURCH
LITTLE ROCK, ARKANSAS

Sermon preached by the Reverend Dr. Dale Cowling

Of necessity there will be a time of uncertainty while new leadership forms and firms into shape to claim our confidence. This uncertainty throws us back upon our dependence upon the God of history who has blessed our nation beyond any in the world today.

Seeing what He has done with and for us, surely we can know in this hour that He will see us through this wilderness.

This sad experience has had some obvious lessons and may God help us to learn them well.

Hate is malignant; to hate is to be guilty of murder.

Let us face the awful truth. The murder of our President is not simply the work of one deluded maniac. It is the product of radicals and extremists from every side of the issues which have torn our nation in recent years. It is true beyond doubt that the influence of all men of ill will joined together to put the pressure upon that trigger last Friday.

If we intend to build a better home, a better church, a better community, a better world, we have no time but now.

Many of us have grown so accustomed to a life of ease that we are scarcely prepared to face reality. Perhaps in the grim reality of this bitter experience, we as individuals may realize that this is a part of life from which none of us is immune.

God alone is adequate. Man alone is never adequate.

American citizens should come to their knees now. From heart and home and church throughout this land of ours should rise a crescendo of constant prayer for the leadership of God.

From: NORTH CONGREGATIONAL CHURCH
OF THE BEATITUDES
PHOENIX, ARIZONA

Sermon preached by the Reverend Dr. Culver H. Nelson

We now, in this house of worship, have every right and—indeed—obligation to inquire "What has happened this week?"

We ought not to mince words in so solemn an hour as this. That fearsome and fatal bullet was not sped on its way by a gun pointed at John F. Kennedy. It was aimed instead at the heart of our government.

Mark you well, the private citizen from Massachusetts, divested of his seal of office, representing nothing but himself, might have been maligned and hated, but that would not have called forth the assassin's blow. It was *because* he stood at the heart of our national life, representing a free citizenry expressing itself through the orderly processes of government, that he was slain.

Now it does not really matter whether the assassin was of this persuasion or that. It does not matter whether he was of the radical left (as evidently he was) or of the radical right. It does not matter even that he may have been plainly deranged. What does matter is the *climate,* the atmosphere of respect we have or lack for our basic social institutions. Only days earlier, in that self-same city, the Ambassador to the United Nations was jeered, physically struck, spat upon, and derided. It is not the city that is to blame; it may, however, be the climate.

Too many words have been too easily chosen and too hastily spoken in recent months, words which have impugned the patriotism and the loyalty of those persons who man our basic American institutions. The Supreme Court has been subjected to contempt. The federal courts and their authority have been called into question. Clergymen by the score have been accused of disloyal temperaments. Schoolteachers have been subjected to the wrong sort of harassment.

I hardly need to remind Christian people that a free society, more than any other, must insist upon a climate of respect and regard for basic social institutions. We must do this even within the context of disagreement, overpassing partisan issues. Criticism is right and proper, indeed a function of a free society, but it must be criticism of an opposition that is *loyal* to the institutions being criticized. When those institutions themselves are called into question—the courts, the Presidency, the churches, the schools, the national government itself—when all are viewed with suspicion and when their responsible leaders are held in distrust, you are but one step removed from contempt. And this ceases to be *loyal* opposition.

What does this have to do with what happened in

Dallas? It has this to do: We have allowed a disrespectful climate to blanket parts of our land. This climate, while created by only a tiny minority, nonetheless affects us all and more especially our children. Thus a fanatic of the left, or of the right, or simply a deranged man, finds an environment which, in his own distorted mind, seems to condone and invite violence.

No President is ever cut down simply because of his humanity but because he stands for something, because he is at the heart of our national life, because he symbolizes to the world the structure of our free institutions. All this is at stake.

This is still the season of Thanksgiving, and though our national standard will be flying at half mast in every corner of the world, still may we be grateful for our American inheritance—and the very pall put over this season by this dark deed may have something of point to say to us.

For example, we must not give way to our baser emotions in this moment of our national life. On the contrary, we ought to thank God that we are a people whose life is rooted in mutual trust and confidence.

This season, though bordered in black, may cause us to give thanks for our national glory, and give us wisdom to see how *we* are personally affected!

Ours is a nation of orderly transition and change. The mantle of the most powerful office in the world has shifted shoulders easily. This is a profound parable for our personal lives.

The American way of life is an experiment in freedom. It is rooted in *change*. There are those in our midst who resist and resent change. But as a people and a government, we have not only been willing to change, but have welcomed it.

How vividly this truth has taken hold of us this week!

The President's very death gives all too eloquent witness to the dramatic changes of our era, and the transition of vast power into the hands of Lyndon B. Johnson gives point to the obvious complexities of modern life.

We only fear change and retreat from it to our own inner disadvantage. We Americans have orderly processes for change, but we must use them and respect them and support them. We have the courts and the ballot box. We have innumerable forums of public opinion and a free press. We have pulpits that are free and community institutions that give sounding to our common needs. Through all these vehicles change is coming. We must not resent the change—only see that it is safeguarded by our democratic rights and privileges, and from violence.

As Winston Churchill so pointedly remarked, "A fanatic is one who can't change his mind and won't change the subject!" The American experiment must resist such a posture. And we must be adventuresome people on a continuing pilgrimage.

With the Psalmist of old, and not unlike our own colonial ancestors, we may turn at this season and declare "God is our refuge and strength!" And in so doing we may touch again the roots of our national greatness: faith in the goodness of God, confidence that we are His children and will be given guidance by Him on this, our pilgrimage.

For us this guidance will not likely be found in high drama but in simple duty. And we shall find ourselves *most* patriotic when we are engaged in the humblest of service: working for a better and more peaceful and more just world—in our homes, in our churches, in our schools, in our communities. The real gift we may offer our nation in this hour is simply ourselves, strengthened with affirmative resolve and nourished by God's goodness.

Rudyard Kipling put the matter quite clearly when he wrote words so fitting just now:

> The tumult and the shouting die;
> The captains and the kings depart;
> Still stands thine ancient sacrifice,
> An humble and a contrite heart.
> Lord God of Hosts, be with us yet,
> Lest we forget, lest we forget!

From: BIG ZION A.M.E. ZION CHURCH
MOBILE, ALABAMA

Sermon preached by Reverend Marshall H. Strickland

KENNEDY—THE DREAMER

These all died in faith, not having received the promises, but having seen them afar off, and were persuaded of them, and embraced them, and confessed that they were strangers and pilgrims on the earth.

A few days ago our nation reeled under the staggering news that the President of the United States had been assassinated. In every city and hamlet pains of grief struck the heart of a nation as people wept and others stared into empty space in a cloud of disbelief. Whether the events of this day can be construed as an act of Providence or the mad reaction of an abnormal age we will never know. But each one of us must live with the fact that our President is dead.

It is fitting that we come here today to share with the world the acknowledgment of our loss. Our solemn hymns, our words of praise—though imperfect—declare our genuine affection for a man who meant so much to so many. Will he be remembered as The President, The Humanitarian, The Politician, The Young Executive? Who can deny that he was all of this and more? But to be satisfied with such a surface definition of him makes too easy the story of his life. Behind his aspirations to be President, behind his benevolent acts to mankind, behind the fact that he used well the vigor of youth and the principles of politics, stood a man who was —— a dreamer.

Thomas Carlyle once wrote "The man who cannot wonder, who does not habitually wonder and worship, though he were president of unnumberable royal societies, and carried the whole Mechanique Celeste and Hegel's philosophy and the epitome of all laboratories and observatories, with their results, in his single head, is but a pair of spectacles behind which there is no eye." Such was not the case with John F. Kennedy. He heard the voice of destiny call to him from the dim unknown, and listened attentively to hear its message. He never wore the badge of doubt within his heart, but made courage and hope his companion. He sincerely believed that truth sustains those who really try, and if a man dreams long enough and hard enough, he can achieve where other men have failed.

His vision of The New Frontier; his declaration "Ask not what your country can do for you, but what you can do for your country" revealed a man who possessed the courage and the faith to seek the goals he had chosen for himself. Truly he belongs to that peculiar breed of man, the patriarchs of history and the scriptures who are the architects of greatness. The writer of the book of Hebrews' memorial to their genius can be applied to him—"These all died in faith, not having received the promises, but having seen them afar off, and were persuaded of them, and embraced them, and confessed that they were strangers and pilgrims on the earth." Let history record today that Kennedy was a dreamer.

He dreamed that man's elusive quest for peace could begin to realize itself in our times. He believed that the cycle of human conflict that has donned the pages of history since the fashioning of the first crude instruments of war could be reversed and men could truly live together. He believed that war was a luxury that mankind could no longer afford, that either we must strive for world peace or this planet will become a mass graveyard. His efforts toward the first Nuclear Test-Ban Treaty was his investment in this dream. Kennedy was a dreamer.

He dreamed that the greatness of the America of the past could produce an America of the future that would be true to the heritage of our forefathers. He believed that such phrases as *The land of the free, and the home of the brave, Government of the people, by the people and for the people* should not be timeworn expressions alone, but actual measuring rods in the fulfillment of the American Dream.

There are those in our race who believe that his passing marked the end to the Negroes' struggle for equal opportunity. This I do not believe. His martyred blood shall nurture the plants that will produce new champions of our cause. Gone now is the voice, and physical presence that identified him, but the dreamer remains.

The martyred body surrendered itself to the fatal hands of death, but the spirit remains. America will rise above the tragedy of this hour. New voices will come to champion the cause of freedom, and all men, of every race and creed, will live in a better world because *Kennedy dared to dream.*

From: TEMPLE B'NAI JESHURUN
DES MOINES, IOWA

Sermon preached by Rabbi Dr. Edward Zerin

November 25, 1963

While much has been said already and so much more will be written by personal friends and skilled commentators about the dreams and visions of John Fitzgerald Kennedy,

In this hour of reverence, let us pause briefly to consider a few of them:

You and I know his dreams and visions—

His dreams of a nation that would be free—not just for one man, but for all men, whether white or black or yellow—whether Protestant, Catholic, or Jew.

His visions of a world in which great and small alike would labor for the peace of mankind, in which the rich resources of the universe might be requisitioned to realize the fullest potentialities of every human being.

These were among his fondest dreams and visions.

How could he help but have a vision for the world:

Who better than he knew that scarcely a day passed in which a sniper's bullet would not snuff out some human life as nations continued to lift up sword against nation?

Who better than he was aware that every night one out of every two human beings went to bed—if he had a bed—hungry?

Who more than he was tortured by the knowledge that boys and girls—not only because of poverty, disease, and physical oppression but also because of the lack of opportunity—were being denied their human birthright?

Who better than he realized how many Einsteins and Galileos, perhaps even another Moses—and a Jesus—this world might have brought forth!

How could he help but dream dreams for our nation?

How well he knew that we were an affluent nation.

How fully he appreciated the fact that ours was the highest standard of living in the world!

At the same time, how concerned he was that between forty and fifty million Americans still were poor—the unskilled workers, the migrant laborers, the aged, the minorities, and all the others who continue to live in the economic underworld of American life.

How could he but dream dreams of our nation and see visions of our world, for his was a life in which he believed, as the poet W. H. Auden has penned so poignantly:

Hunger allows no choice
To the citizen or the police;
We must love one another or die.

Now John Fitzgerald Kennedy can no longer dream dreams and see visions. The hatreds and the ills which he sought to obliterate have shattered his brain and stilled his heart.

But we, who have gathered reverently to mourn, can still dream dreams and see visions.

Dream with me for a moment.

Suppose that all the resources—which during these past four days have been mobilized in death—had been summoned in life?

What wonders we might have achieved for our nation and world!

Is it a dream to ask for a crash program to eliminate poverty, disease, and all the physical afflictions that destroy the human form?

Is it a vision to request a crash program in education, employment, and leisure opportunities which dignify the soul of man?

Suppose the dignitaries of the world had come together so willingly for life instead of death—

Suppose the facilities of television and radio and aviation had been focused so intensively upon the evils and the opportunities of our day.

Suppose the appalling apathy of the great masses of the world had been converted into a committed concern during the life of John Fitzgerald Kennedy as it has been compelled by his death.

How many wonders might have been achieved!

Would that the wonder of life could summon men and nations so willingly as the awful specter of death!

Come, O my people, let us boldly dream dreams and courageously see visions.

The noblest memorial which we can erect in memory of our late President is to reconsecrate ourselves to the American dream of a nation conceived in liberty.

And to the universal vision of a world dedicated to the peace and welfare of all mankind.

From: THE ROTUNDA
CAPITOL HILL, WASHINGTON, D.C.

Eulogy delivered by the Honorable Mike Mansfield

There was a sound of laughter; in a moment, it was no more. And so she took a ring from her finger and placed it in his hands.

There was a wit in a man neither young nor old, but a wit full of an old man's wisdom and of a child's wisdom, and then, in a moment it was no more. And so she took a ring from her finger and placed it in his hands.

There was a man marked with the scars of his love of country, a body active with the surge of a life far, far from spent and, in a moment, it was no more, and so she took a ring from her finger and placed it in his hands.

There was a husband who asked much and gave much, and out of the giving and the asking wove with a woman what could not be broken in life, and in a moment it was no more. And so she took a ring from her finger and placed it in his hands, and kissed him and closed the lid of a coffin.

A piece of each of us died at that moment. Yet, in death he gave of himself to us. He gave us of a good heart from which the laughter came. He gave us of a profound wit, from which a great leadership emerged. He gave us of a kindness and a strength fused into a human courage to seek peace without fear.

He gave us of his love that we, too, in turn, might give. He gave that we might give of ourselves, what we might give to one another until there would be no room, no room at all, for the bigotry, the hatred, prejudice, and the arrogance which converged in that moment of horror to strike him down.

In leaving us—these gifts, John Fitzgerald Kennedy, President of the United States, leaves with us. Will we take them, Mr. President? Will we have, now, the sense and the responsibility and the courage to take them?

From: THE ROTUNDA
CAPITOL HILL, WASHINGTON, D.C.

Eulogy delivered by Supreme Court Chief Justice Earl Warren

There are few events in our national life that unite Americans and so touch the heart of all of us as the passing of a President of the United States.

There is nothing that adds shock to our sadness as the assassination of our leader, chosen as he is to embody the ideals of our people, the faith we have in our institutions and our belief in the fatherhood of God and the brotherhood of man.

Such misfortunes have befallen the nation on other occasions, but never more shockingly than two days ago.

We are saddened; we are stunned; we are perplexed.

John Fitzgerald Kennedy, a great and good President, the friend of all men of good will, a believer in the dignity and equality of all human beings, a fighter for justice and apostle of peace, has been snatched from our midst by the bullet of an assassin.

What moved some misguided wretch to do this horrible deed may never be known to us, but we do know that such acts are commonly stimulated by forces of hatred and malevolence, such as today are eating their way into the bloodstream of American life.

What a price we pay for this fanaticism!

It has been said that the only thing we learn from history is that we do not learn. But surely we can learn if we have the will to do so. Surely there is a lesson to be learned from this tragic event.

If we really love this country, if we truly love justice and mercy, if we fervently want to make this nation better for those who are to follow us, we can at least abjure the hatred that consumes people, the false accusations that divide us and the bitterness that begets violence.

Is it too much to hope that the martyrdom of our beloved President might even soften the hearts of those who would themselves recoil from assassination, but who do not shrink from spreading the venom which kindles thoughts of it in others?

Our nation is bereaved. The whole world is poorer because of his loss. But we can all be better Americans because John Fitzgerald Kennedy has passed our way, because he has been our chosen leader at a time in history when his character, his vision, and his quiet courage have enabled him to chart for us a safe course through the shoals of treacherous seas that encompass the world.

And now that he is relieved of the almost superhuman burdens we imposed on him, may he rest in peace.

From: MT. VERNON PLACE METHODIST CHURCH*
WASHINGTON, D. C.

Sermon preached by Rabbi Stanley Rabinowitz of Adas Israel Synagogue

November 28, 1963

In our reflexive observance of an occasion triggered by the pages of the calendar, we are apt to find ourselves in an embarrassing position. There is an obvious incongruity in the proclamation of Thanksgiving Day this year and the prevailing atmosphere of the week. Moods cannot be controlled by the clock; nor can joy be commanded by proclamation. It is difficult to assume a posture of thanksgiving in the midst of the ravaged emotions from whose ruins we contemplate the aspirations aborted, the vibrancy extinguished, and the vigor defaced.

But not for such somber thoughts has this day been given. The day is clearly designated on the calendar as one of joy and thanksgiving. The proclamation for this day from the very hand whose absence creates our dilemma is the mandate. Of course, we can evade the mandate and give way to mourning, or we can evade the mood and find reason for gratitude. But in either alternative, we must do less than justice to either our emotions or the proclamation of the day's significance.

Perhaps we should look back into the day's begin-

* Delivered in the presence of The President of The United States and Mrs. Lyndon Baines Johnson and their children at a Union Thanksgiving Service.

nings and remind ourselves that life was bleak for the Pilgrim Fathers who designated this day on our calendar in the first instance. For what did they have to be grateful? A few grains of corn, a meager harvest, the promise of uncertainty? The year in which the first Thanksgiving was proclaimed was not marked by conspicuous blessings. There have been other years of adversity, war years, in which men have had to find reason for expressing unto God a feeling of gratitude without compromise of integrity.

Thanksgiving in thankless times provides a real test of faith. It requires no great moral courage to express thanks when everything is well and life is peaceful, and even the price of turkey presents no problem. It is only when the path is uncertain that giving thanks to God assumes an added spiritual significance.

Of course, there is still much for which we must be grateful. We must be grateful for the continuity of the government under which we live. We must be grateful that the crime committed was not in the pattern of those republics or kingdoms where the bullet is the ballot as well as the weapon.

We are not without a President. We are blessed with a President gifted with the talent of leadership and with proven capabilities. Our freedoms remain uncompromised. Our bounties are rich. Our warehouses are filled to overflowing. There is order in the land. There is no cry of distress in the broad places. For all this we are truly grateful.

But even as we find cause for gratitude, we must realize that we have not resolved the dilemma, for these thoughts are insufficient as consolation to a bereaved family, the family with whose grief we must all identify. Every man is a many-splendored thing, even a President. There may be continuity of office, but even with a firm belief in immortality there remains an empty chair in a family compound, a family grouping which itself has become something of an American legend, even in our jestings. One chair is empty.

To think only of our own bounties, comforts, and freedoms is to make of Thankgiving Day a selfish thing rather than a day of empathy.

Yet we must find a way in which we can observe the Thanksgiving proclamation with integrity. If a path is to be found, it will be found in the directives of our religious tradition.

We worship together as Americans. In united worship, we have reduced the barriers between us, but not the diverse paths which are legitimate and part of the glory of our country. But these paths, though divergent, have a common beginning. We are all united by a faith which goes all the way back to the first pages of the Book of Genesis, and if we would dip into the common resources from which we have all derived wisdom and inspiration, we will find an answer that will make us comfortable with Thanksgiving.

But in the days when the terms *Jew, Nazarene, Hebrew,* and *Christian* were regarded as synonyms by the Roman commentators who were contemporaries of Jesus, there lived a man by the name of Akiba—Akiba the son of Joseph. He lived in troubled times. Death and assassination, crucifixion and martyrdom were daily fare and an astonishment only to the victims, but part of the pattern of Roman life, the routine risk of living for both the kinfolk and the followers of Jesus.

Akiba wondered how he could offer a prayer of thanksgiving to God when there was so little for which to be thankful. He found an escape from the uncomfortable horns of his dilemma by offering this insight to his generation: "Just as one must be grateful for the good things of life, so should one be grateful for its evil."

What could he have meant by this? Some of us will find it very difficult to accept this doctrine. Let us see what Akiba did *not* mean.

Akiba did not imply that we must be resigned in the face of evil, nor did he suggest that we must accept evil along with the good as the unavoidable consequence of the natural order. He did not say that there is no such thing as evil or that what we call evil is not really evil so much as goodness in a ghastly masquerade. Nor did he mean that evil is necessary to appreciate the good, or that evil only appears to be evil to our limited understanding. You could not utilize his insight to conclude that war is good because it strengthens character, wipes out slums, reduces excess population, or brings about prosperity. In fact, Akiba was not addressing himself to the nature of evil or to its reality.

What, then, did he intend to teach? He meant to teach that there is something sensitive and creative in man that enables him to take steps to correct a situation that is evil; and that this determination can be triggered by a deplorable occurrence. We must thank God therefore, said Akiba, for that resolve within man that stirs him to action in the face of challenge and that arouses him from complacency in the face of threat. We must thank God, he said, not only for man's ability to resist evil and to rise above it, but also for his ability to extract from it a blessing.

Thus did Akiba proclaim his belief that the good that man can do is more powerful than the evil that we can commit, and his faith that man can convert the reality of evil into an ultimate blessing. There is no evil experience which need remain a final evil, if we have the faith and determination to react to its challenge.

Note how true this has been in history. We do not get

an iceberg patrol until a *Titanic* falls victim to the icy assassin of the seas. The ominous evil that polio has inflicted on man prompts him to enlarge his efforts toward its eradication. Had polio been less of a scourge, we would have complacently endured its proportions.

Akiba taught his generation, and by implication our generation, that misery and pain can alert the conscience of man to advance the cause of ethical progress, that sorrow can arouse man's love of his fellow man, that tragedy can awaken our souls to the evils of our day, that cruelty can galvanize our determination to take action against those evils which we would be inclined to overlook so long as we were not deeply affected.

We are expressing gratitude, therefore, not for evil itself, but for our ability to convert sorrow into a stimulus to action. Thus do we extract from it a blessing. And it is for this element in man, rather, for which we are grateful and for which we must continually give thanks.

The earliest resolutions that came forth from the city of Dallas had an air of righteous apologetics about them. The public statement expressed regret and sorrow, sympathy and compassion. One word was missing, however. The word was *guilt*. Gradually the mood of self-righteousness gave way to a spirit of self-criticism which engulfed not only Dallas, but the entire nation. We all shared the guilt.

For this capacity to realize that we share the guilt of our society we must be grateful. And if this realization prompts us to change our attitude and our behavior toward those whom we ask to accept the responsibilities of civic life, our gratitude must be compounded.

Man's hatred is a dangerous thing and if one man, in the insanity of his hate, could loose so much havoc upon a world, a country, and a family, then should we not be fearful lest some other man, in his hatred, plunge us into war? The awareness of this possibility should impel us to take care lest we bring down the curtain on the drama of our civilization. And for our ability to be alerted to the dangers of the fallout of hate, for our awareness of the harm that man can inflict, we should be eternally grateful.

President Johnson, whose presence gives this Thanksgiving service an added dimension and significance, and for whose achievement we join in fervent prayer, perceptively grasped this ancient truth in his message to Congress, when he stated that from the brutal loss of our leader we must derive not weakness but strength. President Johnson proposed the early passage of a tax measure, of the Civil Rights Bill, and the final ending of the Civil War as the only fitting memorial to the late President. The President quickly grasped the opportunity to convert the shock of the past week into a forward, constructive movement. For this reflexive response we need a thousand thanksgivings.

Not only the President but all of us find times in life when we, like Jacob the Patriarch, are forced to stand at the brink, when we are accosted by a power that challenges us in the darkness of the night. We may emerge lamed, weakened. But if we are resolute and if we have faith, out of this encounter we can extract a blessing.

And once we have found a light that will show us the way to emerge out of the depression of this week, we should be able to focus the light along other paths that will enable us to emerge from the valley of the shadow of despondency whenever we find ourselves in its cavernous depths.

Having perceived this light, we can see in any affliction or sorrow the opportunity to find a deeper understanding of life. Out of illness we can extract a second chance, not only at health but at life itself. It is only after a dangerous brush with death, when living becomes a luxury, that some people discover their God, their soul, or purpose in their work. Illness can make one sensitive. Only then does one begin to appreciate the little things in life which he was heretofore too busy to notice: the flowers, the loveliness of the day, the birds, the smile on a friend's face, the warmth of family love. We frequently take life for granted until it is almost taken from us by some evil occurrence. But for this ability to recoil and to extract from illness something of a blessing we must be grateful.

Sometimes there is a death in the family. Depression follows in the wake of anguish. But perhaps only after a bereavement do we become aware of how much sorrow there is in the world. Then we must ask ourselves, have we added something to the world's sorrow? After a bereavement, we might feel that all of life is nothing more than "a tale told by an idiot, full of sound and fury, signifying nothing." But if we are perceptive, we will finally understand how painful is the brevity of life. Whether death comes at forty-six or eighty-six, few are the days of our years. Let us not squander them. Let us find a heart of wisdom. Out of life's brevity, let us find purpose in life. Out of sorrow, let us learn to be all the more compassionate and tender to those whom God has spared to us.

I would not verbalize evil out of existence nor would I deliberately seek suffering for the sake of blessings that may result. But since evil situations exist, we have two alternatives. We can accept its inevitability as final and say 'tis noble to endure suffering. Or we can say it is more noble to take arms against a sea of troubles, we require a Thanksgiving, even in thankless times.

We today have much for which we are grateful. To

offer thanks to God when all is well is proper. It is religious and it is appropriate. But it is also not enough. To thank God when things are not going so well—that is thanksgiving at a higher level. To be wise enough to be grateful for the opportunity to grow with each affliction and to mature with each crisis, that is thanksgiving at its best.

From: WASHINGTON CATHEDRAL
WASHINGTON, D.C.

Sermon preached by the Very Reverend Dr. Francis B. Sayre, Jr.

The people said of Jeremiah, "This man is not worthy of death."

This is the thought that is burning deeply in every American heart as we mourn our President. There were some who hated Jeremiah the Prophet; some who feared him because he did not shrink from declaring the truth as God gave him to see it. Nor did he fail to live it out, whatever the political consequences at the hands of those who presumed to fashion the nation after their own image instead of God's.

But when it came to a plot against his life—ah, then the reeds are pushed aside, the crabgrass cut. And men look down at the deeper springs of the man's life: the courage underneath; the hidden suffering; the lonely track against the lowering gloom of destiny, the free and shining vapor trail across the skein of heaven.

When the sharpness of death sums up all of a man's

life, then is the inner source known. If it is a man like Jeremiah, or like John Fitzgerald Kennedy, the anguish of sorrow will cry out:

> *This man is not worthy to die: for he hath spoken to us in the name of the Lord our God.*

As the first reeling shock of sadness passes, echoes of sacred conscience remain. We begin to separate the strands of our loss. Out of the very tragedy come fresh glimpses of the truth. Crisis always brings forgetfulness of ourselves, and so a plainer view of God and of His will for us.

I think, first of all, that we have understood that God has shown us our *guilt*. News of the President's death drove us to our knees in national penitence. The weapon that killed John Kennedy was not only in the hand of his murderer, but was in the heart of every one of us who ever hated, who ever set brother against brother by his selfish spirit. Surely we all do repent that shallow and divisive contentiousness which bred an atmosphere in which some ignorant sharpshooter would one day execute our careless threats, and think he served his country well by the despicable crime. Blame not the man, nor the city, nor the region where the deed was done. But let us search our own hearts to see if pettiness or hostility or unworthy anger did not set the stage for the overt act.

Yet, if God has shown us that, has He not forgiveness too in store for us? A purer love, a humbler citizenship, more honest acceptance of one another? May our sorrow prompt us to that prayer this day!

There is another strand that most of us by now have identified, mixed in with our grief. Anxiety for the future! Suddenly a brave and intelligent leader is taken away. What does it bode for our nation at a moment of dread uncertainty and fearful risk? How shall we do without the sure-footed assurance of this young President whose style of manner, whose backbone of responsibility the world had already come to admire and depend upon?

But in the very fearfulness God finds a way to make plain His Grace. I'm sure we've all been led to remember how in another period of awful uncertainty, God knew to raise up a guide for our nation's destiny. After the Civil War, when the wilderness of pain had brought our people's public morals to lowest ebb, another great President was shot. In Lincoln's staunch shoes stood an adroit little politician named Johnson—Andrew Johnson. How would the wounds be healed and the high road be found by such a man as he was on the fatal day? Yet there was in him a reservoir of mettle all unknown to others, and even to himself: Which for the sake of all, God did now reveal. As Andrew Johnson rose beyond the water level of all he knew, he met the challenge laid upon him.

Strange and wondrous is the Christlike power that discovers strength in weakness, new life in the presence of death, and faith that can conquer chaos and dismal fear. Such is the power of God to redeem anxiety and to lift up all that is cast down, to sustain us when we falter, and to give us life again.

Thus the final experience that is distilled from the tragedy that afflicts is that of faith. May it be the faith of our people now. When the whirlwind came for Elijah, the prophet of old, he turned to Elisha, his young companion.

"What wouldst thou receive of me before I am taken away from thee?" the old man asked.

"That a double portion of thy spirit be upon me!" said Elisha.

"Thou hast asked a hard thing," he replied.

But so it was, when Elijah passed to Heaven, that his mantle fell upon Elisha. And he who was now called to fill the holy man's shoes took the mantle and smote the waters of Jordan as he had seen the Prophet do before. Again the waters parted, and the people passed through.

As now the mantle falls from one man to another, let that same faith be in us that was in Elisha. And let us take up the mantle, smite again the waters, knowing that God will help us to push back the specter of hate, the terror of man on every side. And that by the healing power of God we shall safely pass to the other side.

From: THE NEW YORK AVENUE PRESBYTERIAN CHURCH, WASHINGTON, D.C.

Sermon preached by the Reverend Dr. George M. Docherty

At midnight on Friday the twenty-second of November my wife and I left our church. The great bell in the steeple had tolled since early afternoon when the news of the President's assassination reached us. Now it, too, was silent. We walked through the darkness of a mild evening toward the White House bathed in the light of arc lamps splashed across the Avenue. The fountain in the front lawn sparkled a spectrum of color. Little groups of people were standing on the sidewalk or walking silently. Automobiles moved slowly past in a whisper of sound. The policemen stood faithfully on their duty.

We turned back and took our car home, making a detour en route past the Bethesda Naval Hospital where the body of the stricken President was then lying. The lights in many rooms were still burning. At the hospital entrance, ablaze with light, guards were questioning a visitor. Rows of cars were parked on both sides of Wisconsin Avenue.

We made a U turn and came home. In the eerie silence hanging like a great fog around us, I remembered, during the war on the mornings after a night of terror showered from the skies by Hitler's bombers, this same silence, the mind bleached of all feeling, the numbing void as we returned to places known since our childhood and now laid flat in a jagged heap of rubble, buildings severed as if cut down by a giant sword, streets strewn with broken glass and people aimlessly walking around in a similar echoing emptiness.

It is ever thus in sorrow and bereavement—an empty chair, a pair of slippers, a walking stick in the hallstand. The White House, the nation's family home, for almost two hundred years a scene of pageantry and gaiety and music and in our own day increasingly the center to which the leaders of the world converge, now stood like a sad ghost against the night sky. A voice is stilled, a podium stands empty, a desk is bare, and a rocking chair sits solitary and still.

John Fitzgerald Kennedy achieved the highest office in the land at an age when most public figures are reaching for political maturity. Before his election some fears were held lest his years would vitiate the demanding position of a President. Certainly after his first year in office, these apprehensions proved groundless. Indeed he brought to the Presidency the refreshing verve of the young in heart whose eyes are not yet dulled by cynical compromise and who have not yet abandoned the dreaming idealism of youth. In the incredibly short period of four years, this energetic young Senator had stumped the country, blazing a breathless and magnificently organized campaign, meeting political opponents on their own battleground, and always emerging from triumph after triumph in debate.

In American history Presidential campaigns are portrayed in whistle-stopping itineraries across the country and a favorite platform for photography and oratory was the observation-car platform at the rear of the train. Kennedy followed the pattern of his predecessors, yet in addition chose his own medium. Television brought the Kennedy image into every home—the piercing intense eyes, the staccato forefinger of the right hand, the New England accent with overtones of Irish, and the air of knowledge of his subject as if he had done his homework well, which he always did. Comparatively few of the nation saw him face to face, fewer spoke to him, yet all felt through his television appearances as if he were a member of every family. His televised press conferences were not merely delightful but provided the layman with a liberal education of America's place in the world, as he answered the questions coming at him from all directions in that large White House Press Room from the world's leading journalists and covering almost every subject in world affairs. Often he would recognize the questioner by name. We will always recall his pause for a brief moment, the lowering of the head, lifting it again with a pucker of smile around his lips as if tasting privately the humor he was about to share with his audience.

President Kennedy combined three unique gifts which are seldom found in a single political figure.

First, he was a politician in the Greek sense of the word—a student, a practitioner of the art of government. One might say he was a born politician. Certainly the undeviating goal of his life was to serve in the arena of political concern. He possessed that political courage of which he had written so eloquently in his *Profiles in Courage*. He brought Churchillian confidence to the nation when on television he announced that an ultimatum had been presented to the Russians for the immediate withdrawal of offensive nuclear weapons from Cuba.

Secondly, his political shrewdness stemmed from an intellectually sensitive mind. Few great intellectuals make great politicians. The intellectual approach to problems too often cannot see the wood for the trees, deviates from the main issue to the eddies and facets of an issue and as with Hamlet:

> *. . . the native hue of resolution*
> *Is sicklied o'er with the pale cast of thought,*
> *And enterprises of great pith and moment*
> *With this regard their currents turn awry,*
> *And lose the name of action.*

Thirdly, he possessed the saving grace of humor, without which no man is truly a man nor can a public figure become historic. Such humor as he possessed, no doubt inherited from his Erin Isle forefathers, gave his utterances and point of view a sense of proportion, enabled him to laugh at himself, and to be aware of the incongruity of all life. At first we thought the President was a stern man; actually he was, I think, a shy man; and with the years this native shyness was breaking down more and more in the natural breaking through of a clean effervescent and spontaneous sense of humor.

And now at the threshold of what might have become one of the great Presidencies assassination has silenced all. One recalls another prince of men, separated by the seas and by a century, writing his own epitaph, loving life no less nor finding it any more fulfilled. Robert Louis Stevenson wrote these words:

This be the verse you grave for me:
Here he lies where he longed to be;
Home is the sailor, home from the sea,
And the hunter home from the hill.

To focus the entire guilt upon one man, to look upon this as the hazards that must be experienced by any President, is a much too superficial answer. This answer presupposes a law-abiding country, every citizen playing his part unselfishly and costingly for the upbuilding of a nation dedicated to freedom, a God-fearing people with an occasional perverted rebel besmirching an otherwise pure social order. This too-simple answer begs a deeper question. What kind of culture have we created to throw up such a warped and hating individual? Where did the assassin come from? Who were his mentors? Such assassins walk the streets of our cities daily. Street shootings have become so commonplace that outside the local newspapers they are hardly mentioned in the national press. In the eruption of the President's death we had to remind ourselves indeed that a policeman had died as so many others have died, fulfilling his duty. What makes this particular shooting so heinous, and therefore makes us aware that every shooting is dastardly, is that the victim was a beloved President of the United States. The conscience of the nation is not to be eased by polarizing responsibility upon this madman or gangster or rightist or leftist or Communist, in Dallas or in any other city. The solidarity of our involvement with each other in obedience to the law is the obverse of our solidarity in sharing to greater or less degree responsibility for a society that produces such thuggery.

The glitter of the highest standard of living in the world will not dazzle us from the awareness of an underworld of violence and hate and fratricidal struggle for power in high and low places.

To what Providence of God can we relate this assassin's bullet? What meaning is there in this shot? Not all shots were meaningless. The shot fired at Concord Bridge, reverberating around the world, was a call to arms and freedom, the initiation of a new era of a young nation. But a sniping gangster's shot—where is the sense in this?

With reverence one can only answer "Only the Lord knows." These matters lie inscrutably in the heart of the Providence of Almighty God.

Yet in fumblingly seeking some light in our darkness, it is not without reason that I turn, not to the professional theologians, but to another President who also fell before an assassin's bullet and this too upon a Friday. Abraham Lincoln bore in his life the tragic agony of man. In his Second Inaugural he shared with the people the contradiction of unendurable suffering with a continued belief in God who is both Judge and Father. Lincoln did not deny the existence of the war—he carried the rifle of every boy, he wept the tears of every bereaved mother, he suffered the hardships of every citizen. Neither did his faith in God wilt under the strain of suffering. Rather he faced the fact that the Providence of God must be seen against the canvas of the life of the nation, and however long the journey, people must go on enduring the consequences of injustice. In Lincoln's day the nation was divided by two views of human personality—slavery as an institution reflected a concept that some humans are less than persons, some persons have a claim on others, body, life, and even soul. This violation of the dignity of personality Lincoln in the

Second Inaugural expressed as "the woe" of the people.

"The Almighty has his own purposes. 'Woe unto the world because of offenses for it needs must be that offenses come; but woe to the man by whom the offense cometh!' If we shall suppose that American slavery is one of those offenses which in the Providence of God, must needs come, but which having continued through His appointed time, He now wills to remove, and that He gives to both North and South this terrible war, as the woe due to those by whom the offense came, shall we discern therein any departure from the Divine attributes which the believers in a living God always ascribe to Him? Fondly do we hope—fervently do we pray—that this mighty scourge of war shall speedily pass away. Yet if God wills that it continue until all the wealth piled by the bondsman's two hundred fifty years of unrequited toil shall be sunk, and until every drop of blood drawn by the lash shall be paid by another drawn by the sword, as was said three thousand years ago, so still it must be said, 'The judgments of the Lord are true and righteous altogether.' "

Despite the war and its tragic suffering, despite everything that seemed to contradict sanity in human affairs, God still reigns and God rules and until men obey and follow and love and seek to fulfill His will in their affairs, both private and social, economic and political, the judgments of the Lord remain true and binding. We bring upon ourselves the consequences of our blind injustice.

The shot fired in the Dallas street is a dramatic symbol of the slumbering hatred and fear and will for power that stalks the life of the nation as a whole. We bring upon ourselves the consequences of denial of and indifference to the Providence of God.

Yet God does not forsake His people, nor stand by idly, nor exist as an aloof absentee. This shot is not the devil's laugh of victory over the Providence of God. A President dies, but what he stood for cannot be destroyed. The leader of the nation is laid low but the nation will rise again to fulfill his dreams.

Hope lies in our awareness that buried among the variegated individualism of our society, amidst the contradictions of this many-state enterprise united as one yet preserving the sovereign rights of each state, inextricably mixed in this melting pot of the world's peoples vociferously asserting rights and privileges, amidst this mixture of spiritual blindness, expediency and self-sacrifice, selfishness and service, God still rules and reigns. We live "under God"—under His grace and favor, and under His judgment. God can turn even the wrath of men to praise Him, can take our imperfect schemes and our dreaming hopes and dare to challenge us to incarnate them in the life of the nation.

In a torrent of silence and sorrow and shame and bewilderment, the nation at this moment is mourning. Never before, perhaps since the last armistice closed the second world war, has there been given to the nation such an opportunity for rededication. A new frontiersman has gone beyond the frontiers of this earthly life to the eternal glory of God that knows no limit. The grave has not silenced his unbounded belief in the American system of government and the place of a believing people in the affairs of the world. Down the years his words will be read. On television we shall hear them spoken again to us.

This is an historic moment to be alive. In the years to come, we will tell our grandchildren that we indeed lived in the days of Kennedy.

He brought youth to the helm of the Ship of State and like a good sailor went down in a squall that struck the skipper but did not founder the ship.

And tomorrow he goes home.

Home is the sailor, home from sea,
And the hunter home from the hill.

From: THE JEWISH COMMUNITY
WASHINGTON, D.C.

Eulogy delivered by Supreme Court Justice Arthur J. Goldberg

November 25, 1963

In the Book of Ecclesiastes, Chapter 9:12, it is said, "For man also knoweth not his time: as the fishes that are taken in an evil net, and as the birds that are caught in the snare; so are the sons of men snared in an evil time, when it falleth suddenly upon them." Friday was an evil time. Sunday was an evil time. Today our country has engaged in a day of national mourning; it has also endured a day of national shame.

It is a cardinal principle of our democracy derived from biblical teachings that it is an inalienable right of man, as a child of God, to have human dignity. The assassination of our great President on Friday was a supreme violation of human dignity; the killing of a man charged with the assassination Sunday was a violation of human dignity too, for on Friday life was taken —the great commandment "Thou Shalt Not Kill" was violated—and on Sunday too a life was taken without due process of law. Human dignity on both occasions was violated.

Today's day of mourning was different from that day of mourning when we buried our great President Franklin Roosevelt, because while our grief today was equally great, it was compounded by humiliation—humiliation lacking when Franklin Roosevelt was buried. If, in a new country in a remote corner of the world, the head of state was assassinated and if the man charged with the killing was himself assassinated a few days later while in the custody of the police, we would say to ourselves in all self-righteousness that the country was not fit to govern, that it was uncivilized. What are we to say to ourselves as a nation?

John F. Kennedy, two weeks before his inauguration, stood in the assembly of his native state of Massachusetts and gave a speech in which he quoted Pericles' statement to the Athenians: "We do not imitate, but are a model to others." An assassination is not an act of a people; a wanton killing is not an act of a people, but in a very significant sense, we are all responsible for these terrible happenings—all of mankind is responsible. The dominant characteristic of the present age is the lack of respect for the human being—our forgetfulness of the human dignity with which God endowed every human being. More people have been killed, more exterminations have taken place, more massive barbarism has occurred in the world since the beginning of World War II than has ever been recorded in the history of civilization.

There is another saying from Ecclesiastes—"Sorrow is better than laughter: for by the sadness of the countenance the heart is made better." Let us use the occasion of the sad passing of our great President to make the heart better, to make the heart more responsive to what is needed in the world. And what is needed in the world more than any other thing is Love and not hatred, because, in a real sense, hatred is what caused the terrible events of the last few days.

Our late President, John F. Kennedy, was a man of love; he was not a man of hatred. He devoted himself in international affairs to the elimination of hatred between nations, to the cause of world peace and world justice. He devoted himself, in domestic affairs, to the elimination of hatred between the people of this country, to the cause of equality and brotherhood. The President is a victim of the unfinished tasks of his own administration. Would that he had lived out his full days and his full time, so that he could have witnessed a more peaceful world and, in the words of our Constitution, a more perfect union. But he was snared in an evil time, and he knew not his time—as, indeed, we know not our time.

We owe it to the memory of our martyred President to rid our nation of the evil forces of hate and bigotry and violence. In the book of President Kennedy's speeches which he called *To Turn the Tide,* he wrote: "Neither wind nor tide is always with us. Our course on a dark and stormy sea cannot always be clear, but we have set sail, and the horizon, however cloudy, is also full of hope." Today, our course is on a dark and stormy sea, and the horizon is cloudy. We must make it full of hope, full of hope for a better world, full of hope for freedom, for justice, for order, for peace. These are the ends of organized society; these are the ends for which President Kennedy gave his life; these are the ends to which we must all rededicate ourselves.

From: THE EPISCOPAL THEOLOGICAL SCHOOL
CAMBRIDGE, MASSACHUSETTS

A letter from Dean John B. Coburn to his son Mike at preparatory school

Written November 23, 1963

Dear Mike:

We have been thinking of you particularly since hearing the tragic news of President Kennedy yesterday. It is beyond belief and yet there it is—something we have to take in, a dreadful event for our country and for all mankind, a terrible loss for Americans and especially for those who felt about him as you did. I am glad you have that letter and signature to keep forever.

Your mother and I have just heard President Johnson declare Monday to be a national day of mourning. That is a great thing to do for all of us, not only as a nation but as individuals who have lost someone who is really part of ourselves, the way a President is. And it is right to mourn, to grieve and to cry. There have been no dry eyes around here for the past twenty-four hours.

I feel a little the way we did when our Cynthia died. This seems like a member of the family.

There are times when if you cry you are a baby. But not this time. This is what you do when you love somebody and then that person is lost. So I hope you haven't been ashamed to cry.

But the crying—this kind of crying—is really for ourselves. It helps us. It doesn't help President Kennedy, though it is a tribute to him. He really doesn't need our help, though, because now he has God's help and that is all he needs.

We've had a lot of talks in this family about life after death and where Cynthia is and what she's doing, and all that kind of thing. It's probably good for us to do this once in a while, if we don't take our own ideas too seriously.

The fact is of course we can't be certain about any of those details. The only thing we can be certain of is that God is God and everybody with God is safe.

So Cynthia is O.K. and President Kennedy is O.K. and so is everybody else who is with God—and that includes us so long as we are with God.

So we can weep all right and it's a good thing for us to do. But we don't have to weep for the President. He's with God and he's all right. As a matter of fact I even believe that some day you can count on seeing him and telling him about your letter.

Anyway, seeing President Kennedy is going to be one of the good things about dying. There are a lot of others it's going to be good to see. You can imagine seeing Caesar, for example, so you'd better get moving on that Latin. I'm only kidding, Mike, about the Latin but a question you might ask your roommate is "What language do you speak in heaven?" Dr. Guthrie says it's Hebrew, which is going to make it tough for most of us.

There are two other things I want to say about this death. The first isn't pleasant, but it's real and has to be faced honestly sooner or later, so I might as well spell it out now.

This is that there is a power of evil at work in the world, and it is an active force against all that is good and lovely and true. You see it when some evil man in an office building kills a President, or when death comes to some innocent baby, or when I lost my temper and knocked you on top of the head, or when I booted Tom in the seat of the pants, or when people suffer pain, the way Professor Batten did, or when some fellows are lonely all the time and nobody accepts them or is nice to them, or when wars break out, or when white people slam doors in the face of Negroes, or when big kids tease and beat up little kids. There is something going on which is evil in the world, and it's got a lot of power.

And what is worse, some of it gets into all of us. We can't just separate people into the "good guys" and the "bad guys." There is something of both good and bad in all men, including nice people like you and me, and it is this mixture which makes life and its different battles so complicated.

Now, the other thing I want to say is that this power of evil, strong as it is at times, and apparent victor every once in a while, as when the President is shot—this power of evil does not have the last word.

Love does.

Decency does.

Truth does.

Honor does.

Not cheating on an examination does.

Giving your life for your country in time of war does.

Keeping your temper does.

Keeping your word even when it is to your advantage not to does.

In one word, God is more powerful than everything set against Him. And I'm using the word *God* now in the biggest sense possible, as that force in the universe which is responsible for all creation, which undergirds all man's discoveries and which calls us all to a life of nobility (or honesty, if a less fancy word is better) and service.

And if I had to add it all up I'd say this is the life

which was in Jesus of Nazareth. Stick around him, try to live with his spirit, ask God for His help by praying, and gradually all the disjointed bits of life begin to fall into place.

Friendship is more fundamental than loneliness, life than death, and love than hate, because all of this is the character of God.

What this means for all of us I guess, right now, is that we don't get discouraged or afraid or give up hope. We know that we are on the right track because President Kennedy really was "a great and good man," as President Johnson just called him. And his greatness and goodness was from God and cannot therefore ever die.

So all Americans can respond to the best that is in them now because this is a great and good country—not because it is ours, but because it is God's. And we can make it more God's now than ever before as all of us in some small way become a little greater and a little better ourselves.

That means I have to be a better dean than I've ever been, and a better father and husband.

And you have to be a better student.

I won't say a better son, because you're a good one now.

I won't say you're a good student. Your mother and I were pleased with the last marks because you weren't flunking anything, but we agree with you that they weren't great and that you can do better. So get on the stick and work at those books—not really for our sakes, though you know we'd be pleased, but for the sake of all of us in this country, and for J.F.K. and all he stands for, and for God because he is as ready to help you as he is those who now live with him forever, and of course for your own sake.

Well, I don't want to turn this into a sermon, though I must confess you've always been kind in your remarks about my sermons, and I appreciate it. I really just want you to know we are thinking of you, and we love you, and wish you well as a person living and growing up in a great and good country in a great and good generation to be alive.

It will be wonderful to have you home for Thanksgiving. We are planning to meet your cousins late in the day and then go see the Bruins play (I think) the Rangers. The poor Bruins are having a miserable season and need our help. Judy will be home for dinner, but has to return to school that night. Tom will meet us at the Cape on Friday with Sue.

We hope all goes well these next few days. Sarah sends her love. So does your mother. So do I. God bless you.

Love,
[*signed*]

. . . world sentiment was perhaps best summed up by T. S. Eliot in these lines from "East Coker" *

We must be still and still moving
Into another intensity
For a further union, a deeper communion
Through the dark cold and the empty desolation
The wave cry, the wind cry, the vast waters
Of the petrel and the porpoise.
In the end is my beginning.

ACKNOWLEDGMENTS

They cared—and shared

The Reverend Robert Nelson Back
Richard Berlin
Ralph Carson
John Clements
William Dozier
Frank Di Marco
Martha and Henry Federman
Frank Fogarty
Harold "Hap" Kern
Frank King
Stanley Marcus
Howard Mendelsohn
Sandra McPeake
Marcus Morris
Alice Shea Patterson
Ann Kissel Reisman
Barbara Rosenquest
Betty Rosher
and
my wife Pat, for invaluable
criticism and support.

Troubled Lovers in History

Troubled Lovers in History

A SEQUENCE OF POEMS

Albert Goldbarth

Ohio State University Press
Columbus

Library of Congress Cataloging-in-Publication Data

Goldbarth, Albert.
Troubled lovers in history : a sequence of poems / Albert Goldbarth.
p. cm.
ISBN 0-8142-0813-4 (cloth : alk. paper). — ISBN 0-8142-5015-7 (alk. paper)
I. Title.
PS3557.O354T76 1999
811'.54—dc21 98-39035
CIP

Text and jacket design by Paula Newcomb.
Type set in Usherwood by Tseng Information Systems.
Printed by Thomson-Shore, Inc.

The paper used in this publication meets the minimum requirements of the American National Standard for Information Sciences—Permanence of Paper for Printed Library Materials. ANSI Z 39.48-1992.

9 8 7 6 5 4 3 2 1

ACKNOWLEDGMENTS

The author is grateful to the editors of the following journals for first providing the poems in this collection a home:

The Alaska Review: Substratum
The Bellingham Review: In the Bar in the Bar
The Beloit Poetry Journal: Natural History
Black Warrior Review: Travel Notes
Boulevard: "Of Course They're Strangers. They *Aren't Me."*
Crab Orchard Review: There, Too
The Georgia Review: Imps
The Gettysburg Review: Against; Two Weeks, with Polo Chorus
The Iowa Review: Dog, Fish, Shoes (or Beans); The Number of Utterly Alien Civilizations in *Star Trek* and *Star Wars*
The Kenyon Review: ***!!!The Battle of the Century!!!***; The Fiction Shelf; In
Ontario Review: Con Carne
Poetry: Ancestored-Back Is the Overpresiding Spirit of This Poem; True; Various Ulia
Poetry Northwest: Alternative Uses
Quarterly West: Complete with Starry Night and Bourbon Shots; Directional; "Duo Tried Killing Man with Bacon"; *The Lost Continent* (1951); Squash and Stone; What We're Used To

and for reprinting certain of these poems:

The Best American Poetry 1997: Complete with Starry Night and Bourbon Shots
Harper's: Ancestored-Back Is the Overpresiding Spirit of This Poem
Poetry Daily: Dog, Fish, Shoes (or Beans); *"Of Course* They're Strangers. They *Aren't Me."*

and a special thanks to Mindy Wilson at *Black Warrior Review* for using "Travel Notes" in that journal's chapbook series

and, for other special editorial generosities, thanks to David Baker, Susan Burton, Stan Lindberg, Joel Lovell, Pattiann Rogers, Margot Schilpp, Marion Stocking; and to Ellen Satrom, for her fine eye.

These poems attempt to look at what we've learned by this time in our century to call "relationships" (romantic/marital relationships for the most part, although the section titled "Generations" includes poems about child and parents). Their group notion is that the ups and downs of our contemporary hearts can be amplified by historic reference: from the *Travels of Marco Polo* to the hokey delights of 1950s horror films, "othertime" attempts to speak with, and for, *our* time. There is, necessarily, a good deal of estrangement and bickering in these pieces, and much of human components that won't happily cohere; but in between are small moments meant to be more idyllic, and *those* of course are

for Skyler.

The most beautiful of pairings come from opposition. . . .
Consider the bow and the lyre.

—Heracleitus

CONTENTS

Travel Notes

Travel Notes

introductory section

This sad first line presents somebody
sitting at the window, in her seventh year of marriage,
in a fall of early morning light
so new—so yet untouched by any texture—
it's incapable of artifice:
everything shows. And so
her disappointments and frailties
are obvious in this introductory section
—in the way her hopes of seven years ago are on display,
are an unmediated beaming, in the photograph
she keeps on the credenza ledge.
And by the space between these two far faces
we can measure a journey, something
like the passage that Monet provides his haystacks.
—Not in miles; but in deepness
over time. —And not in shoeleather,
no; but hour by hour, sun by cloud,
in the ripening weight of experience.

1.

"A new day's march, the tins of biscuit gone
last night to thieves. So be it. We wade
through our fatigue as if it were only another
infested stream to cross. . . ."

Wait: Did he say
only? "Oh, that. That's merely Bloodsucker Creek."
"That's just Deathrattle Canyon."
Ambling casually across the leechy muckholes
of this scary planet, humming *Rule Britannia*. . . .
"To his credit, he uttered no word of regret."

The greatest travelers never kvetch. For them,
the application of potentially fatal Saharan heat
to flesh is—"vigorating," one called it.
How can you be something so sublime,
so *monumentally* sublime, as "stoic,"
if needles of ice *won't* work their way into your feet,
if swarms of stinger-gnats *won't* boil up
out of the jungle brush as thickly as spewed-up gruel?
"This proved a tonic, after our days of restful confinement."
Adversity burnishes them to perfection.

So: in 1887, thirst reduces the robust party of British explorer
Sir Francis Younghusband to the extremity
of lapping the blood of a freshly beheaded rooster,
then of a throat-slit sheep ("immediately it coagulated
into a cake"), and finally "Islam and Yoldi
collected camel's urine, mixed it with sugar and vinegar,
held their noses, and drank." By night they struggle ahead.
By day they bury one another up to the gizzard in sand,
for the feeble extra degrees of its cool. Eventually the thirst
"did not torment us, as it had done . . .
for the mouth-cavity had become as dry as the outside skin,
and the craving was dulled."

And what *is*
Younghusband's summary? "It is a curious fact,
but when real difficulties seem to be closing around,
one's spirits rise . . . difficulties seem only to make you
more and more cheery." Somewhere else,
concomitantly, an arctic adventurer rolls
the rotted soles off his feet as if peeling a tangerine.

"There was, of course, some initial discomfort
as we kept on toward our goal."
Of course. Of such intrepid mettle
are the High Lords and Ladies of Wanderlust.
But

~

I prefer the more roundedly human touch
of a grandiose sniveler, who *knows* an inconvenience
when he sees one, and vituperates it accordingly.
Thomas Manning is a nineteenth-century master
of this arch effect. "Turning my head back towards the west,
I had a noble view of a set of snowy mountains
collected into focus, empurpled with the evening sun. . . .
I heartily wished I might never see them again."
His room in Phari-dzong, on the road to Lhasa,
is "low, long, dark, narrow, windowless, full of smoke.
Dirt, dirt, grease. Misery." Simply: "I find going uphill
does not agree with me."
Or Dickens, on his first night
in a canal boat through the Alleghenies:
"I found suspended on either side of the cabin,
three long tiers of hanging book-shelves, designed apparently
for volumes of the small octavo size. Looking
with greater attention, I descried on each shelf
a sort of microscopic sheet and blanket; and then
I began dimly to comprehend that the passengers
were the library, and that they were to be arranged,
edge-wise, on these shelves, till morning."
Of tobacco juice and its being so freely spat, and
of the various "zephyr whisperings" that emanate their richness
from the other thirty beds, he rises to rhetoric
impassioned and ornate enough to otherwise be chronicling
the battle of Masada or our touchdown on the moon.

Well what does Dickens *expect?* "Have got a diarrhoea,"
Byron says in one of his earlier letters, "and bites from the mosquitoes.
But what of that?
Comfort must not be expected by folks that go a pleasuring."

2.

When his eyes can focus, my brother-in-law is lost
in reading a book about the European mapping of Australia
—sandstorms; sunsets like a smear of iodine dye;
bone-jangling thunderstorms; betrayals.
When his eyes can focus. . . .
Sometimes, though,
the M.S. won't allow that small coherence;
much less walking. Then a day is a matter
of thought and dream; and of the half-state progeny
of thought and dream; and there are places
wholly independent of geography and time,
to which we'll spirit ourselves.
And surely if a man can exit
his skull without anywhere shattering it,
the roof of a house on Nathan Road in Edgemoor, Illinois,
is no impediment, nor the sunlit, swaddling
atmosphere of Earth.

~

" 'On what am I walking?' she asks.
And the table replies: 'On a world—Mars.' "
This is the seance of late November 1894,
and the "mediumistic astral peregrinations"
of Miss Élise-Catherine Müller of Martigny, Switzerland,
(named Hélène in the literature) begin here, and will last

five years. Five years of intricate trances, and their
on-the-scene reports from that neighboring planet.
Mitchma mitchmon mimini tchouainem mimatchenig
masichinof mezavi tatelki abresinad navette naven navette
mitchiichenid naken chinoutfiche: "Hélène

herself will speak Martian." In the company of friends
as well as under the scrupulous scrutiny of psychologist
Théodore Flourney, this seemingly ordinary
middle-class silk-shop salesperson undertakes
the episodes of what becomes a startling psychic odyssey
in the annals of "disincarnate travel" (or,
I would also argue, of travel literature of any kind).

Look, the sky is all red . . . a rose-coloured fog. . . .
Quick, please, give me paper!

Of her spoken and written Martianese:
"It is, indeed, a language
and not a simple jargon or gibberish of vocal noises
produced at the hazard of the moment without any stability."
 From out of the fog—he is riding in a miza,
 a "moving house" without wheels or horses—
"It cannot be denied the following characteristics—First:
It is a harmony of clearly articulated sounds,
grouped so as to form words. Secondly:"
 —with a beast, a "pet," with the "head of a cabbage"
 and one great eye in the middle, like a peacock feather
 that moves on paws—
"These words when pronounced express definite ideas.
Thirdly, and finally:"
 and aquatic creatures, they look like giant snails
 —meanwhile, Astané has a grotto for meditation
 carved out of the mountainside
"Connection of the words with the ideas is continuous; or,
to put it differently, the signification of the Martian terms
is permanent and is maintained
from one end to the other of the texts which have been collected
in the course of now three years."
 —and a hall of infants set on yellow moss;
 and there are animals, almost hairless,
 and with the large soft eyes of seals—and these
 have tubes attached to their udders by the men,
 and these infants are fed on the milk
"It is the complete fabrication of all of the parts of a new language."
 —and I was there.

one red fantastic corpuscle
at the center of her brain,
one red amazing impervious corpuscle,
three inches in;
                three zillion light years

~

My sister returns from her shit job; phonecalldemeaning
deadlinedemeaning teleconferencedemeaning shit pay.
The kids the dog the evening meal the laundry
the bills the pills to pick up at Drug Rite,
and Dannie—*pecktothecheek*—he'll rise now
from a day of M.S. reverie and greet her.
"He *tries* to help around, but—" (shrug). My sister

isn't the woman I've invented
for the introductory section, she
of the quiet disappointments, who speaks
for so many of us. And maybe my sister here
is only "my sister"—one more fiction;
this isn't meant to be autobiography.
Still, I understand what she's thinking tonight

as she stares in the mirror and dabs
the day's mascara with her cleansing pad:
this isn't the life she'd planned on having
(that commonest of American misgivings).
It may be strengthened by the invisible struts of love
in any number of viable ways, and yet . . .
this isn't where she thought she'd arrive.

My brother-in-law on the living-room sofa.
My brother-in-law how many mental-states-of-himself
removed from the living-room sofa?
how many alternate Dannies, alternate
chronologies and galaxies, does he get to explore in exchange
for being unable to press
the gas and brake in the Honda?
Question: how far could you fall if you fell
like energy into a microchip?

And how far has my sister come
to stand at this bathroom mirror
in its unconcealing light?
There is no standard unit of measurement for this,
but I think */she looks, and looks/*
the face can be an odometer.

3.

And he will describe for you these numerous wonders,
of Lands and divers Peoples, and of heathenish Customs,
also of the Creatures of these places.
—Marco Polo. Ah, yes:
". . . a hidden city as profligately topped
with golden domes as a bakery table might be with dollops
of eclair cream." ". . . an ascension of mist
that begins at the foot of the waterfall, so vast it seems
as if an entire town were created of vapor."
/*numerous wonders*/ It's a craving for this gawk-response
in the face of the sheerly amazing, it's
this goosebumps of the retina, of the breath,
that kickstarts most of us out of our sedimentary slew
and sends us posing for those Ms. (or Mr.) Zombie
passport photos. Surely we want to think of wonder
as Parnassuslike in scale—*a parade*
before the Empress of a thousand temple dancers
on a thousand temple elephants—but
just as surely it can be a single life
in size; on the lonely tableland of northern Tibet,
explorer Alexandra David-Neel sees a distant moving dot:
a *lung-gom-pa,* a lama whose mystic way
is "wonderful endurance," is a "tramping
. . . without stopping during several successive days and nights"
across that normally empty limitlessness.
The lama (in a trance; that is, "with the god in him")
approaches, closer; she writes, "The man did not run.
He seemed to lift himself from the ground,
proceeding by leaps with the elasticity of a ball.
The right hand held a *phurba* (magic dagger)
and moved slightly at each step as if leaning on a stick,
just as though the *phurba,* whose pointed extremity
was far above the ground, had touched it
and were actually a support." At which
description, a wild frisson of awe shoots through me.
—*Not* the reigning sensibility

in the letters
of Thomas Gray. In 1739 he travels from Great Britain
to the Continent: "There are Trees, & Houses
just as in England." And writes of himself, laconically,
"Goes into the Country to Rheims in Champagne.

Stays there 3 Months, what he did there
(he must beg the reader's pardon, but)
he has really forgot."

Some do best
rooted. (Gray, for instance,
back again in London, gives posterity his grandly visioned,
vastly moralizing *Elegy Written in a Country Churchyard*
—"The paths of glory lead but to the grave," etc.).
Dickinson made a circuit of Einstein's universe every day
in her garden in Amherst. And this barnacle
on a wheelchair, its fourth-dimensional mind out touring
post-Einsteinian hyperspace . . . ?—is
Stephen Hawking, stationary lama of the millennium.
His travel is into the endless viridian-manganese sea
of phosphenes in the eye, and then through it,
and into the subumbilicus of Everything and Nothing,
of the proto-breath of the proto-word
of the cosmic Open Sesame.

That's a looooong way

from the level at which the contrapuntal rhythm of things
for most of us gets played out. In this city
this morning, the dawn sun glints pristinely
off the clean lines of a building where the blueprints
of the cyberzip electrotechno future are created
out of silicon and wish. And in the shadow of this building,
not a two-block walk away, the Middle Ages is finishing
one more piss-pants night. You can tell
by the burnt cat on the hood of a truck, and by the zonked-out
teenie hooker sweetly singing glory hallelujah
through her caked puke, you can tell
by the ten billion eyes of a plague as it waits for its chance
on a needletip, and by these guys who are whipping each other
drunkenly with ripped-out car antennas,
and by the stabs of love, and by the love of stabbing,
you can tell that as the supersonic cruiser
slips across the sky, it passes for a heartbeat blur
above the year 1000,

where we still live,
in an everpast.

grafitto
in the courthouse john:
goin nowhere
fast

finish

"On 27 February 1914, shortly after midday,
we started down the River of Doubt
into the unknown."
—While Theodore Roosevelt explored this
sprig of the Amazon, and Alexandra David-Neel
entered Lhasa disguised as a Tibetan beggar woman
(1914 too) and Sir Aurel Stein discovered the Cave
of the Thousand Buddhas (1907) and Robert Edwin Peary
arrived at the North Pole (1909) in a flurry
"of dogs, sledges, ice, and cold"
—Claude Monet
was painting, and had been painting, and would continue
faithfully painting, water lilies and light
in his garden at Giverny. You can see
by the way the petals are as indefinite as flame,
and by the way their watery filaments seem to drill
so deep they suckle on a broth at the heart of the world,
what a lifetime pilgrimage this was
for him, though not one
of mobility.
While I think
of his haystacks series I first saw when I was seven
at the Chicago Art Institute (1955)—and
how these great lumps move
from being on fire at sunbreak,
through the color-chart declensions of the light,
to their late-in-the-day reserve,
gravid with plum and indigo—
Monet is leaning,
stick-man that he is by now, on the rail of a bridge
across his lily pond, and thinking
backward into time, to a confluence of many
earlier waters:
Venice, Amsterdam,
the dazzling chop of the Seine, and ocean water churning
into white carnations on the sand. . . .
And at this point, our introductory-section woman
enters the poem again, returned to us
over so much time like an object
lost in the sea, and then suddenly washed to shore,
back into the light we live by.

Without ever speaking to us, or reading these words,
she thinks it too: that she's been lost
for years in mysterious travel,
turned in its current, worked
a molecule at a time by this.
And now she's beach glass—now she's something
beautiful but reduced.
Yes, that's it: beach glass.
With her soft hues.
With her awkward, glossy finish.

Trouble, with pleasant interludes

Against

In the medieval village, "decisions respecting plowing,
planting, weeding, harvesting, pasturing,"
were based upon community consent: the entire
adult population was a part of this agreement.
Or think of nation-states eventually coming to terms
beneath a truce flag. But in the Center
for Marital Counsel today, these two
refuse agreement on the budgie's plastic water dish,
on a sprinkle of salt, on a nose hair, on a nail head.
There's something almost admirable
in the obdurate integrity, the *purity,* they bring
to what would otherwise be petty spite.
They won't agree on a button-snap, on a postage stamp,
they couldn't on the same day both say *yes* to the same coriander seed.

~

T's father, eighty-one, was only shut in what the children called
"the care home" by a week before a tumor-laden X ray
of his wife's meant that the children swiftly placed her
in that euphemistic, wretched place as well. Now
they were roommates, after sixty years of marriage.
And you'd think that, in the disinfected shadow
Death casts there, they'd ease their sixty years
of differences, of bickering, with a front of united defiance.
Ha. "It's TOO WARM, do the thermostat." "Don't
TOUCH it! It's CHILLY in here." "Yeah, in your head
it's chilly." Maybe it *is* defiance,
is the flag most drenched in the spitfire raging of life
that they can yet wave. They become a salient lesson:
We will go to our graves contending.

~

I was seventeen, and making goofy googoo talk
to Lyla Rolker, sixteen, who was miles of untouched whipping cream
and a beaconlike dollop of civet musk and several feet
of artfully batted eyelash. That's when Nate Yblonsky,
eighteen years and 218 pounds of football practice, sidled up
and taught me something intense about the idea
of territoriality. Ah, the always powerful I/Thou, Me/World
interface! In medieval villages every spring,
the village boundaries were recommitted to memory
in a walk around the perimeter called "a-ganging."
And to emphasize this lore for them, they'd dunk
small boys in boundary brooks, and knock them
into especially important configurations of boundary rocks,
and smack their silly heads against the trees.

There, Too

I'm not the dapper man in the lambswool overcoat.
I'm not the woman unfolding the mail, lost
in a lozenge of light by the vase of roses and ferns.
I'm not the man with the cocky swagger
and fresh dirt under his fingernails.
I'm the triangle—that's right, I'm the triangle

that they make, the way it's made every day
in movies and cheapie self-destructo novels:
steamily, greasily, and I protest this
smutting of my self. I was there

with the square and the circle, originally,
when shape was something pure
and transcendental—long before
the borders-smudging confusion of human affairs.

Whenever you're with another person
—even with who you think of
as *the* other person—I tell you

that the mind and the heart are too bountiful for fidelity,
and I'm there, too.

Ancestored-Back *Is the Overpresiding Spirit of This Poem*

If only somebody would drill with a finger-long rig down
into my skull, and saw a tiny circle out of its bone,
so pools of acid antsiness and angst can steam away;
so all of the great in-gnarling, all of the bunched-up
broodiness can breathe; and so at least the day's
accumulated ephemera, its fenderbender squabbles,
its parade of petty heartache can evaporate in writhes
of sour mist—this spatting couple, for example,
in the booth across the aisle as I'm chowing on a burger
and their every more-than-whispered perturbation is,
this afternoon, a further furrow worked into my mind. . . .
You know I'm kvetching metaphorically. But literalist
Amanda Fielding, wielding a scalpel and electric drill,
bored a hole in her skull in 1970, filming that self-surgery,

~

and zealously thereafter promoting the benefits of this
third eye, finally "running for Parliament on a platform
of trepanation for national health." The operation
was successfully conducted in the Stone Age (72%
of the skulls we've found reveal that the patients far survived
that crisis moment), and the Chinese medico Thai Tshang Kung
(150 B.C.) was said "to cut open the skulls of the sick
and arrange their brains in order." A Roman physician's
effects from the second century A.D. include a trepanation kit
in bronze, its tooth-edged bit and driving-bow
as finely produced as any machine-tooled apparatus
a surgeon in 1996 would wish for—when the bow unfolds
it's as intricate in its simplicity as a line of true haiku.
I've read a book whose major pleasure is its breathlessness

~

in gasping at the ancientness of various devices,
flushing toilets(!) condoms(!) hand grenades(!)—the book
is a grove of invisible exclamation points. These
green glass beads like rain-splats on a leaf
—4,000 years ago. Bone dice, the same. The ribbed vault
in this early Gothic church is a masterly hollowing-out
of space—but houses of *literal* ribs, of mammoth bones,
were sturdy dwellings 15,000 years ago. Rhinoplasty(!)
soccer(!) odometers(!) "Butter" (a favorite sentence)
"spread everywhere, once it was discovered." Though we don't know
poot about the urgent stirrings in our own hearts
or the dreams irrupting nightly in our own heads,
we've been diagramming stars on plaques
of tortoise plate and antler, we've made sky maps,

~

from before we even understood the link of sex
to birth. And if our coin-op slot machines
can be ancestored-back to that Greco-Egyptian
contrivance of Heron of Alexandria (by which
a dropped-in-place five-drachma bronze piece
starts the portioned flow of a worshiper's ablution-water) . . .
if *ancestored-back* is the overpresiding spirit
of this poem . . . we *are* the progeny of stars,
we *are* their original core-born elements
in new recombination, densed and sizzled into
sentience and soul. I can't imagine the interior tumult
driving Amanda Fielding and her followers, but
I'm not surprised our smallest human units were created
in explosion, speed, and void. My friends

~

are not the kind to drill their heads and rid themselves
of troubles by decanting. Even so, I've seen them consider
their restless faces in the mirror and wish for *some* release.
Our daily dole of woe is unrelenting. In this burger joint,
in the Booth of a Thousand Sorrows across the aisle,
they're arguing still. Outside, the snow provides each tree
with a clerical collar—this couple is arguing. Outside,
the setting summer sun makes each tree a flambeau
—this couple is arguing, they'll never stop, their joys
have been prodigious and their anti-joy will balance this
or more, the hands with which they make their hard points
in the air are hands of oxygen and nitrogen and argon
older than dust or salt. It's midnight. How
emphatic we can be. How long they've been at it.

Imps

Fire isn't allowed, for the sake of the books.
The lean monk-copyist who scribes the books is slate-blue at his fingertips
this steely late-November day in the year 1000. Brother Ambrosio
huffs some perfunctory warmth on his stiffening hands,
then bends again to his goat's-horn of ink. For every line,
he believes, he's forgiven a sin. And now he's at his heavy
uncial letters, and will be for nine hours more,
until a slab of bread and a beet relieve his transcriptual ardor.
What he copies?—psalter, missal, hagiography:
the predetermined and sanctioned community passions
of a religious culture. Nothing like the twentieth century's
prevalent kneejerk "self-expression." Nothing like the priest,

excuse me: *former* priest, and former nun, on daytime talk TV,
who live, she tells us, in a "trinity of love" with the former
creator-of-tourist-ashtrays-out-of-catfish-heads. This is,
she insists, the final and jubilant stage of a lifelong "quest
to feel belongingness" initiated thirty years before
by parents skittering cross-country with the military: *they*
were wholly rootless, and so *she* grew up "unable to commit." The following day,
a man confesses to pedophilia because of a lesbian aunt.
A woman says she robbed the Sack-N-Save of $13.42
"because of what they're dumping in the water supply, it makes me
go all freaky." Steve was bounced out from The Chicken Shack
"because I'm Scandinavian." The culture

of blame is *so* completely exterior in its search for cause,
some days I wake to think I'll find most people laboring
under the weight of sci-fi-style mind parasites, like fleshy turbans
spewing in, and feeding off, their brain blood. This (by "this"
I mean of course a recognition of the magic of objective correlative
boppin' about in the spotlight) is, to some length,
understandable: you can't beat the miniscule carry-along
convenience of a silicon chip invisibly set in something,
BUT for sheer persuasive visual power, *that* can't touch
a 1940s generating plant, its giant Alcatrazian shape
against the sky, and the enormous wrestling electrical crackles
snaking its rooftop pylon. In the scriptorium, even

—such an isolated unit of human endeavor, its limited range
of reactions surely is pure—when Brother Ambrosio
nods off, sleepy in his long day's long eighth hour
of thickly nibbed and careful letters, he knows
it's imps in league with Satan that keep pulling down his eyelids.
If in scratching his flea-measled thigh he spills
a hand's-expanse of ink across the vellum page, the fleas
are tiny devils on a guerilla mission from Hell.
And once a devilkin took lodging in his belly, and there
created "rumbling noises like a toad, and which, for hours,
spoiled the concentration of all of the other Brothers."
We find parchment scraps with appropriate exorcisms:

"Away! you flaming sow, you poisoned udder,
you arse of the arch-fiend, shit-fly, stinking he-goat,
out out out, away, back into thine infernal kitchen,
you bestial puke!" We also find
those charming marginal doodles (sprigs in flower,
unicorns, seemingly every songbird in Creation): such
diminutive external bodies given to the longings of these
cooped-up men. And when they came to drag my friend Jess
screaming to the ward, because he was beating his head
on the lawyer's steps, it was clear to us all that the chemicals
in his mind had turned against him. It was clear to Jess
that he was being hunted like prey by hounds from the moon.

The Number of Utterly Alien Civilizations in Star Trek *and* Star Wars

He *likes* to be touched—it must be
it reminds him of his mother's nightly
fussy tuck, her brush-of-his-cheek,
and all of the other subsequent formative contact
from the world: the jockly high-fives in the gym,
an early girlfriend's sweetly puckered smacks
along his inner thighs . . . as if his life has licked him

into hale shape, from out of no-shape,
like a dam bear overseeing its cub. Then
he weds. And *she?*—well, let's say
that her childhood is a series of sudden
physical encounters best left undetailed here.
From these apart approaches, we can predicate
endless scenarios, but I don't mean marriage

only. For example, on Christmas Eve in 1100,
the Lord of the Manor of Upper Gooseholm
adjusted his rabbit-and-squirrel-trimmed tunic
about his girth, and at a table lit at either end
by silver candelabra, sat to a dinner of calf brain,
flank of deer, roast wood duck, honeyed ale,
and upland eels simmered in buttery ewes' milk; while

the annual treat bestowed upon his villagers
was breadsops and a slice per house of baconfat,
most likely shared with the rats that lived in the thatching
—a distance of style as psychologically vast across
as is the Great Red Spot of Jupiter ("three Earths could fit
inside it"), astronomically. When archeologists
spaded up the artifacts of Gooseholm,

they discovered a Roman outpost under those
and, under *that,* the stony hints
of an Early Bronze Age settlement still in place,
still meaning a time and a people, as if
the later layers above—straight up to Crazy Maisie's
Super Pizza & Video Shack—
were only so much weather. There's no such thing

as one planet. It's all science fiction.
It's all a billion planets.

"Of Course *They're Strangers. They* Aren't Me."

I'll tell you about "the Major" three doors south of here,
he fashions birds of candle wax—sparrows, jays—exactly
duplicated around a complicated copper-wire armature,
and then he convincingly jackets them in feathers from actual
dead birds that we find it especially convenient not
to ask about. At Donut Diner, the Widow Sloane
will dolefully inform you of "the button" in her left
(or right: it varies) ear, through which "the masters"
speak and make her shudder so, that once she wet
her good pants in the taxi. And I'll tell you, too:

I've made them up, to represent your officemate
you interrupted yesterday in going back to grab an extra folder,
who was whipping at his bad left thigh
with a strap in his Mother Superior of a left hand,
who was whimpering, who represents the woman
at the bus stop with a past she drags behind her
like a conga line of corpses, and she'll share with you
the name of each, and the special handmade sorrow of each,
and how the particular worm in the heart of each one
burrows into hers. As if she's saying: *you'll* understand.

~

Where do we come from, out of what smouldering crevice
in our brainstems do we crawl, to bear
such furred or scaled lumps to one another?
—like coal miners, only
self miners. Only spelunkers,
only bathysphere explorers,
of the psychological lamb's-foot jelly
shivering at the core of the id. But all that's
metaphorical, like the pool balls we see
atoms as. Where *do* we come from? Kansas

countryside won't hold the eye. You're always aware
of the sky heaped heavily over it, past air, past where
the o's of *ozone* empty into that sweep of void
and scattered pinpoint fire we call the empyrean.
I've idled on the clay and gravel roads that sprig these fields,
watching distant towns so drowned below the heavens,
so beneath a comprehension, they were relics
in a kind of archeology no one's invented yet.
It's like—we come into one another's lives
from Atlantis, we rise from so deep.

~

Native of India, Fred spoke singing Americanese
in that beautiful bird-inflected flutter
they never lose. He told me about his work
on the Browning collection, and the stiffly formal details of his visit
to the Queen Mother, to note the Browning Jubilee.
"Not bad," with a wink, "for someone who isn't Christian,
Buddhist, or Mohammedan." So I made the obvious
joke, and extended my hand for a shake: "A fellow Jew!"
"Oh no," he corrected me very
very seriously; I was speaking with the only

practicing orthodox Zoroastrian in Kansas.
"Ahura Mazda is The One True God. You would like to see
my undergarment?" This, in the third-floor offices
of Kansas Book Recycling, over Lin Foo Chinese Carryout,
next to the Greyhound station. Fred continued
processing used textbooks as he talked at me.
"And when I die, they will set my body atop
the Tower of Silence"—now his eyes took on a dreamy light,
as if he were describing the glowingest heaven—
"and vultures will pick my bones clean!"

Complete with Starry Night and Bourbon Shots

Morgan's father will be mailed to her,
they've said in a letter—now that every bequested
dole of his body has been banked away,
the residue in its factory urn will be mailed.
She says Stephanie sometimes wiggles her fingers around
inside *her* father, so the bone chips
clink against the fired clay, and I suggest
the final char of Bob Potts be sealed inside maracas;
"He'd like that," Morgan says, especially if the Texas
Sexoramas used him percussively, his favorite
country-funk group. What she'll really do
this June is scatter him into the air
of Mount Palomar, "because he loved his telescope." Let him
circle and settle, circle, circle, and settle.

~

He also loved his drink, but no one mentions
touring the Pearl Beer plant and surreptitiously adding him
to a vat. The stories are legion,
legend: for instance Bill English of English's Bar
in one clean squeeze deadeyeing a shot glass
off his pate. Though now that's decades gone.
When I met him even his *teeth* were grizzled
—up at the bar surrounded by all of the gleaming
palomino hotpants twenty-year-olds of Austin, Texas;
reading Kipling's *Kim* in the sonic boomboom rock.
I first ate pit-cooked cabrito at one of his parties,
lank and sharp and good. Then doing our names
on the lawn, from the bones—in the light,
and in the easiness, before anything like that seemed symbolic.

~

The Wild West–style saloon doors of "The Hall of Horns"
(the brewery's tourist annex) open grandly on its choice, thematic
gawkables: a map of the United States entirely
done from snake rattles; sturdy desks, and chairs, and armoires
completely or near-completely from antlers and hooves.
Also the monstrosities: the Siamese-twin calves
with braided horns, like a Swedish Christmas candle;
the calf with horns that horribly loop forward and enter
its eye sockets. Yes, and there were those Victorian museums
of human residue: the brains of criminals floating like compote,
the gold-cased tibias and jaws of saints. Our wonderment
can seize on something commoner than these, without
diminishing: a skeleton of an owl, and the ribs of its digested
field mouse suddenly tumbling out.

~

Because he loved his telescope . . . he's being flung under
everything above, the whole night sky is called upon
to be his memorial marker. Maybe our obligation
is finding lines from star to star up there:
the new bones of his new, if metaphysical,
existence. Etc., etc.—sky and bones, the stuff
of sonnets. Some people like calling the heavens
star-complected, to some that's "precious" odium. Tastes
differ. *My* father was heavily lowered into the earth,
is earth by now, is the dry click of ants in the grasses.
Still, I think that they might meet at the horizonline,
Bob Potts and my father. Maybe they're having a metaphysical
quaff right now, remembering how one's son and one's daughter
divorced each other—one of the copious little deaths.

~

Even microscopic radiolarians have skeletons, and this
alone can jolt our cogitation meters into the red
astonishment zone—what then to make of Morgan's parcel
flying through the mail? Not that comedy, say, or bereavement
are matters of size. And still it's the whale I think of,
washed ashore in 1564 on Nod Thwaite's property:
yes, the whale would do, as a unit for Morgan to measure by.
Thwaite cleaned each stave, and on a brisking autumn day
when his buffing was done, began to charge admission to that osseous
parthenon. Hundreds took the tour. By night a fire
threw the vaulting into flickery relief. By day they clambered
their midget way among these ruins. I like them mostly
in the skull; as if a whale were dreaming of what it had been
before it turned from that and chose the sea.

~

I'm sorry, but this gray vase bearing gray debris,
this poof and its stringbean pieces of bone, is no
Bob Potts in his cardigan flecked with pipe shag
holding court at The Cedar Door or Mulligan's.
No. This vase is Nothing; its contents, Nothing.
And Nothing can't be counterbalanced. I'm sorry,
there isn't a fact that can do it, there isn't
a richly glitzed-up fiction in the world, not God,
not no-God, there isn't a memory that means anything
to Nothing. And Morgan says, with a tender shake of her head,
"That man," as if he might have been some feathercrested
platinum-shitting prodigy, "was something."
Even without his eyes he was something, without
his legs, and in the final sour bubble of breathing: something.

~

Because he loved his telescope . . . he's given away
to that emptiness now, he's sprinkled from a daughter's fingers
into the galaxy pinch by pinch. As physics knows,
and so as endless poems these days repeat, we're all
constructed of the particles of stars. The service
may as well go *dust to dust, and astra to astra.*
Not that any rhetoric really comforts.
Not that any glint of wit or thundered scripture
suffices for long. But since you've asked for a poem,
my ex, my sweet and troubled one, I'll give you this
attempt, complete with starry night and bourbon shots:
Here,
I'm lifting a beer
for Bob Potts.

In

the text:
& then the author's life

behind the text:
& then the preexisting

psychic fundament behind *that:*
always further layers penetrable

or not:
the word & its origin

& its intention
& its several dozen possible meanings

in several dozen heads:
not to mention the moment

& the moment before:
not to mention let's say love

& then the word "love"-(a)
that's painted over with "love"-(b)

very impasto
very very impasto: always text

& overtext: always
& overtext

~

He hiked the strenuous trails—and above.
He did the Stätzerhorn (8,593 feet)
and the Lenzerhorn (9,703) and the Piz Bernina
(13,284). There would be storms at times
—the ice axe and the crampons little help in this
opacity, as Alpine snow *became* the air—but mostly
it was the clarity of vision at these supernal heights
that lifted him like a pocket's lining
out of himself; and he could see
the glitter of a river in some distant glacial valley,
every pock of a boulder along its twists
as obvious as the alpenroses and edelweiss beside his booted feet.
—The way (and now he remembers) that he was ten and leaning
observantly over the lucid waters of the Grift, and staring
straight to the river's utterly evident bottom muck: the feeling
was that he could peel that dirt back now
and stare with a similar potency at
the living chthonic heart of the world. . . . Remembering this.
Wilhelm Röntgen. November 1895: what should he call this
ray that he's discovered, this mystery force, this X.

~

This is how we fought: we rubbed the skin off
one another's minds. Because we were married,
because we'd learned through intimacy
the weak link and the likeliest archeology-point
for quick unearthing, this is how we did it:
we worried the top skin off the mind, and then
the underskin, we reached inside with eyes that saw
through history, and lifted from out of each other
the oiliest, inch-squirm maggot-thing-of-an-idea
we could find in the gnarls, and held it
to the light. It was on one of those days
I thought back to the fluoroscopes so popular
for viewing the fit of kids' shoes in the early 1950s.
I was . . . five, I'd guess. Across the store, a girl of five
was ushered in a pair of deeply lacquer-looking party shoes
to the huge machine, for her regiment of bones to be put
on parade for the world—her inside life, her own.
I'd never seen such frightful screaming. "Albert,
you're not a baby like *that.*" Oh, maybe; maybe not.
I know I understood her shock at that radiatory undoing.

~

When you invoke the grand metonymy,
when you ask for a hand in marriage . . .
oh

it will stroke you, gently/sexually;
it will hammer your back, a ballpeen fist;
and often it will be one part of the shrug
that says our every attempt to fashion something
shared between two people is laced with a basic
unreadability . . .

he was silent,
as if he had left his mind in the laboratory. . . .
He picked at his food without enjoyment. . . .
She began to worry. . . . She asked. . . .
He made no reply . . . apparently had angered him. . . .
He disappeared through the open door,
walked along the hallway and entered his study. . . .
She went to bed alone, leaving him in the laboratory. . . .
(W. Robert Nitske, in *The Life of Wilhelm Conrad Röntgen*).
Evening: December 22, 1895:
"Bertha, may I have /

~

. . . her hand / in its consent / her hand
in all of its physical "hereness," yes, but also
in all of its new "new physics" insubstantiality /
holding still for fifteen minutes on the plate /
amid the induction coils and pear-shaped Hittorf-Crookes tubes
and the Lenard tubes and Ruhmkorff coil and Raps pump /
here: her hand: her famous hand: the famous fingerbones
showing up with the jointing and elegant length
of bamboo done in a gray wash: here: her fingerbones
like the legs of the deep-sea spider crab /
the famous photographed enterable flesh /
and the famous two resistant rings:
those dark and obdurate things:
as if all of the hesitant pleasures
and go-for-broke hell-bent inanities
and desecrations and choked-down hopes and heavings
of a marriage
here were locked to the bone
in mineral form so concentrated, nothing, *nothing,*
could light their essential privacy.

~

there's an airplane in this poem
that won't go away, it circles

insistently, is shooed off
but returns, is here like a fly

in the room in 1995
as the two of us bicker and icily stare,

and is there in 1895 somehow
before its invention at Kitty Hawk,

it's in the thin blue winter air
as Röntgen walks with Bertha

in their fur coats
to the mailbox on the Pleicherring

with copies of his initial report,
it snaps them

and it listens in,
its lenses and its microphones

are overhead, relentless
in the way that the author and reader are

as the characters step to the therapist's all-ears couch,
as the characters start to strip

~

. . . and the bones in his wife's hand. No doubt it was this last capability that made Röntgen's discovery the first modern scientific breakthrough to spark banner headlines in newspapers around the world. Some anxious people even began taking baths fully clothed, convinced that scientists were lurking about their houses peering at them with these mystery rays.
—Marcia Bartusiak

She wants, she says, "more sharing" in this
relationship, more swappage of our days' individual freight.
Okay. What *I've* been doing is reading
about the application of Röntgen's uncorked power.
In 1925, forensic detective Edward Oscar Heinrich had
"the corpse sent to his laboratory and X-rayed.
He immediately observed that a molar was missing,"
and, soon enough: case closed! It's similarly handy
when a jewel thief's nabbed in flight and slyly swallows
the incriminating diamond. Maybe my favorite
tale is someone stopped when airport security sees
the X-rayed shape of a gun in her carry-on; and
she pleads with increasing intensity as they open her bag
for the snooping world to wonder at
her steel-cored dildo-*cum*-balls. —And how
was *your* day, where have you been? At that,
my wife's face storms protectively
around some inmost selfhood of the night, and this
gets ranted: You/can/NOT/know-
EV/'ry/SIN/gle/thing/that/hap/pens/in/MY/MIND!

~

. . . And I watch her sleep. I study her in sleep
until I'm hypnotized, and think that I can see
our trouble feeding on the reeds inside her (even as its sister
swims in me), a bloated, scales-covered thing with fearsome
beauty of its own. In the book of "radiological photographs
of nature," every leaf of chard and every balled-up grub
becomes a reliquary rayed to reveal
extraordinary interiorscapes: a minaret,
in a water lily; the swaddled hooded-cobra-head of the clitoris,
in a cowrie shell; my grandmother's sinuous intricate
hook-and-eyelet leather strips along her orthopedic boots,
in the length of the rat snake. . . . Strangeness,
loveliness. In Röntgen's early study of a custodian,
the clothes and then the flesh have drizzled transparently
away and leave the metal keys on either hip
like a schoolboy's catch of minnows after a day at the stream.
We all have fish in our chests. We all have
rings of keys, and knots of barbed wire, and jellyfish stingers,
and overblown roses, and shake our sediments up
and we all contain an undulant wing of lees.

~

When I watched them wheel my father into the lab
(I wasn't used to—then—a hospital's visual rigamarole),
what struck me hardest wasn't the vividly purple-green
tarantula the needle bruised into his skin;
or the dolly the bag rode on, that accompanied him
like a gaunt and silent retainer; or even the catheter tube
that seemed as thick as an eel set to drink his pee . . . no.
No, it was the G-string—except, about the size of home plate—
made of lead, that they hung at his crotch
as they placed him inside what looked like a toll-guard booth.

The booth's front side is glass: the "private dancer"
faces out, then there's an immediate akimbo
display of the goods. Some dancers obviously resent
their work, and some take powerful pleasure from
its muff-and-money mix. But *this* never varies:
"Where are you from?" "Connecticut," she says
(she's from Montana). Former job? "Uh—waitress"
(a courier for Trans-Send). Kids? "Yeh, two of them" (no).
It's her lead shield. There are places
even your goddam hard-earned dollar won't let you go.

~

He was meticulous, and cautious; when the badgerers
from the newspapers all demanded he prognosticate some marvelous
applications of his discovery, he demurred: "I am not
a prophet, and I am opposed to prophesying"; it wasn't
marvels that he sought, but what was
measurably there. His world was one of verification
won in small and graphable increments. And yet
with Bertha gone—she died October 31 in 1919—
sometimes he read aloud from the newspaper
or a novel they had liked, or mail received, pretending
that she still shared her thoughts with him.
(Whitman has this two-line poem from his old age:
"These carols sung to cheer my passage through the world I see,
For a completion I dedicate to the Invisible World."
I think of Röntgen completing himself that way.)
And so this is where we should leave him, yes?
—Sitting there,
                    rocking,
                              intimately speaking
into the gateway of X.

~

Sentences have a noun phrase as the subject followed by a verb phrase as the predicate. That rule is needed to account for such sentences as The woman wept. *Note that* The gun wept *also follows this rule, but it is not an acceptable sentence.*
—George A. Miller, in *The Science of Words*

Under the rubble of World War II is the rubble of World War I.
And under that is a layer of struggle-to-make-ends-meet
and yet bucolic, warless village-and-shepherding life. And
under that, intact, is a circle of dwellings structured
out of tusks and reinforced mud. And under that, some
bones—like accent marks distributed in the Earth—
including some earliest human skulls. And in them:
tiny figures, each with tiny skulls of their own,
and brains the size of garden snails' bodies that,
like any brains, are larger than the universe that holds them.
Out of yours, we took a hatchet that mewed my name;
and out of mine, we took a perfectly innocent-looking freestone peach
that was a grenade. So easy—once the monstrous pain
from sawing the skull-tops off was numbed. And we arranged it
all on the table: the gun that wept, the tear that burnt
like a spill at the foundry, a clock of teeth
and sexual lubrication, an open sore that winked
just like a flirting eye, a lightless sun, a pastry made of pins.
And we said: Here is the marriage, I hate you,
here is the marriage, heal it, heal it.

~

There's an airplane in the skies, from somewhere
out of poetic eternitime, it hides

between the couplets, it disguises its noise
in the general human buzz, it lands

some pages back, in the Alps, and deposits
a microsurveillance device in one of those alpenroses

you read about. Yes, you
—you're being watched. We know all about you.

As a compensation, of course, you get to voyeurize
this couple in their most distressed extremes;

although another way of saying them right now
would be this tender evocation Rembrandt has done

of a woman in difficult contemplation, as she sits
on the rim of her bath. X-ray analysis

shows an earlier composition
under the current surface, shows us really

another woman inside this woman.
It's late afternoon; the day folds up.

Another head is in her head,
and wearily rests against it.

More Trouble with Pleasant Interludes

Squash and Stone

> *Like so many men of his time, he was after a grand principle that would explain a universal truth. An element that he called "septon" was, he declared, the instrument of decay and the cause of most diseases. He lectured on septon, wrote papers on it and even composed a long poem called "The Doctrine of Septon," in which his doggerel blamed septon for cancer, leprosy, scurvy and ringworm.*
>
> —on the nineteenth-century naturalist Samuel Latham Mitchill, collaged from Joseph Kastner's *A Species of Eternity*

And so it is, with the physicists' need
to find a simple, nonexclusionary Supertheory that gathers
the "weak," "strong," gravitational, and electromagnetic
forces into a single "field." And so it was with the marriage.
We wanted its failures in a single word
that ends in -ism or -phobia. One thumb to suck.
One wilted plant to mourn for or renurture.
Isn't it difficult enough, to be a "me" in a world
of daily half-price sales at the Chooz-a-Self?
We wanted the flaw in "us" to be a single, lucid wrongness
(that would require a single righting).
Of course we wanted this; the Supertheory is meant to be
completion raised to beauty,
the way the ocean is both the ocean and the sky.
I'd see her sitting in the kitchen some days staring
at a random still-life basketful of leeks and summer squash
as if this might comprise a read-out screen, a Ouija mechanism,
to the planet of The Single Reason. Once, she said,
she watched me in the dusk light try to squeeze a stone,
she said I really looked as if . . . she thought
of a film noir private detective trying to make a suspect talk.
I remember a day when the mill across the county line
in Nestorville caught fire, and I wished the arm of char
it raised across the sky
would write some Answer, something brief
the way the elementary is by definition brief, and irreducible.
Give us our god, our needle.
Give us our theory, we thought to ourselves,
as if it were a Constitutional right. Give us our septon.

Dog, Fish, Shoes (or Beans)

"I was a shmooshled little girl," my Aunt Elena says.
"I'm seventeen, I have a shape from a matzoh ball,
boomp boomp boomp I walk. So no wonder, Glicka
with big soft eyes like stewed prunes
has a boyfriend, he would jump through hoops of fire
for her if his wizzle was dipped in kerosene first,
and Pearl has a boyfriend, Misha does, Rebekka
whose body goes in and out like an accordion, hooy
she could walk down the street and the trolleys
fall out of their tracks. But poor Elena, me,
boohoo boohoo with the tears all shpritzing, don't
laugh from my story, it's very sad. So what
does Elena do on Saturday night, with everybody else
in front of the radio holding hands to ukelele songs?
Elena, the poor shmo, baby-sits for people
in her building. On the third floor are the Morrises,
with a dog a cocker spaniel—like a bowling ball
of dirty fur and always yapping, I
hated it—and a goldfish. And so for *them*
I don't even *baby*-sit, they would hire somebody
I swear to wipe the dog's tush if they could.
So I stay up there, I feed the fish and the dog,
I clean the box, I listen like an idiot
to the ukelele serenades like everyone else, and I cry.
Good; so this is my Saturday date. One night,
does it *rain?*—like Noah's Flood of a rain.
From nowhere, a Noah's Flood all of a sudden.
I run to close the bedroom window—*whoops,*
and down the three floors goes the goldfish bowl
with Miss Goldilox, which the name is a joke,
like lox the fish, but a goldfish. It lands
in a puddle. I think to myself, 'In a puddle?
Could beeeee . . . this little fishy's heart still beats.' So I

run downstairs—" "—*But,*" my Uncle Mo
takes over, "she leaves the door to the apartment open.
This Is Important: remember. Meanwhile,
a certain very handsome young man—" "—oh, handsome
like a *blintz* that got run over—" "—is delivering
a wagon of shoes from the Jewish Poor Relief Fund—"
"—shoes? it was canned goods—" "—listen
in *your* story maybe it's canned goods, *mine* it's shoes—"
"—okay, Mr. Memory, but I'm telling you I see
these little cans with the pears and the whaddayacallem beans
on the labels—" "—shoes, it was shoes, it was shoes,
up past your winkus in shoes, do you hear me—"
"—don't laugh—" "—so anyway—" "—feh!—" "—where
was I—" "—don't interrupt—" "—and I said
'Pardon me Miss but is this poor shivering
cocker spaniel yours?'—" "—and here we are to tell you
this story Fifty Years Later!" Then we always said:
Did you go upstairs and kiss? And they always
never answered: "The fish, by the way, we never found."
"So you see?" she'd add. "Nothing is hopeless."

In the Bar in the Bar

Someone's voice, made haughtier by her rum-on-ice
than necessary, says "I can see right *through* you," and
I think of that population in the paintings of previous eras
we've subjected to twentieth-century X-ray study:
a world of interior bodies, whole unto themselves,
that are caught torqued contrariwise
to the turn of their outer bodies; of women staring beseechingly
out of the eyes of men—and men, of women—night and night again
at the window; of downswept necks bent in submission
or devotion, like a counterweight
inside the upthrusting faces of prideful defiance . . .
some seem no more than a clever inner puppet show, but others
shriek with the urgency of the prematurely buried. . . . Blurry,
earlier selves. . . . In the oil on panel
Portrait of Edward VI of England, radiography
shows us that the boy-king was a girl once: how
the roundness of her Netherlandish skirt has been
subsumed into his raiment, how her loosely held carnation
has become a tasseled dagger in his grip; how she remains
in him, the living underpinnings he began as. . . . Everybody,
yes?—would seem to be a new home for this old, old cricket
rubbing the ancient music out of its legs. So
when I hear some hombre's slurry bravado
loudly lobbed from a corner (*I fuckin said NO WAY, Miss Kiss-My-Ass*),
I know "this Chinese vessel, a *fang ding,* of the eleventh century B.C.,
shows extensive interior damage under X-ray light,
and clumsy attempts at soldering; a liberal application
of false patina attempts to mask this." When I hear
a woman's martially jolly *OF COURSE I'm happy,*
I TOLD YOU I'm happy, and don't you EVER forget it,
I know "beneath the chest of this tenderly rendered
'infant suckling' set scene, is the breastplate of a warrior
that analysis shows as the painter's original study." Everybody,

yes? In the face in the face. In the bar in the bar.
And it turns out, beer is a kind of crystal ball;
you don't look *into* it, you take it into *you*.
In mine, by midnight, I can read the past
as it rises like mist in front of me. I can read the text
in the text of the wedding. Two of us, saying
eager *yes*, and *yes*, in front of the witnesses. And already,
a head in each of our heads, a mind in each of our minds,
beginning to slowly shake itself
against the thick of the current—*no*, and *no*.

Alternative Uses

> *While exploring a branch of the Victoria River, in North Australia, we halted, as usual, at noon, with scanty rations, which Mr. Gregory improved by taking from his hat a stout sewing needle, softening it in the fire, and bending it into a fish-hook, baited with grasshoppers.*
>
> —nineteenth-century travel account

It will often be found useful to carry a bottle
of cold tea, nothing is so effectual for thirst.
Experienced travellers frequently carry in their holsters,
instead of pistols: in the one, a tiny
teapot with a paper of tea, and in the other,
a cup and a paper of sugar. And in those days
friends would always seem amazed when they suddenly
opened my refrigerator and found—because
I ate my meals in neighborhood cafés and hated to see
good shelf space wasted, and because I wanted
these stacks of nuisance out of sight
as rapidly as my red pen could complete them—
mounds of graded Composition 101 assignments. (And
once, in 103°, a lover's folded lingerie.)

~

He needed to pretend to be straight, in order
to be promoted; and she had a proven record
of being exactly that, with a skillful ardor.
She needed start-up backing for the catering shop
she dreamed of; and, the heartless bastard,
he'd devoted his life to squeezing money out of others.
He needed a legal reason to stay in the United States,
once his card expired; she needed a father for the baby,
any father. She hated her overrestrictive fundamentalist
parents; he was surely a pile of nasty habits
looking for a container to stain. He
had his agenda, she had hers, and they coincided
along a delicate line. And so they took each other
in holy matrimony.

~

Hoping this finds you well. There is so little
in the way of news I am almost ashamed to write,
but for the obligation I feel to one who is
himself such a prompt correspondent.
The garden is declaring itself already
this season in butter-yellows and blues that look
as if they want to wave hello all the way
to Turners Crossing and Hill Fork. Oh,
there is a new pastor, sorrily NOT a real rouser
of a sermonizer. Yours, as ever, Imojean T.
The postcard is from 1912, and brittling enough
so that its penny stamp is chipping off, and the spidery
message, hidden under it, says
Hot kisses to my honey boy.

What We're Used To

Or the woman who, after the seeped stink of her death
had slapped the neighbors into attentiveness and then the cops,
was found to have shared the dungeon-dark of her backlot shack
with (this was by actual clicker count) 548 rats, that
(who?) she'd made her confidants—had fed,
and built a gamy junkparts playground for, and nested with
in sleep (perhaps by then could *only* sleep with the familiar
tictac dance of their garbagey paws across her body). And
"familiar" *is* the keynote word: that dankness
was the comfy psyche-soup in which she lazied back
and happily dissolved at the end of a day. For her,
this was natural. In the Hanzai Valley, the villagers

~

live with ghosts around them as commonly as oxygen
is around them—ghosts, cospatially with the air
they breathe, the air that rides the blood, the air we'll all become
one day, one way or another. "Rounded [cosmos/sky-container]"
(their ritual greeting) they say on meeting any of this invisible
and thronging population. For them, it's natural. The spectral selves
of animals and plants attend the hunt and the fields. Stars,
the various intimacies that occur at night in those fields.
Ancestral spirits see through the dark, of course, and so
not even the fevery knots of the sexual union are secret
from them—if anything, their up-close sidelines cheering
is expected, is part of the order of things. In Rembrandt's

~

engraving *Het Ledekant,* of a couple in coitus (he's on top
between her legs, in a billowy, canopied four-poster), the woman pictured
in this otherwise realistically rendered bedtime scene is given
three arms; to this extent, the viewer is given two choices.
If we ask to accept the arm that laxly sprawls at her side
(presumably paired with one out of sight, on her other side), then
the woman's nearly asleep, or swoozled on too much wine.
If we ask to accept the hands that clasp his ass in tightly,
the woman's actively passionate: dark lines beneath one hand say
fleshly pressure. Whichever. Neither reading's "wrong." Each
has a naturalness, depending on the lives, and on the thousand
constituent details of their time together. Once I loved

~

in the way I thought love worked: you made
life easier for someone; made it into a calm continuum,
sans burden or suspicion; you were free of frowst and bitterness,
and you trusted that life would buoy you in return. For her,
each day Creation started up from zero again, tough brick by brick,
and debt by debt; attack was ever immanent, defense was ever
hammered-on in thick emotional sheet metal. So it
didn't last. And both of us felt betrayed. I remember . . .
the sun through the bough, like a loading ramp into infinity . . .
I explained my idea of life, and I could see it wasn't material
at all, it was a phantom life, and she could put her hand right through me:
I was supernatural.

The Lost Continent *(1951)*

The purse-snatch in this 1568 painting of Bruegel's
squats behind his victim in a clearly absurdist rendering.
He wears—he's *in*—a cagelike sphere the size of a balled-up person,
and it gives him the look of a toy man someone
jammed inside a gyroscope. But, after all, he *is*
"the world"—he is, for Bruegel's purposes, the whole
deceitful globe. Yes, much the way the view of Antwerp
out the window of a prison in this other one, from 1562,
becomes the world—becomes a distant light-tinged scene,
so unattainable (the sails on the bay, the hovered gulls)
it comes to feel comprehensive of each single pleasure
life affords in every bend of land, in every friendly lump of bedding.
Melville's "Pequod" is intended as the world. And in the upstairs ward
the orderlies called No Return, I listened as a woman,

with enormous generosity, guided a tour through the stains
of her ceiling and walls, and through the abstract pattern
of her patched chenille bedspread—these, a detailed map
to the planet Eterna, and all of its seas, all of its basilica'd cities,
had their weighty, populated histories. "And this," she switched
attention to the lose-yourself-inside-it endless-viridian of a lamp's
ceramic glaze, "is outer space." She knew the birth and death
of every thumbprint galaxy. And the desk lamp
in Elizabeth Bishop's "12 O'Clock News" is wittily
transmogrified into a full moon; and the typewriter
into a terraced "escarpment" rising on "the central plain";
and a spilling pile of manuscripts, a landslide: as if *any*
of the Earth's minutiae might be DNA for replicating
Earth full-scale. This is why my marriage

disparages anything less than a Chinese New Year Dragon
(a beast of the gods as long as a city block, a whiskered river
with the bebop in its belly and a fire in its mad jaws) as a symbol;
and why we argue until the first pearl light of dawn hits
like a car crash on our skin, we're made that sensitive; and why
sometimes we're gentle the way the lid is to the eye. Because
we do it for you. Because we bear your grief and celebration
in our own, your dulling wits, your verve, your human juice.
Because our fury is Fury; and our woe is Woe; our love is Love.
John Hoyt was asked to remember thirty-five years back
to the set of that lo-budg quickie. "We had six or eight rocks
and some dead trees. We kept walking around and around them
while the prop men rearranged them," he said.
Eventually it was a continent.

Substratum

The Black Lagoon is turbid—is an inky egg-drop soup
of mysterious antediluvian matrix—and its famous Creature
doesn't rise up *from* it, but more accurately
is it, in the way a genie is one with the smoke in the lamp.
There's so much socio- and psychoacademic jaw-breeze
solely devoted to reasoning out the tropes of this
impressive ichthyterror, this ornately scaled and gilled
half-fish-half-man, that it's a challenge to reanimate
the goofy wonder of 1954 when I was six, and "wreaking havoc"
meant—I thought—the Creature stunk. But I remember,
with a clarity four decades hasn't darkened,
its balletic underwater scene with the beautiful
(and therefore, natch, imperiled) Julie Adams; as well as its slow,
forebodingly thunky lumber on land. And also
It Came from Beneath the Sea: a *giant* octopussish horror,
released from the aboriginal sea-ooze ("out of primordial depths"
the poster says) to smack the San Francisco skyline
into bloody rubble. And also *The Phantom from 10,000 Leagues.*
And also *The Beast from 20,000 Fathoms.* Lesson:
the substratum of things is seemingly everprolific
in monstrosity. It *squanders*
ogreish shapes, and can afford to. In *The She Creature,* Andrea,
standardly "gorgeous hypnotist's assistant," is regressed to her
most atavistic past-self: talons,
bony hooks, fangs, wings, antennae, fins, and a stomach cavity
framed in hokey tusklike teeth. *Forbidden Planet*'s stunning nemesis
—a hungry, abstract "field" of "force" that kills—
is the scientist Morbius's unconscious mind
projected into the everyday light of exterior space:
an id
with the physical presence of Kong.
Well, that's the function of Hollywood (another way of saying
the function of myth): to *make* a thing

that large, to make it the size of a culture.
Once I drove with Ed up the Northwest coast, from sunrise
into stars: so there was time
for our initial series of wiseass, zinger badinage
to deepen. After one especially
empty silence, he said: "One night
when I was driving the old-time gin-joint back roads
in Kentucky—this would have been, geez, this would have been the spring
of 1983—I looked in my rearview mirror and saw a face
was floating in the darkness of the backseat. It was the face
of a demon. A virulent sulfur-green; and a malevolent grin.
I wasn't drunk or drugged or sleepy, the weather was clear.
And there was that face, as plain as a fist or an apple.
I'd turn around, and it was gone. I'd look in the mirror again,
and there it was again, as if some factory worker in Tokyo
had fixed it into the air of the car to begin with. Just silent.
Watching. Don't ask *me;* it came with me all the way
over the state line, and it stayed until the sun came up
outside of Cincinnati. That was the only time." We're quiet
for a while after that, my sane
and rational and civilized compadre Ed and me.
Our conversation shades away to the usual
rants, the usual guy enthusiasms, the usual instances
of highway philosophy over a styrofoam coffee cup,
the usual florid memories of women. Then we're quiet
again. Ed says: "When Helen and I divorced . . . shit,
when I found her fucking Gus in our bed that time,
it seared my mind for a long long while, I did some truly
malicious things in return. That spring when I lived in Kentucky,
I heard her mother died, and Helen needed me there
at the funeral. In fact I'd loved her mother too. And what
I did, out of spite?—I drove to see
an old ladyfriend in Ohio. A lot of ugliness
was trapped inside my brain, and needed *out.*"
It's then I share with him my hazy recollection of the story
of Paul and Annie Smith—and when I'm back home,
I look up the details. Three days after their marriage,
in April 1972, in Yorkshire, on their way to deliver
leftover wedding cake to a friend, their three-wheel mini-car
slammed straight-on into the rear of a truck, "went underneath,
came out and somersaulted several times, hitting a bus stop
and landing square on its nose." The couple survived, and in fact
had presence of mind enough to film the car immediately

for insurance purposes. Annie Smith: "When watching the film
for the first time, I saw someone in the passenger seat,
distinctly. It was terrifying." . . . *came to believe the image
was of a "crisis apparition" of Mrs. Smith, imprinted out of her,
onto the air, by her sharp, primal fear of death.*
And the eight grainy minutes of weirdly sinuous
something making lengths of sunset-gilded s's on the black scrolls
of Loch Ness. The giant golden turtle of Hoan Kiem Lake.
The dragon of Banyok, 250 miles northwest of Moscow,
ascending giddily from the depths of its liquid midden
for the timely tourist camcorders, snorting once
with Mesozoic hauteur, and then diving cleanly out of sight.
If *Creature from the Black Lagoon* is "a seminal,
even a monumentally seminal, cinematic text to study" . . . then
these jittery and blurred home-movie testaments are the graffiti
that our neighbors scrawl in their genuine way
around that monument's base. They always have,
from the beginning. When Leviathan arose from the waters.
When Snake Mother came from the [waves?] [sea?] (water sign).
And then does Tiamat rage (up) from the (place of) water,
from the First Abode, and the people are scattered,
their dwellings and their stores of grain are scattered,
they moan and Tiamat rages,
they beat at their breasts and Tiamat comes,
they beat at their heads and Tiamat rages.

Various Ulia

Did we say it out loud? Eventually
we said it. Cancer. Somewhere someone else
said AIDS. But only toward the last,
near the end, when the dying was
the fear—and not the dying's being invited.
For such is the power of utterance.
Susie says that even ten years since the divorce,
she refuses to drive alone at night
—that's when the words come back.
Although the infamous Mercury Theater production
of *The War of the Worlds* (October 30, 1938)
was intended to horrify, still,
"CBS cut the cries of the invading Martians
('Ulia, Ulia Ulia') as too frightening."
A song comes on; she won't say why, but
she needs to turn off the radio.

Two Weeks, with Polo Chorus

> *Every culture has its own distinctive features; Chinese windmills turn horizontally; in Istanbul, the scissors have hollow blades, and the luxury spoons are made of wood from the pepper plant; Japanese and Chinese anvils are different from ours; not one nail was used to build the boats on the Red Sea and the Persian Gulf, and so on.*
>
> —*The Structures of Everyday Life,* Fernand Braudel

She's upstairs assembling the lounga-recliner.
Strut C . . . into knob-slot A . . . then tighten . . .
From the dormer window, she can see him,
Mr. Mechanic, clucking over his bike—she can *observe* him
maternally tending its frailties, oiling it, and buffing it. . . .
Two weeks now, that they've known each other. Usually
it's a goofily pubescent thunkathunka loveorama feeling
filling her, but . . . just now, somehow,
watching as he lobs his toolbox
over the stone ledge into her bed of nasturtiums . . .
it's a fundamental *strangerness* she senses,
as his own needs and itineraries stake their alien claim
to the day . . . and suddenly this *uno-a-uno*
xenophobia won't let her go.

~

And Marco Polo says, in the city of Hormuz
ships are fastened not by iron nails but thread
from coconut husks, and caulked with fish oil
which we do not do here, and the Tartars, when they sit
to eat, they take their graven god and smear a lump of fat
around his mouth and the mouths of his wife and children
which we do not do here, and the idols of Cathay
and Japan and Manzi have the heads of cattle,
pigs, and dogs, and sheep, and some have three faces or four
and some a thousand hands *and these are not our gods,*
and in Cathay at the time of betrothal of marriage,
certain matrons especially deputized by both of the parties
will prove the bride's virginity (or not) by the test
of the pigeon egg *which we in our Christian land do not.*
—In Haiti in 1937, Royal Geographical Society member
Ian Sanderson wrote "I found here three bicycles
left by a stranded Circus that went broke,"
and the locals were using them to power their local
electrical dynamos: a savvy and almost familiar
otherusefulness which we do not do.

~

The story I want to tell you is one of hair in the sink,
of clock alarms that chitter someone else's
daily schedule through your sleep—of things
as minimal as the scribble of shit a guppy trails,
adding up unbearably. / She feeds his fish, and watches
the wavering drapery of flakes descend. . . . Alone upstairs,
he notices the lounga-recliner. Renee,
his ex, enjoyed a similar penchant
for unfolding the instructions (pidgin Martianese),
then flurrying into a wrench-and-lugnut tizzy. . . .
Renee, her ginger-speckled shoulders, and
her matching towel-and-loofah sets . . . That's history,
though. *This* lounga-recliner he's sitting in is
. . . and he drops through its ill-fit seat with a crash.

~

And Marco Polo says, in the city of Hormuz are professional
mourners, women who bewail the dead
on hire *which to us appears strange,* and
in the island Japan the dead are buried
with a pearl in the mouth, white or sometimes red
which is not our way, and among the Tartars
the practice is this, that when a boy will die
and in another family a girl will die of similar age,
a deed is arranged and the two are given
unto each other in matrimony *and this is not our custom,*
and in the city Sa-chau the dead are cremated,
and horses and camels of paper, and pieces of money of paper
are burnt so that the dead may have these
truly with them in the next life *even though*
this is peculiar to us, and in the city Khan-balik
the money is made of the bark of mulberry trees,
and in Kaindu province the money is loaves of salt,
and in the province of Toloman the money is cowrie shells,
and more, and further, and ever else, *and this is not*
our way our righteous way our sweet familiar.

~

Words—not a quarrel exactly, but . . . words
with edges. He slammed the door (a kind of overword)
and now he's out riding. She's here, she's watching
three beautiful fecal ideograms three guppies drag,
some untranslatable statement through the water.
He's out riding . . . he's out burning it away
on the bike. *Away* is the point: the piling up of distance.
But a psychic thread connects him
to her house and can't be shaken off; the farther he goes,
the fiercer he pedals, the stronger is its wirey pull
and the more his energy seems to light the house
he leaves behind. Two weeks, and already they make
a system. He remembers eighth-grade science: how
the term they use to measure electric current is *resistance.*

True

Of Devotion / John Donne

There is, in ev'ry Temple to Our Lord,
A Portion of His worshippers who raise
Their voices, where from Deep Within is pour'd
Into the world Great, Tributarie Prayse;
The whiles their Thought is contemplating Else,
Of Merchantry, or Spite, or Carnal ways;
And thus, their song of Reverence is false,

—speaking of which, I'd better stop here and admit
(not that I necessarily think it was a world-class con)
I wrote those lines. No one likes being lied to
—though with history behind us, and with politics to left and right,
we're used to it by now. We know that Plato would bar poets
from the gates of his ideal state, essentially because they "lie"
(see pseudo-Donne above, as current evidence); about the time
that Vasco da Gama reached India, the Chinese
made construction of an oceangoing junk a crime, and burned
the logbooks of earlier ships, because explorers trafficked in
"deceitful exaggerations of bizarre things." Don't we all,
as the night grows thick around our tongues, and the face
of the clock on the wall of the bar refuses to flinch, no matter
what full crock it overhears. What Plato fears

is accurate enough: unchecked, our natural attraction
toward embellishing (or outright whopperstyle re-creating)
what a friend here calls "the actualfactual true poop"
will confound our lives past any sane decision-making.
"THIS," a woman screamed out, fueled by enmity and whiskey sours,
"this," and "this" again, as if the noun to come were too foul
to approach without a sputtered string of buffering, "this
'marriage' is a *fiction,* is a goddamn Halloween-mask SHAM!"
Though the party guests ducking her room-trajecting highball glass . . .
was real. If this smacks of glammy TV shockumentaries,
it's had its quiet counterpart in every heart I know: a lonely
moment when the I.D. card of Who We Are Inside at last
won't match the face we daily show the world. Then
endless floatingdrowningfalling in our myriad ways. And yet

the truly nutso charm of fakery can't be denied:
the faddish rich in the middle of the nineteenth century
had their landscaped grotto installations decorated with old men
dressed as "Gothic" hermits moping around in retro-fashion cassock and cowl.
And some of this less-than-verity is *hilarious,* by which I mean
for example the phone-sex caller who complained that when he dialed
the "Hear Me Moan" line, what he got was a recording of a woman
nagging her husband. (The telephone standards committee then ruled
that the tape met its title's criteria.) Some lies not only nubble
extra texture in our lives, they *save* our lives: I know
a couple in their eighties now who snuck from Hitler's Germany
as corpses, in a rattling van of many hundreds of *real* corpses
being hauled for fertilizer: "We rode into life in the arms
of the dead," he says. "In the *smell* of the dead," she adds,

and then: "For years I dreamed that I *was* dead. I would wake up
screaming and not understand—for how could a *cadaver* scream?"
Extreme—but representative of that faceted thing
we call the human psyche. We'd better get used to it,
aren't we all collagework, every "me" complete
with zip-out not-me lining, every "solid" "thing" a fizz
of void and quantum physics hocuspocus, isn't the green we see as "leaf"
the light the leaf refuses, not the light it *is?*
You needn't be the Prince of Bigamists or a Secret Service plant
in an enemy embassy to understand instinctively
that "you" is forever a lie to every equally credible
"alter-you" . . . and *then*
what's verifiable, what senses do we trust? A story
from out of the life of Donne, as reported by Izaak Walton:

round with child, afeared, Anne Donne allows his travel to France
on an ambassadorial mission with a faint
"unwilling willingness." The second night in Paris, Donne looks up
from the table and sees "my dear wife pass twice by me,"
hair in wild disarray "and a dead child in her arms."
A servant is sent back to London and twelve days later returns
with the news that "Mrs. Donne [is] very sad and sick
. . . she had been delivered of a dead child." Yes, and *did*
Donne "see" "her"? Water into water, and who can tell
the demarcations? Snow in more snow, and in yet more snow,
and dark poured like an unguent into dark, and time
on top of time, and "truth" spilled into "history."
I picture him in a study that night, remembering an incomplete
erotic sonnet he started for her, so many life-upheavals ago. . . .

We hie to bed, the way that they go Forth
Who seeke New Lands, who test the falsitie
Of Rivers running Gold, and test the Worth
Of tales of Beasts that Speake. And if they then Bee
Lost inside this New and Rich Countrie,
They have their Lodestone. We have ours and we
Do not fear therefore. Love is our True north. . . .

Directional

↓

The level where the bits of frizzled-out satellites orbit
isn't "high up"—not in a universe that reaches unboundedly out
to the flimmering skins of forming and dying
stars, the ghosts of stars, the great creation-wisps of stars . . .
it makes the swifts, this April evening, as they dive
and lift in zippy bug-gulp passes that we think
should trail scorchmarks through the air . . . it makes
these remarkable flyers ("overhead," "in the sky")
mere bottomgrubbers, not markedly different from us,
from everyone bearing the umpty-ump impossible tons of atmosphere
per square inch on their bodies. And the rain
"falls" "down." The leaves, in their season. The snows.
The light on this page has been falling for 93 million miles.
Think of everything it carries by the time it lands.
In Kansas, in the flatlands here, a farmhouse sits in the middle
of such emptiness, such morning-misted and borderless space,
below such *outer* space, that from the distance of the interstate
it looks like a corner of sunken Atlantis,
tilted a little, weaved through by the sea-floor things
that have no eyes and live on flakes of sediment. And even

~

↑

here, the idea of "up" is alive, and people wake—or, as they say,
they "rise"—routinely from a dream of flying. Some
of them levitate casually, as if they sat on top
of an invisible pillar elevating. Others run and flap their arms
like one of da Vinci's apprentices strapped to a hinged contrivance.
One friend says: "I met him in midair, we fucked
in zero-gees like . . . dandelion-fluff with a sex drive!" These
are the secular versions of what we see in the varnish-browns
of a sixteenth-century Flemish oil: people's bodies
sprawl the ground like shrimp husks, broken open
with a single cracking twist; and from this shell
a hazy spiral floats, that starts itself to take the shape
of a body; only, a spiritual body. See?—its eyes
look inward, it ascends with boneless pliancy.
The painter seems to say that what are wings
on other creatures are internalized for us
as sweet and aching alleluias in our breasts, and there
will come a Trump, a Judgment, and a Night of Din and Lightning
by which these will be released. And so the gravity
that claims us, and a counterbeckon heavenward, achieve

~

⟷

a tensile balance: we're complex enough for these to coexist
in us. The late tenth-century Magyar ruler Géza
"continued to sacrifice to his ancient idols while,
at the same time, praying to Christ and sincerely taking the sacraments,
saying that he was rich enough to serve
two different gods." —As are we all, if *rich* is daily measured
by connection-dots that blip inside our brains, or by
the quicksand in our hearts. And though it's true that monotheism
makes a lesser thing, a "devil," an "evil prince," from what was once
in the older religions a god—an equal-powered god—that new demotion is only
taxonomy: our *real* lives, as we feel them in the small raw
human yolk at our psychic centers, always offer themselves to more
than one force at a time. This snappy, street-sly
six-year-old, as one example: scampering the alley
with a kite and roll of string; *and* with a gram of asskick coke
crimped into her sneaker. Her daddy's at home, "getting high."
Her momma's on the shrink's couch, "feeling low." This
diametric pull-apart we see graphed-out in her
so vividly is only a single instance of (truly) everybody's apposite
and simultaneous weathers. When the main electrical plant

~

for the entire city died, *kaput,* and some blocks went ten days
until that juice returned, and people lived
a huddled-at-the-fireplace existence that was barely
twentieth century, "have you got power?" soon replaced
"how are you?" as a greeting until it took on the loose and mystical
aura of having a capital *P;* and in the unlit night,
they'd catch themselves unconsciously looking away from the city generator
across the bay, and up to the fires-spotted expanse of the sky,
as if *this* might be the source of their answer.
So it goes. We bury our parents, deep—and think that they continue
to instruct us from "on high." We bear the weight of one more year
each year, we shlep our day's frustrations on our back
—then fall in love and "walk on air." The crazy evidence
is everywhere. At the bend in the alley I came across an old
abandoned floor safe, of the kind that might have once stored
the entire office assets of an 1890s robber baron: sizable and heavy
enough to hold the deed on every swatch of deforested land in the continent.
Someone had tied it up with kite twine; maybe that girl I saw.
It won't fly. It won't ride the wind. Yet, somehow . . . even
here, even this, smacks faintly of resurrection.

generations

"Duo Tried Killing Man with Bacon"

—headline, *The Spokesman Review* (Spokane, WA)

At tornado force, a full length of uncooked spaghetti
has skewered a heart, and killed. A falling block
of frozen urine. A trout, that leaped precisely
into a yawn and thrashily lodged until the breath stopped.
Endless ways. Perhaps each death is as unique as the life
it ends, to whatever extent that is. I do know
when they found the fourteen corpses in the rubble
of the pipe-bombed synagogue, that mass of broken and indistinguishable flesh
was still divided equally into enough for fourteen burials,
and each of the families' griefs was its own. My father didn't need this

immediate neighborhood drama: fear of what the world could do
to his family was a living writhe inside him; once I doodled it
as a liver fluke that could mimic the face,
as needed, of my sister, mother, self. Because Chicago
offered its perils in generous headline-shrilling quantity
(and some—like the parts of children they always seemed to be finding
dumped in shallow graves—were fiercely lurid) and because
the cells of the body so often and fatally
rebel against the whole . . . he lived his days out in a series
of preventive ceremonial gestures, alternately sacred or tepidly humdrum,

as a situation called for—or, as a character in the gypsy slums
of nineteenth-century London says, by way of exemplification, "I made warding signs
and said 'Garlic!' about a dozen times" (Tim Powers, *The Anubis Gates*).
Garlic guards against the evil eye, as does (depending on where you live)
a desiccated frog, a shamrock, bezoar stones removed from the stomach of llamas,
handsigns like the "horns" or the "fig," or ritual spitting.
Beeswax candles. Lamb's blood over the door. My father
set my weekend curfew, and heeded the vast refusals of kosher laws,
etc., sternly certain that these self-set limits saved us from the limitless
predations of the universe. I think of what Tim Meiseneltzer felt

—the "victim"—manacled, ankles and wrists, on the floor of the woods,
and a bagful of fat-edged rashers spread around his body
to attract the local wolves. He lived. And it was even comic
in its way. But what did he feel, *then,* with the kicking
hoof of death in his chest. With the fist of death in his rectum
slowly opening up. Its taloned glove. What promise did he breathe
to what protector-god. I *can't* think into that
alien fear. But I remember a version of its minor key: my father
accidentally biting into a BLT, then kneejerk spitting it out
in a cafeteria napkin, while the whole world watched, and the heavens

stared down, as if our lives depended on this.

The Fiction Shelf

The Swiss watch isn't ticking for a week, before
a credible Hong Kong knockoff's on the market.
Fraud has always been a close, close shadow.
A blink or two after there's money, there's
counterfeit money: the fake of a silver coin
from the island of Aegina is sixth-century B.C.
In medieval Egypt, an inspector called
"the censor of morals" oversaw quickie eatery stalls, where
mystery extender in the rolled meats wasn't rare.
Presumably Eve would sometimes mimic the crescendo
of pleasure, and Adam his longing—anyway
certainly *after* the Expulsion. It's always pacing us,
it's always almost *ahead* of us: some shrewdly suited,
loitering imposter awaiting an impostee.

~

This ochered spoke of bone . . . This bony hole
it *nearly* fits, but doesn't fit . . . *Is*
Piltdown Man the greatest hoax of the twentieth century?
—all of those high minds brought to low blows
in persnickety scholarly tiffing. No,
a friend insists, the absolute whopper of all would be
that great granddaddy of "pyramid schemes"
the dapper swindler Ponzi perpetrated in 1920. . . .
Whatever. We pay the check, go home
to our respective simulations of daily contentment.
I have friends I love whose marriages are compounded
of cosmetics, aluminum siding, and scripted avowal . . .
then the curtain drops, their audience leaves, and in an itchy aversion
they unfasten their intricate happiness masks.

~

In 1897, when Peary returned to New York from another
triumphant Polar expedition, he brought six visiting
Greenland Eskimos, too—a sort of informal and very "proto"
cultural exchange trip. Four of the Eskimos died,
but a child, Mene, and Uisakavskak, an adult,
returned to their people in the spring of 1898.
Uisakavskak regaled the tribe with his tales
of "houses as big as icebergs; people
live up in the air like auks on a cliff.
There are so many of them, when people make breakfast
the smoke rises out of their chimneys until the sun
is eclipsed." And the elder angrily shouted at him,
"Uisakavskak, go tell your big lies to the women!"
He had lost their respect, and was given the name "Big Liar."

~

Do we need *more* newsreel footage?—bodies
tossed in carts like sheaves of shitted rags,
and the bereaved in the dirt. They've been led here,
of course, by one of the various Great Untruths
the sachems of our world dispense like penny candy.
Other untruths are smaller but kinder, and one
of the newsreels features lines of weary, war-torn
refugees passing a gaudy gypsy wagon,
where a healing tomorrow is hokily predicted
for a pear or crust. I know a man who lives in lavish
Xanadus of lies lies lies, self-mesmerized,
believing them, they're such a heartstabbingly beautiful
contradistinction. We've been hurt enough;
the right lie is redemptive.

~

18 people in a room. "I love you" each says to another, meaning
18 different things . . . 1,800 different things . . . 7 *continents*
of different things. . . . A public word is already only
a fiction of its referent. This spatting couple, up
all night in talk made from divisiveness . . .
What do I wish for them—some monolithic verity
to share? You know there isn't one. You know
that it's a world of slippery relativism we fumble through,
a universe of subatomic "here" and "not-here" blips.
But I can wish, at least, they share a lie—a single
and emollient lie, like a bottle of herbal Cure-All Wonder Waters
from the gypsy wagon; thus do we calm and anchor
our lives, that the periodic table of elements
ceaselessly reinvents.

~

"*Poo-jok,*" their Eskimo guide said—"mist."
But MacMillan and Green were sure they witnessed
"hills, valleys, snow-capped peaks," at last
the fabled Arctic Atlantis, "Crocker Land," that Peary
recorded having seen just a few degrees from the Pole
in 1906. It was eight years later now, and they headed
relentlessly toward it—over shifting, grinding
crash-ice, and into a wind that sometimes halted
the forward-straining dogs like a wall. Their party
required four more years to return. They were 14,000 1917-dollars
over budget. Green had shot Pee-a-wah-to,
the Eskimo guide, to death in an ice-blind madness.
And of course there was no Crocker Land.
Deluded by *poo-jok*—broken by mist.

~

So many moments leave us feeling emptied-out
and helpless, while the con-game packs its shill-stuffs
into the idling van. . . . My mother lightly places
her hand on my arm: *Opnarn iz keyn kunts nit,*
she says: "Deceiving others is no big trick."
I find this homily consoling somehow—its Yiddishy
sense of community, her attempt at comforting
contact. Then: *Der bester lign iz der emes,*
she says: "The best lie is the truth." I don't really
understand that; still, it has the ring of something
solid and true. I'm glad she's visited. But
my mother is dead. I've mumbled over her gravestone.
Now her touch disappears from my arm
—she's spirited back to the land of isn't.

****!!!The Battle of the Century!!!****

the handbills shrill, in searing orange-crimsons. *Any* century.
There will always be these two opponents, circling for a throat-hold.
Call them Plus; and Minus. Call them Void; and Matter
(from before there even *were* "centuries," or any creatures
capable of notching an antler into a lunar calendar).
Sperm; and Ovary. Belief; and Doubt. Thrift; and Bounty.
Steady-state; and Ever-expanding. Curse; and Blessing. *Versus*
is the only engine possible under the physical laws of our universe.
Slyly hip to this most elementary of verities,
the carny barkers are briskly pitching the wonders
of that asterisk-heralded titular battle scheduled for noon
in the center tent, twixt Dragon Sam, the Great Exhaler
of Gouts of Amazing Flame (whose claim
was, he could "conflagrate to the length
of four bull elephants trunk-to-tail," and for a coda
"thrust a white-hot coal inside his fundament, as a suppository"); and
Liquid Dan, the Living Geyser, Fountain of Fantastic Feats
(and who, in fact, could down a hundred mugs, then spout
a grandly arching shower into a silver basin twenty feet away,
"and you will see this stream change into a series of rainbow colors").
Fire; and Water. The ancient story. And so
the tent can barely hold the crowd.
And isn't this—because it's 1800—just a sideshow version
of the clash between the Neptunists and the Vulcanists
at scholarly colloquia? Such contumely
heaped like buckets of rhinoceros dung by stammering men of letters
over one another's anger-reddened heads!
". . . will clearly demonstrate, for all time, and beyond *all skepticism*"
[here, a glare of poison spear-tips at his colleague with the whiskers]
"that the agents of geological change have been—since the Creation,
to the Present Day—the rising and recession of the Waters,
and the work of Rain and of Rivers upon the land.
As to the specious, vapid, dunce-expounded theory

of the primacy of" [forcing out a jackass laugh] "volcanic action
evidenced at all . . ." [*Rah! Rah!* and *Bah! go soak
your beanbrain in your Waters!* and *Tell them, Chauncey!*]
at which, the bewhiskered proponent of Lava and Magma leaps up
to the podium, as heated as his subject, and: "You demonstrate
the intellect of a tuber!" [*Huzzah!* and also some *Boo!* and a single
Let them go at each other with rowboat oars!] "The work,
the immemorial work, of the Fires . . ." "Charlatan!" "Pestilential lout!"
[*and then it all breaks down beneath the weight of assorted professorial
catcalls, thrown tomatoes, hoots, and mooshed-in noses*]—
Scene: A Farmer; and a Cattleman.
Monotheism; and Pantheon. Electric; and Acoustic. There will always be
the bringing forth of Light, from Dark, and then a cosmos built
on that division. There will always be two sixteen-year-old lovers
screwing madly, for the contrast, on top of a grave.
Scene: He's back at the house, from the pasture. There's
this moment in his day—the sheep are tallied-up, and penned;
the silo, locked; the children, safely, even quietly,
at their various indoors busyness—when everything seems to fit
foursquare in its own ordained container, and the sky is the color
a rose is, and the dusk against his face is like another face,
familiar, soft. And then—what does it? a kind of sound?
some reminiscent whiff?—he has an image of the cattle ranchers
surging over everything, and suddenly aversion is a sickness
in his belly, is *a taste,* and hatred roils through his forehead
from a place in him so deeply lodged in Time, there aren't solids yet,
or sentience, and protein wars with protein.

~

There's nothing. Then there's something. In terms of narrative
this is a rudimentary plot, this is The First Plot. Then
uncountabillion years go by: the story is the same now,
but the players are gods and primal monsters:
"Nothing existed, there was nothing," says the *Popul Vuh,*
"and in this nothing the Creators waited, the Maker,
Tepeu, Gucumatz. They planned the whole creation of everything,
arguing . . ." Yes: *arguing.* For energy requires
a polarity, define it how you will. When two millennia go by
it's 1939, and *Marvel Mystery Comics* #1 is on the stands
and introduces its credulous adolescent audience to The Human Torch
(whose body is that, essentially, of a Superman flambé;
who hurls his fireballs—like snowballs, see? only fire—
with force enough to burn through steel, and can ensnare
the nefarious crimelords of his day in webs of fire,
or trap them in barrels of fire, etc.; who's solemnly sworn
to use his combustible powers "for justice!"; who can fly, because
"the combined blue and red flames made The Human Torch
lighter than air," a surely physics-revisioning concept) AND . . .
to The Sub-Mariner [as in *marinate,* not *marine*]
(who is really Prince Namor of Atlantis, undulant son
of the subsea royalty, ocean-breather, and commander
of the waves to do his bidding—and by extension, waters
everywhere—as well as his endless subservient conscriptees
of true fish, shellfish, and the occasional ocean-dwelling mammal, and
who can fly because of tiny wings on either heel).
Each premiered in a separate sock-and-pow adventure, of which he was the star,
but unlike calls to unlike, over barriers
of distance and time, with the undeniable inner pull
of gravity or magnetism: Matter; and Antimatter.
Cops; and Robbers. Done; and Meant-to-do. By July of 1940
the two are sparring with a grim, persistent hydro/pyro-inevitability
that so far—with lapses and revivals—has lasted over fifty years.
The ill-tempered Namor could *never* be lazily plotting any aqueous mischief
in his "self-appointed castle, the Statue of Liberty," *without*
The Human Torch, on serendipitous patrol above, besieging him
with fireballs, their snakily prehensile tails of cartoon-red
across the cartoon-blue of the New York skies. "I'll douse you yet,
you raging hothead!"—with a shaking fist. They made a holistic system.
Point; and Counterpoint. This hectoring, from a single issue:
"You flaming fool!" "You water rat!" "This is the end of you,
my little glo-worm!" "Here! I've got you at last, my fine
water-moccasin!" "Fire-bug!" "Water-bug!"—shibboleths

by which they know each other in a world they both find alien
(after all, they're both a super-brand of freak) or almost,
almost like the babytalk of lovers, or the weird, parodic
babytalk of lovers when their lust and loathing grip the same
whipped nerves: "Come on, you big fish!"
"I'm coming, Flame!"—and they're indistinguishable.
Continuing that interrupted sentence from the *Popol Vuh:*
"They planned the whole creation of everything, arguing
each point until their words and thoughts crystallized and became
the same thing." Though I earlier fashioned a comic scene
of rivalrous exchange between the Neptunists and Vulcanists,
the partisans of each were sober men engaged in sober labor
over years of thought, and of scrupulous fieldwork—the nascent labor
by which our comprehensive twentieth-century understanding
of geologic change was formed. To imagine these seasoned scholars, volleying
their invective—! "It is indefensible. . . ."
"Even a child would laugh at such impoverished reasoning. . . ."
Finally, posterity wedded them.

~

For forty years, my mother lay down at my father's side each night.
Now ten years after his death, we lay her there again.
If "her" is a viable construct, under the circumstances
—or "there." And what about "self"? And "who"? For instance,
to "who" did my sister talk, those several gray and rainy minutes
after the shovelwork was done and the dirt was level?
You can say a dozen different things, and none of them will change
the biochemical fact, the noise we are, the silence we become.
No matter *what* the question is, the real answer
is death. So: 2 + 2 = death. The major export of Fill-in-the-Blank,
and who did I see you with last night, and the number of feet in a mile:
death death death. It's surely the answer to where
we go in sex, the way our concentration
on the body—all of its anthers lit like Vegas,
all of its cellar kitchens spooning up a funky musk-alfredo—
pulses suddenly, and empties us out of our "us,"
out of our "here," and into some free-floating "where"
so atemporal, we could be motes in the sun
of Sumeria, or the dander of the twenty-fifth century
thermaling over the rocketports . . . wherever, it's the unguessable place
—if "place" is a viable construct—that my mother went
as the nurse held her wrist and the tiny molecular fuelpile
finished its countdown. This is vague,
I know, but no worse so than the rational alternative
that traditional Science offers us: the swarming
entomology necropolis, then a redistribution
back to the world as combinable protoparticles. Okay,
swell. Or Religion: those delicate human-headed *ba*-birds
hovering over the chests of the recently entombed
in ancient Egyptian art are charming images, equally so
are the willowy ectoplasmic shapes escaping like bouquet
from uncorked wine, in medieval and Renaissance scenes, but . . . none of it's
going to comfort my niece as she walks from her grandmother's funeral service
dutifully to the waiting limo. None of it means
a thing to the skin she lives in. On the homemade bier they carpentered
for Dragon Sam, a circus poster artist painted perfect scroll-like flames
around the panels, as a tribute to his famous, florid talent,
but this, as always, is eloquent more of our need for ritual
than it is of our understanding of what's "beyond";
the mourner's Kaddish we said in that afternoon rain, we said
for ourselves. And when it was over?—I lingered
as the limo's windows misted and its engine purred pure silk.
I listened, hard. Two voices fought for attention. "The Emperor

Q'in Shih-hunang-ti was buried with life-size terracotta figures
of an army of over 1,400 warriors (including a section of cavalry
with chariots). It's amazing here, in me, where your mother is
now. There is no death here; only the dead, which is different.
Only the bones: the stopped batons. Only the music
written for scarab-shears and petroleum forming. I'm the one weight,
and she's a part of that weight. Look down—" and the other voice
broke in, "Look up." I did: the sun was like a gold yolk
being folded into gray dough. There were morphing shapes,
as usual, whatever I wanted: continents, fantastic beasts,
continual reorganization—"Everyone was here at the first,
and is here at the last," this voice said, "and then here at the first
again: do you understand?" "No, no; look down, and breathe
the nearly carnal richness from between a mushroom's pleats. . . ." And so
they vied this way, they wanted me, as if the shitty penny
of belief that I could offer were the universe's treasure.
—Each, beseeching allegiance.
Earth; and Air.

Con Carne

We might also follow fashion in food through the revealing history of . . . "good" and "bad" ways of roasting meat—but that is another, and very long, story.
—*The Structures of Everyday Life,* Fernand Braudel

My father had worked ten-hour days from when he'd turned sixteen,
he lugged the blending tubs, then finally sold accounts,
my mother had disciplined herself to the needs
—the nearly pre-electric needs—of a 1940s kitchen
for that long as well, but this was new, in fact
this was The First Time, on The First Day of their real life
together, that he drove the bumping 1947 Chevy home
to a wife along an imagined thread of the odor
of pot roast she had done, for him, as he
had shmoozed the sorry shit of the world for her, for only her,
with the lovingcare of a meisterjeweler
sculpting a diamond under his loupe. / That hunger
was here at the start. We've found the shankbones
charred in the hearths of *Homo erectus,* "Peking man,"
400,000 years ago, and it must have been common
protoculinary practice even then. The bones
—they're human bones—were roasted, and then cracked
to reveal the yellow oily glisten of their marrow inside:
the last, perhaps the richest, of the body's held-back secrets
to be fingered out into the emberlight, as if
this early lesson is that the music *is in* the baton,
the magic *is in* the wand,
and embodiable. / For some, the sudden
cochineal jungle at the center
of a medium-rare filet mignon. For some,
their strip of Reser's Bull Whip Pepper Stix, *a yard*
of jerkied whatsit beef. In the year 1000,
"people ate cranes, storks, swans, crows, herons, and loons,"
and the monks of the abbey of St. Gall "treated their guests
to the barbeque of a complete horse." When the Traveler
reravels his way back home to the England of H. G. Wells
from the year 802,701 A.D., "For a time
my brain went stagnant. Presently I got up

and came through the passage here, I saw the *Pall Mall Gazette*
on the table, I found the date was indeed today,
and looking at the timepiece, saw the hour was almost eight o'clock.
I heard your voices and the clatter of plates. I hesitated
—I felt so sick and weak. Then I sniffed
good wholesome meat, and opened the door on you."
/ The browning we see in roasting occurs
when certain amino acids and sugars are subject to dry heat
—this is called "the Maillard effect," and this
is what's responsible for the typical enticing aroma
that gets the mouth wet like a lover. / "My ass
is what got me hired," my cousin Deedee once said of her summer job
as a carhop at Teddybear Burger—the shirred skirt always eager
to billow a peekaboo froth around her hips—
"and got me *boocoo* tips" if she would only titter at the obvious
sophomore wit surrounding "buns," and she did, she was always the frisky,
risky, high-hormonal, lust-struck baby of the family,
I never saw her waste good indignation
on a problem that her estrogen
could handle much more keenly, "but all that ended," and this
is the closest I ever heard her approach a principled feminist ire,
"when I wouldn't suck off the night manager, and
they put me on day shift standing out in the street in 98°
in the Burger Bear costume." / Tartar warriors
stashing a slab of the day's kill under the saddles
of their sturdy steppes-bred ponies, and then after another
long-ridden day of marauding . . . *voilà!*—automatic supper
of coarse-ground game, served raw (from which,
our "steak tartare"), discreetly seasoned
"with oil of saddle and sweat of horse's rump." What
won't we relish. "The liver of a walrus
is a delicious morsel. Fire would ruin
the curt and pithy vitality which belongs to its uncooked pieces."
"The flesh of the rat is here considered an able
hair-restorer." Starving in the Gobi,
Lord Dunn-Nulworthy boiled a camel's hoof
"for three days, until it was serviceable." / He
could picture the sanctum awaiting him; at least
that's how their two-flights-up apartment near the el tracks asked
to image itself at the end of a day of snafus stacked
past bearing—belts of sprockets torn,
the time sheets stolen . . . *cheez louise*, a chunk of granite
would drop its stoic demeanor and kvetch at *tsooris* like this.

And after all, my father was only human. He was at the corner
of State & Division, idling in back of a semi and thinking wistfully
of the checkerboard linoleum in their kitchen, and a beckoning
weather of roast-scent in the air there, and a woman who would take him
somewhere inside of herself a thousand miles away
from daily tumult . . . when the Chevy, with a sludge-glupped
mind of its own, bucked forward into the truck, unhousing
over fifteen crates of very startled chickens into the blattering
crawl of rush hour . . . and, by the time he finally,
wearily, entered their living room, he didn't need to hear
that her First Supper of Their Marriage had come to resemble
a pile of hockey pucks and carrot-colored marbles. Nor
did she need his mood. No, neither of them
really needed the looks of the other. / Marco Polo
reports that the Tartars boil their meat
in an animal's stomach, "and then they eat it 'pot and all.' "
On the other hand, he reports that "those who are called by this name
of *Yogi* would not kill any living creature,
neither fly nor flea nor louse. They do not eat anything
fresh, not herb or root, until it is dried, and only then;
because while they are green they have souls." / Exquisite,
these: The softening petals of boiled brisket
wafting off the soupbone. Near-black, leathery
shingles of pemmican. Nuggets of flank steak
carmelizing inside a glaze of onion baste.
A mound of chile-powdered *carne* as vibrant as henna.
The Olduvai layers of sausage-and-eggplant lasagna.
Goulash. Schnitzel. Hobo hash.
The obelisk of gyros. / It was a woman,
Elizabeth Rosin supposes: "Evidence seems to indicate
that the primitive olfactory brain is more highly developed
in females." So it happens: as the band of hominids
straggles across the savanna, their she-leader's sense
of smell is snagged by something new this afternoon,
it masses, pops, and thickly shimmers off the carcass of a young gazelle
that snapped a leg and roasts now in a dying heat
left over in these lightning-blasted grasses.
And the drip of its sweet succulence is smeared across
the grins of human faces
for the first time. Now whenever they can repeat this
happy recipe of fire and prey, they will. With an eel.
A squatty kind of hare. A calf. An eland.
With the prisoner they take from a similar band

of hominids and kill with stones. / He'd shoot them
with a gun if he could, but there aren't guns yet
(there are barely—by the standards of time a rock keeps,
or the breathable air—opposable thumbs yet). Terrified
and snuffling, he peeks out over the cover a brushy mound provides.
They've killed his cave-kin, Ta of the Quick Tongue, and he watches
as they gather to divide the corpse, while one
stands guard for even larger predators than they are. Rah
is weak now from the recent battle—he'd barely escaped—
and, tentatively safe in the brush, he slips off into a spasmy sleep. . . .
Then wakes. They're gone; some boar or lion has scattered the group.
Rah sniffs: an odor is in the air, a fragrance . . . something
greasily luxurious and undeniable lures him
to snatch at those lukewarm remains, to lift them (gingerly
at first, and then with educated frenzy)
to his lips . . . and does he know, does he suspect . . .
in any case, he can't refuse this thing that calls to him
as flesh calls flesh, what Charles Lamb
a gazillion years in the future will term "a kind
of animal manna. . . . [F]at and lean . . . that both together
make but one ambrosian result." / And what *does*
the Traveler find in 802,701 A.D. that makes his homecoming scene
so sharp in contrast?—"The place, by the by,
was very stuffy and oppressive, and the faint halitus
of freshly shed blood was in the air. Some way
down the central vista was a little table of white metal,
laid with what seemed a meal. Even at the time, I remember
wondering what large animal could have survived
to furnish the red joint I saw. I had a vague sense
of something familiar. . . ." / Stir-fried.
Curried. Teriyakied. Coiled in tortellini: a garden snail
of ground round. Also the *Kobe* beef of Japan:
beer-fed and hand-massaged, until the flavor is beyond
the tongue's ability to comprehend. And who can forget
that pair of five-feet trumpeter swans at the Levinsons' wedding,
sculpted out of chopped liver. / "*Would you like fries
with that?* I said it a stinking thousand times a day,
to every asshole with eighty-five cents. So when he answered
No, I'd like the cash in the register, and waved a gun, I knew
I was in love. I grabbed the money, I ran to his car with him,
and for two weeks after there wasn't a burger shack in Louisiana or Oklahoma
that was safe from us." / Norman was divorced in '67,
and in these thirty years he's never remarried; the other three

are widowers, Sol, Leroy, Yablowsky. Every morning at 7 A.M. they meet
at the Golden Arches, where they kvetch and kibbitz and generally opine
and put the shine on the jive, for at least two hours. *Every*
morning. Snow up to the nutskies doesn't stop them,
neither did the midtown flood in the spring of '80. "It's more
my home than my *home* is," Sol once said, and Norman
added "Yeah, and fewer of them cockroaches." If you think perhaps
the universe is founded on the basic elements oxygen and hydrogen,
or on a crystalline lattice, or is sturdily borne on the backs
of a series of turtles-on-turtles, I give you instead
its true, eternal square of infrastructure:
four coffees and breakfast patties. / Dickens
says of a novice butcher: "His very hair
seemed to have suet in it, and his fresh complexion
to be lubricated by large quantities of animal food."
One hundred years later, that boy, and his sister, are still parading
—as flecked as ever—around the Yards in Chicago.
"Me, I'm in Sliced Bacon. That's what some girls get,
it's lighter and cleaner. But some girls get Dry Casings,
where the pickle water eats away their nails, and eats
salt ulcers in their skin. One girl I knew was in Wet Casings,
where they string the pig guts over a pipe and run cold water through them,
she stood in that water past her ankles all day,
and the stink was still like a pomade stuck in her pores on Saturday night.
The men work Hog Kill, Beef Kill, Sheep Kill,
one man cuts off the head all day, another pulls fat off the carcass
and packs it into vats. A job like that,
it gets between your teeth, it gets in your eyes like sleep,
it makes your own children gag. And then at a Company picnic
we'd be scrubbed for once, with a pat of perfume . . .
the foreman grabs at our asses, like we
was cutlets being inspected." / Okay, so Norman
divorced her. Or she divorced *him*. By now the bridge of tears
and disappointment is so *looong,* she can't look back and see it
clearly. Okay, so now what? Now she's bought a little
carhop burger drive-in, and her friends are up past midnight with her
trying to rename it. "Belly Burger." "Biggie Burger."
"Buster Burger." "Hey, how about Bathos Burger?" "How about
next time you buy a brain, you thump it to see if it's ripe?"
"Brain Burger." "Teddybear—nah." Wait . . . yes,
yes, *Teddybear Burger,* and someone dressed like "Burger Bear"
enticing traffic into her lot! / Haiku:
A bar of Brahms.

A line from Dante.
A skewer of perfect kebab. /
I have nothing against the tofu burger. It doesn't,
however, sing to us in our dreams, and say those things
that fill the mouth with drool and pull at the blood
the way the full moon draws the cresting waters, it isn't
a synonym for our own dear flesh. / *Creamed calves' brain*
—from the recipe book of Apicius, circa 30 A.D. /
In Cairo, in 1400 A.D., "they cook a whole sheep,
and after it is done, a man will carry it
on his shoulders, with a table on his head,
and he goes through the streets in search of patrons, crying
'Who wants to eat?' " / Its aroma is a pleasure
to the nostrils of the Lord. Its aroma could ascend
on pillars of smoke as thick as the pillars of the Parthenon,
and still the Lord—not unlike His created ones—
would ask (or roar as if the very heavens spoke as a lion)
for more. "The fatted calf the people brought to the stone,
and it was an offering." This beef upon the altar is what
the gods elect to smell from us
instead of a rose or a bundle of fennel—*this,*
"the choice of the flocks," is what they grab up,
what they bend to. As do we, of course,
in their image. / "Well, the mood didn't last." But
neither did it dwindle in a fingersnap. They
joked and drew together, then some modicum of injured pride
in one or the other uncoupled them, and then they drew together again
—like magnets with their poles in erratic reversals, that's
the way I see my parents on this night so long ago,
I'm something floating in the iffy, misty realm
of possibility only. "Finally we were silly together.
We got out the dinner your mother had ruined—" "Had
ruined! I'll have you know—" "—and there were pieces of roast
so hard, like pucks, like *hockey pucks,* we sat down
on the kitchen floor and played checkers on its tiles."
Something sweet in this: my parents have always represented
the strengths of a standard middle-class family unity
that so many friends of my own have found elusive. And
one day, quite a while after my father was dead, my mother
(she must have already been in her seventies, I don't know *what*
sassy bug got into her) repeated the legend
and added, with a thespian wink, this ending line:
"*Strip* checkers." / And not only do we use them

to appease our gods—they *are* our gods. The bison
on the cave wall is depicted as the size of a typhoon,
and is a force that we could enter
and be transubstantiated. Also the cattle skulls
of Anatolia, reenfleshed with clay, and positioned
in shrines in the wall. The sacred Apis bull of ancient Egypt,
when it died, was embalmed with a process using
natron salts, and oil injected into the anus, and buried
in a sarcophagus of rose granite, and the mummy linen
adorned with gold, and the priests mourned sixty days,
and why?—"The Apis bull was said to be engendered by a ray of light
descending on a cow"; its soul was at one
with that of Osiris. And of the Yogi, Marco Polo says
"They worship the ox, and most of them carry a little ox
of gilt copper or bronze in the middle of the forehead.
They burn cow dung and make a powder of it, with this
they anoint various parts of their body with great reverence."
Someone making an ostentatiously splashy show of burning cow poop.
Someone else—an agéd, hump-bent woman let's say—
more modestly hobbling across the late, faint lilac shades of fading daylight
to her ancestors' graves; she carries a wooden bowl
with a symbolic cut of pork-fat in its center; and she kneels,
and feeds the dead, and makes the casual conversation
with them of an intimate talking to trusted friends.
All night, for long after the distant village candles darken,
they share the old tales. / My cousin Deedee
used to date (if that's the appropriate term)
a muscle-lumpy fuckrock bass guitarist given wholly over
to '60s-style neopimpflash clothes and peppermint schnapps
she'd pour at parties directly into his mouth
from hers, his fans all called him Dr. Meat;
but that, as my reticent family says when pressed,
is another story.

Natural History

Natural History

Pliny the Elder says pearls are formed by
drops of dew falling into the oyster when
he is yawning. Can't something be done
about that man?
—Will Cuppy

1.

As for the elephant, "it is the largest of land animals"
(which is verifiably true), and "it mates in secret because
of its modesty" (debatable at best), and
"it is attested-to that an elephant has learned to write with its trunk
in Greek" (which is surely a ring-tailed doozy).
And an ox *can't* speak.
The bodies of crabs do *not* transform into scorpions during a drought.
And what of the "stars
that alight on the yardarms and other parts of a ship,
with a sound resembling a voice, and hopping
from perch to perch in the manner of birds"?—well, yes:
St. Elmo's fire, a "real" "phenomenon."
That's the way it always is with Pliny, and probably
everybody: first, the dry, inarguable display
of his metallurgical knowledge, term by term, ore by ore,
and before long "there are men with dog's heads"
introduced with insouciant assurance—"they bark
instead of speaking and live by hunting and fowling,
for which they use their nails." Pliny
inveigles—in*finagles*—our trust
by toe-dunk stages into the warm bathwater shallows of what's
soon oceanic depth. I've been in his books-length history over my head,
amid the snake that suckles at a cow's distended udders,
and the rain of milk and blood, and the Astomi
"who have no mouth, and so no food or drink,
but live from the emanations of flowers and apples that they carry
(they can be killed by a vigorous odor)." And:
"For speech, the dolphin moans like a human being."
T ( ) F ( )
"A copy of Homer's *Iliad* once was writ on parchment, small enough
so that it was stored inside a nutshell."

T ( )   F ( )
"The pelican feeds its young its breast-blood."
T ( )   F ( )
"The crocodile bird struts into that monster's gaping mouth
as it sleeps, and cleans its teeth and its throat."
T ( )   F ( )
"Through drinking of wine beyond a specific limit, the secrets
of the heart are revealed."
T ( )   F ( )
—And so
we see veracity is compromised by dubiousness
in increments as subtle as infant breath;
and only our own
nose-in-it experience is dependable
—if that.* *Do* I believe
that "boiled cabbage prevents insomnia"?
No—not at Casa Goldbarth, it doesn't. Do I believe
that "the eyes connect to the brain by a vein,
and also to the stomach"? Probably
—Goldbarth and Pliny say medical research
sorely lags behind in this embracingly explanatory notion.
And that "Marcus Lepidus . . . is known to have died
because of the stress occasioned by his divorce"?
Yes, *that,* at least, is ascertainable, *that* one verity
I can swear to. I have burned at the base of that great
asbestos heart, I have sat beneath the tree
whose seed is a flake of ash, its leaves are ashes,
and its flowers, I have sat in the ashen fall of its pollen
deadening the air. And there are friends of mine,
a painter of airy lakescapes and his mergers lawyer wife,
whose interior world just now, if translated
into the images of the nightly news, would be a nest of snipers
and the wounded being carried away in long lines over rocky ground.
"This alone is certain," Pliny says, "that there is no such thing
as certainty." Yes. And as for "the vapors
the Nile does" (or doesn't) "give off," and as for "the rays
like minds beam unto each other,"
I'm sorry but none of it,
no matter its attractions, is beyond sane disputation

---

*From a 1940s hard-boiled detective story: "He had gotten to the point where he didn't believe what he heard even when he was talking to himself" (Norbert Davis).

. . . any more than the accepted definition of *I love you* is engraved
on a bar of plutonium in a hermetically sealed tubule of eterno-gas
in an underground vault in Stockholm
under Truth Police surveillance.
—No.

2.

The lake's an oolong brown today,
and gives itself away in rising mist. He views it
thoughtfully, this painter of water and shore; or
anyway, as thoughtfully as overriding marriage angsts allow.
And we can roll our eyes in tight ironic circles
at this common, sitcom-style brand of grief, but
no one's pain has ever registered
any less urgently for that. He thinks
Who's Right (or Wrong), Who's Guilty, Who's the Stinkeroo in All of This
—those categoried ponderings that seemed as architecturally defined
as a row of obelisks or equestrian statues
yesterday as they devastated each other with gall-and-adrenalin bombs,
but now . . . somehow . . . it's all more
like the lake, a scene of fog and indeterminacy,
a moil of accusation, noodgying, disaffection, and longing
they've been walking through as if through billowed haze
until they're both half-haze themselves. Now in the midst
of a life he once thought he could thunk with his knuckles
and hear ring back in an absolute way . . . today
he lifts his hand and almost sees it
flicker, reappear, then flicker once again. . . .
                                        And so tonight,
part-dozed on the back-room bed, he's not surprised
to see a smoky spectral-self rise out of himself
and float off, with an ever-extensive tendril
of smoky connection remaining between. (From Pliny:
"Hermotimus of Clazomenae used to leave his body
and wander about, reporting many things from afar.")
The journey is long and fast—the planet
smudges by, below—and then he lands at the edge of a meadow
men are walking across (it's late noon here), their catch
of wood duck and ptarmigan tied like skirts about their waists
. . . these snouted men with the sensitive, tentlike ears.
He's here in the land of the Dogfaces. Wow.
                                        They lead him,
not ungently, to their village (his necessary thread
of attachment-back-to-home still trailing from him). None
speaks "words," but they have throaty rumbles, aspirates, and yips
that are clearly a pliant and intricate language. Soon
he learns to distinguish individual members of the packtribe;
and, as in the world he comes from, brutish looks can hide
a sympathetic heart, or open faces mask conniving.

He meets the sachem of these people, a gaunt and ocher-eyed
old dogman; and he's given a room in the sachem's
sprawling mega-hut, with walls of mud-daub thatch
made appealing by tapestries showing hunting scenes,
some amorous entwinings (a tug of the home-thread here,
a sad, insistent tug), and what appears to be war
with a scatter of humanoid enemies. He never "gets"
their other-larynxed language, quite, and yet a mix
of body-moves, goodwill, and mutual grunts and sighs
allows him understanding enough to walk the village
comfortably and accepted.

With the royal house's
seneschal he indulges in smoking "dream leaf"
out of a shallow-bowl ceremonial pipe. With the childrenpups
he chases ribboned hoops along the rough streets.
With the women he learns to pound meal. When the sachem's
lady (something like their queen) falls ill with fever,
he's able to ease her plight by humming TV theme songs
at her cot. The sachem's concern is a grave
and admirable thing. (So then, again, that gossamer
pull of his "real body," toward his "real home.")

One night
he sees the warriors stuffing woven bags with shit.
A truce is broken, they're at war once more
with their age-old foes the Astomi—who are fierce and sly,
but pungent smells will fell them as surely as spears will.
He can join the men in battle, but first he needs initiation
at the god-hut, to symbolically remove the skins
of his earlier life—the mall-skin (*hei!*)
and the clock-skin (*hei!*) and the job-skin (*hei!*)
and the book-skin (*hei!*) and the wife-skin
—and before he can tell them *no!* the home-thread
snaps; and he's abandoned here.

Do *you* believe in "the rays
like minds beam unto each other"? He
still doesn't fully understand their doggish talk,
but some days it's as if he's stopped at a light
and one of the Dogfaces pulls up right alongside,
they're listening to the same song on the radio,
both singing it, both of them seeing
that they're singing it, so singing it louder
and crazier, rocking the wheels now, *baby, oh, oh, bay-beee,*
howling it, and howling it.

3.

Do *you* believe
that Danny Harper, blind for sixteen years,
regained his sight "when he was hit on the head
by a falling chicken carcass"?* —*Well,*
maybe. In any case, my friend, the *Daily Telegraph,*
Europa Times, and the *Daily Mirror* reported this.
Do you believe that lightning fatally blasted a woman
in Scotland when it hit her metal-wire-reinforced bra?
Okay; why not? Do you believe her name
is Elotta Watts? *No I don't; do you?*
I'm reserving judgment. Do you believe
it bounced from her and struck her friend
who had been confined to a wheelchair from multiple sclerosis
for twenty-four years, and she rose to her feet and walked?
—a Mary Stryke. *That crosses the line.*
What *is* the line? The little green men. . . .
The fall of raw meat from out of a clear blue sky. . . .
"I do not for a flame-ass minute believe
my own seventeen-year-old daughter is capable of driving
a stolen vehicle *at all,* much less a car
with a thousand dollars of stolen jewelry in the trunk,"
said Lady Kaye, the topless dancer at Obsessions,
in a fluid mix of tequila and tears, and with
such monolithic conviction as surely withstands
the scowls of the dunderheadedly doubtful,
why?—do *you* not believe it?
Angels. Water of Lourdes. Perdition. Antimatter.
Satan. Neutrinos. In Omiya, a suburb of Tokyo,
"in 16 separate incidents, 150 pigs' heads
have been found by puzzled residents." "BullSHIT,"
he says, "if you think I'M going to swallow
men ever walked on no moon." We can only
keep our credibility wary (open),
open (wary), and walk the dappled light of our time
with a show of appropriate
wonder.

"The one who wonders,"
Admirans, is what the king of Spain as a joke suggested

**It smelled a bit off,* said the woman who'd dropped it from her tenth-floor apartment.

Columbus should be called (instead of *Almirante,*
"the admiral")—such was the effect
of the seemingly endless New World marvels
on his toughened sensibility;
yes, empirically pragmatic though his purpose was, Columbus goes
continuously gaga over every further twist of possibility
on these shores. It's from about this time
the notion of a "curio"—a souvenir of grandeur or of freakishness—
is born; and *fifteen centuries*
after that oh-so-compendious Roman observer's inaccuracies,
the pastor/explorer Jean de Léry in 1578 could say
"I have revised the opinion I formerly had of Pliny
and others when they describe foreign lands, because
[he's just returned from Brazil] I have seen things as fantastic
and prodigious as any of those—once thought
incredible—that they mention."
If the rhinoceros: why *not* the unicorn?
If the manatee: why not the merfolk?
If the flying squirrel: the griffin, the roc.
The armadillo: *anything.*
Is a buffalo any stranger than a basilisk is, *really?*
Or for that matter, is the amoeba?
is the ovary?
are your spouse's dreams?
Do you believe these marriages
announced in daily papers?—Storm-Flood;
Beers-Franks; Long-Cox; Sharpe-Payne; Stock-King;
Good-Loser. I've seen the clippings. Do you believe *this*
marriage?—annulled in 1995, when one Bruce Jensen
of Bountiful, Utah, discovered Leasa Bibianna Herrera,
his wife since 1991, was truly Felix Urioste, a man
who "had enrolled as a female student
at the University of Utah and had worked as a doctor
in four Salt Lake City hospitals, alternating
between male and female aliases" (The *Fortean Times,*
as culled from the *Ogden (UT) Standard-Examiner* and *Meriden (CT) Record-Journal*).
Ah!—there is no woolly poppycock, no tommyrot flambé,
to match the straight-to-the-astonishment-gland details
of actual happenstance. One of the Egyptian king Merneptah's
victory monuments in 1300 B.C. lists 13,240
severed penises from conquered Libyans, Etruscans, and Greeks
presented as trophies. / Lee Herman, entomologist:
"We sometimes dissect insects under a microscope

with scalpels we make from tiny pins. Sometimes
the pulse in your thumb will cause the scalpel to jump. . . .
You learn to dissect between heartbeats." / "The gecko's
[pupil] looks like a string of four diamonds, the skate's
a fan-shaped Venetian blind, the fire-bellied toad
an opening like a piece of pie, the armored catfish a horseshoe,
the penguin a star that tightens into a square, the green whip snake
a keyhole, and others resemble teardrops,
bullets, buns, crescent moons, hearts, hourglasses, boomerangs" (Guy Murchie).

So why do we heap such retrospect contumely on this man
who said that "lettuces . . . increase the volume of blood,"
who said "the hair will grow on a corpse," and who,
among his best encyclopedic tries, gave us the manticore:
"the face of a man, a lion's body, a tail like a scorpion's"
—in *this* life, in *this* world,
a not unthinkable proposition.

4.

As to painters' verisimilitude, Pliny tells us:
"In a contest between Zeuxis and Parrhasius," the former
"produced so successful a representation of grapes
that birds flew up to feast there." Plump with pride
at this deception, Zeuxis very disdainfully indicates
the curtain hung in front of his competitor's inferior entry
now be drawn aside—*then* realizes the curtain *is* the painting;
"and he conceded the prize."

My wife says
"You're not *listening* to me," when of course I am,
I'm just not *agreeing* with her. This
makes her mightily pissed, and I can't blame her:
all of us, everybody, little two-bit
zeuxises and parrhasiuses, expecting
that *our* version of reality will be,
in any contest, all-persuasive. This explains
the martial loggerheads of nation-states,
as well as the deep assumption behind most "couples counseling,"
sure; and even so, such knowledge doesn't assuage
a man up walking late one post-misunderstanding night,
a man who's tossed in the crosscurrents ambience
of totaling his transgressions, and hers (first gingerly
separating them out from each other) . . . if he's anything
like me, he'll stare this conscienceful endeavor
straight in its stony face, and try, he'll *really*
try . . . but after a difficult while of ethics,
anger, melancholia, the heebie-jeebies, sneers, nobility,
mean-spiritedness, and sighs, it segues
into escapist fancies. . . .

He's an artist,
remember. So here's what he does. With globby smears
of animal fats and oils as a base, he trial-and-errors together
a make-do range of paints by mixing-in various berry juices
and riverbank clays. The hairs and handles for some brushes
aren't difficult to rig, and he talks the tribal skinner
out of a tattered length of her scraped, tanned hides,
that he primes with his own chalk goo concoction. Now
he's ready. One night he slinks off to the woods-edge
with his tools and enough for a stuttery, furtive fire.
Goodbye, you Dogface-ones. Goodbye, goodbye.
Even as he works, he looks toward the village with something

akin to fondness: not an obviating fondness, no,
but a real one nonetheless. And after several
strenuous hours, he's completed a miniature version of his body,
stretched as if in sleep, and done impeccably
trompe l'oeil . . .

                                        and he funnels back
into it, back in time, and place,
and materializes—*corporealizes*—back
in their own late twentieth-century troubled American bed.

5.

She's a mergers lawyer, remember.
That's an expertise as unyielding to me as brick
or an understanding of escrow. I can't even claim
much access to her dream life, to her wishes
—I'm weary with discord of my own today,
and far from any authorly omniscience. But
I *do* know—it's easy to see, by a flicker of pensive wryness
over her face as she kills time sorting bric-a-brac
in the attic, in its dim watts—that she finds it
especially ironic, the "mergers" part at which
she's supposedly so damn blow-your-eyes-out good;
not in this house, she isn't, they aren't, not
at merging lately in any viable way. And yet . . .
She idly flips through a stack of his unframed canvases.
This one, the day the lake became a steaming witches' cauldron,
or a kettle of fuming hobo stew. . . . And *this* one,
she remembers the day, they'd had a vivifying if cheap
white wine and cajun sausage, and he'd showed her
how the "blue" of it was dozens of colors, really,
if you really looked. . . . She knows
that you can't love a man for his art any more
than for a tight tush or a fatass roll of banknotes.
Still, . . . (*and now she's lost in reverie*) . . .
She has /not good but hopeful/ news from the clinic
about the lump. *He used to hum those TV theme songs*
by my side when I took sick
until I smiled through the hurt. And she goes downstairs
to the back-room bed as he opens his eyes from sleep,
and he says—*a weird thing, almost*
as if he'd been away on a journey—
"I'm back home now."

~

What *are* we going to do with that man?
He'll feed us any gee-whiz scrap of balderdash
and he won't go away, he won't remove
his ancient foot from the door of the twenty-first century,*

---

* From the February 5, 1996, issue of *Time:* "Writing his *Natural History* in the first century A.D.,

he knows the tiny oh-wow-bone in our ears
is evolved exactly to relay */zap zap zap/* astonishment
that the other bones, the payroll-bones and the mortgage-bones,
reject. Because of him I've looked in a woman's face
and seen the ox that speaks,
and the people who turn into wolves, and the bees
that by their flight predict the future.
I've looked in the mirror and seen
the proof of that great truth of his,
"the heart is the seat of the mind."
The two-inch goby fish attaches to a rudder
and stalls a galley ship of four hundred rowers.
The human embryo wears hair, like a beast.
The Arimaspi have but one eye; that, in the middle of the forehead.
There are days when I can almost believe
the marriage will last, will seam itself
and last, and stars will sing of this
to starfish, in the language that they share
because they share a shape.

~

Today they browse together through one of his books
of fifteenth-century art. The anonymous painter
shows us Pliny's dog-faced tribe the only way he knows:
as credibly rendered, yes
and set with weight and history and desires
in the hill-land of a credibly rendered world.
They trade their formulaic greetings and they sell their busheled grain
no more implausibly
than the hundreds of thousands of fifteenth-century saints
conduct *their* nimbused business.

Pliny the Elder reported that when water rises into the atmosphere to form rain clouds, it sucks up with it shoals of fish and sometimes quantities of stones. Fish and stones hover above us in the sky. Elsewhere, Pliny offered an item about a woman who gave birth to an elephant. He was, occasionally, a supermarket-tabloid sort of Roman. A Pliny pattern persists. The scientific side of the observer's mind demands objective evidence, as the great naturalist usually did; but the brain's mythopoeic, magic-thinking side is lured to marvels—to alchemy, to spells, to bat people on the moon or aliens on other planets. Can these matters be addressed with a whole mind? Can the two instincts of the brain—Einstein and Elvis-sighting—be made to fit together like compatible spoons?" (Lance Morrow).

On the next page, a companion piece—and equally
convincing: Pliny's

"headless people,

they have their eyes in their shoulders, and their mouths in their chests."
And once we're past a sort of pink cartoonishness
attending them, we see that they're complete
unto their needs and their fashions—simpering, valorous,
dour, gleeful, every one of them
somebody's child, somebody's neighbor,
every one of them rumpled at night one way or another
by love. The nipple-level smiles are genuine
endorsements of a happiness, for some; while others
wear theirs as a burglar might his mask.
Some are slovenly, others are dapper; voluptuary;
teetotaling;—consider the spectrum of "character"
run through fully. They argue the merits of the printing press,
and other abrupt newfangledness. They can't
believe it. They rumormonger. They have
their dragons and seraphs and pucks. A few of them
are walking out of the frame of the painting
hand in hand, among the lemon-yellow flower-bearing trees
and spaghetti-like grasses, they're going to test the line
between endurance and mismatchment.
Haven't we all, at some time, lost our heads?
They go their own encoded way,
like any confused human beings.

Albert Goldbarth is the author of several volumes of poetry, including *Popular Culture, Marriage, and Other Science Fiction*, and *Adventures in Ancient Egypt*. He is the recipient of numerous awards, among them the National Book Critics Circle Award, a Guggenheim fellowship, fellowships from the National Endowment for the Arts, the Chad Walsh Memorial Award, and the Ohio State University Press/*The Journal* Award in Poetry. He is currently Distinguished Professor of Humanities in the Department of English at Wichita State University.